First World War
and Army of Occupation
War Diary
France, Belgium and Germany

15 DIVISION
Divisional Troops
Royal Army Medical Corps
47 Field Ambulance
9 July 1915 - 9 July 1919

WO95/1932/1

The Naval & Military Press Ltd
www.nmarchive.com
Published in association with The National Archives

Published by

The Naval & Military Press Ltd

Unit 10 Ridgewood Industrial Park,

Uckfield, East Sussex,

TN22 5QE England

Tel: +44 (0) 1825 749494

www.naval-military-press.com

www.nmarchive.com

This diary has been reprinted in facsimile from the original. Any imperfections are inevitably reproduced and the quality may fall short of modern type and cartographic standards.

© **Crown Copyright**
Images reproduced by permission of The National Archives, London, England, 2015.

Contents

Document type	Place/Title	Date From	Date To
Heading	WO95/1932/1		
Heading	15th Division 47th Field Ambulance Jly 1915-1919 Jly		
Heading	15th Division. 47th Field Ambulance Vol I. From 9th July To 31 Aug. 15 Vol I		
War Diary	Marlborough	09/07/1915	09/07/1915
War Diary	Southampton	09/07/1915	09/07/1915
War Diary	Havre	10/07/1915	10/07/1915
War Diary	Sanvic	11/07/1915	11/07/1915
War Diary	Stomer	12/07/1915	12/07/1915
War Diary	Moulle	13/07/1915	15/07/1915
War Diary	Hazebrouck	16/07/1915	16/07/1915
War Diary	Connehem	17/07/1915	17/07/1915
War Diary	Houchin	18/07/1915	03/08/1915
War Diary	Noeux Les Mines	03/08/1915	31/08/1915
Heading	15th Division 47th Field Ambulance Vol 2 Sep 15		
War Diary	Noeux-Les-Mines	01/09/1915	30/09/1915
Heading	15th Division 47th Field Aug. Vol 3 Oct 15		
War Diary	Noeux-L-M	01/10/1915	01/10/1915
War Diary	Haillicourt	02/10/1915	03/10/1915
War Diary	Lillers	04/10/1915	12/10/1915
War Diary	Lozinghem	13/10/1915	15/10/1915
War Diary	Labeuvriere	15/10/1915	16/10/1915
War Diary	Haillicourt	16/10/1915	21/10/1915
War Diary	Noeux-Les-Mines	21/10/1915	30/11/1915
Heading	15th Division 47th F.A. Vol. 4 Nov 15		
Heading	15th Division 47th F.A Vol.5 Dec. 1915		
War Diary	Noeux Les-Mines	01/12/1915	13/12/1915
War Diary	Auchel	13/12/1915	31/12/1915
Heading	15th Div 14th F.A. Vol. 6 F/147/1 Jan 1916		
War Diary	Auchel	01/01/1916	05/01/1916
War Diary	Flechinelle	05/01/1916	07/01/1916
War Diary	Auchel	08/01/1916	13/01/1916
War Diary	Noex-Les-Mines	14/01/1916	31/01/1916
Heading	47th Field Ambulance Feb Mar 1916		
Miscellaneous	Programme of Training Tent Division Rest Period		
Heading	47th F.A. Vol. 7		
War Diary	Noeux-Les-Mines	01/02/1916	29/02/1916
Heading	47 Field Amb Vol 8		
War Diary	Noeux-Les-Mines	01/03/1916	26/03/1916
War Diary	Auchel	26/03/1916	31/03/1916
Heading	15th Div. ?. 47 F. Amb. April 1916		
War Diary	Auchel	01/04/1916	07/04/1916
War Diary	Rely	08/04/1916	09/04/1916
War Diary	Auchel	10/04/1916	24/04/1916
War Diary	Verquigneul	24/04/1916	30/04/1916
Heading	15th Div No. 47 F. Amb. May 1916		
War Diary	Verquigneul	01/05/1916	31/05/1916
Heading	B. 47 F.a. June 1916		
War Diary	Verquigneul	01/06/1916	16/06/1916
War Diary	Fouqueres	17/06/1916	30/06/1916

Heading	Confidential War Diary. Of 47th Fld. Ambu R.A.M.C. June 1st July 1916 To 31st July 1916 (Volume 12)		
Heading	A.D.M.S. 15th Division.	01/08/1916	01/08/1916
War Diary	Fouquieres	01/07/1916	22/07/1916
War Diary	Heuchin	23/07/1916	26/07/1916
War Diary	Wignacourt	26/07/1916	27/07/1916
War Diary	Villers L'Hopital	27/07/1916	28/07/1916
War Diary	St Hilaire	28/07/1916	31/07/1916
War Diary	Flesselles	31/07/1916	31/07/1916
War Diary	Confidential War Diary. 47th Fld Ambulance R.A.M.C. From 1/8/16 To 31/8/16 Volume.		
War Diary	Flesselles	01/08/1916	04/08/1916
War Diary	Molliens-Au-Bois	04/08/1916	05/08/1916
War Diary	Lavieville	05/08/1916	08/08/1916
War Diary	Becourt.	08/08/1916	31/08/1916
Heading	Confidential War Diary Of Lt Col. T.F. Ritchie. RAMC OC 47th Field Ambulance From 1st Sept 1916 To 30th Sept 1916 Volume XV		
War Diary	Becourt	01/09/1916	14/09/1916
War Diary	Contal Maison	14/09/1916	19/09/1916
War Diary	E.7.A Albert ()	19/09/1916	19/09/1916
War Diary	E.7.A.	20/09/1916	30/09/1916
Heading	War Diary Of Lt Col. T.F. Ritchie. R.A.M.C. O.C. To 47th F.A. From September 1916 To 30th Sept 1916 Volume XV		
Heading	15th Div. Confidential. War Diary. Medical Service. 87. Lt Colonel T.F.R Ritchie RAMC OC 47th Field Ambulance From 1-10-16 31-10-16 Volume XVI		
War Diary	E.T.A. Albert Cant Shut.	01/10/1916	01/10/1916
War Diary	Henencourt Wood.	01/10/1916	08/10/1916
War Diary	Becourt	08/10/1916	31/10/1916
Heading	15th Div. Confidential. War Diary. Of Lt Col. T.F. Ritchie. R.A.M.C. OC. 47th Field Ambulance From 1st Nov To 30th Nov 1916 Volume IV-17		
War Diary	Becourt.	01/11/1916	30/11/1916
Heading	15th Div. Medical Service. War Diary Of Lt Col. T.F. Ritchie O.C 47th Field Ambulance From 1-12-16 to 31-12-16 Volume 19		
War Diary	Becourt	01/12/1916	11/12/1916
War Diary	Esbart	11/12/1916	28/12/1916
War Diary	Warloy	29/12/1916	31/12/1916
Heading	15th Div. War Diary. of Lt Colonel T.F. Ritchie RAMC. O.C. 47th Field Ambulance From 1.1.17 to 31.1.17 Vol. 18		
Heading	G.G. & Q.M.G. 15th Division	01/02/1917	01/02/1917
War Diary	Warloy	01/01/1917	31/01/1917
Heading	Confidential War Diary of 47th Field Ambulance For February 1917 by Capt J.V. Brown OC 47th Field Ambulance		
War Diary	Warloy	01/02/1917	13/02/1917
War Diary	Bretel	15/02/1917	15/02/1917
War Diary	Fortel	16/02/1917	16/02/1917
War Diary	Hericourt	17/02/1917	17/02/1917
War Diary	Neuville Au Cornet	18/02/1917	26/02/1917

Heading	Confidential Medical Service 15th Division War Diary of Lt Colonel T.F Ritchie RAMC. OC. 47th Field Ambulance From 1.3.17 To 31.3.17 Vol 21		
War Diary	Neuville Au Cornet.	01/03/1917	09/03/1917
War Diary	Habarcq	09/03/1917	21/03/1917
War Diary	Arras	22/03/1917	22/03/1917
War Diary	Nouveau And Arras	23/03/1917	24/03/1917
War Diary	Arras	24/03/1917	26/03/1917
War Diary	Nouveau Quai. Arras	26/03/1917	26/03/1917
War Diary	Arras	27/03/1917	31/03/1917
Heading	War Diary For. April 1917 By Lt Colonel T.F Ritchie RAMC. OC. 47th Field Ambulance. Vol 21		
War Diary	Arras (Nouveau Quai)	01/04/1917	01/04/1917
War Diary	Arras	02/04/1917	12/04/1917
War Diary	Arras Ecole Normale	12/04/1917	13/04/1917
War Diary	Arras	14/04/1917	30/04/1917
Heading	B.E.F. Summary of Medical War Diaries of 47th F.A. 15th Div. 6th Corps. 3rd Army. 18th corps From May 6th 19th Corps from 22nd May. Western Front Operations-1917-April-May.		
Miscellaneous	B.E.F. 47th F.A. 15th Div. 6th Corps.3rd Army. Officer Commanding-Lt. Col. J.F. Ritchie. April 1917	00/04/1917	00/04/1917
Heading	War Diary For May 1917 of 47th Field Ambulance By Capt J.V. Brown RAMC A/OC 47th Field Ambulance Vol 22		
War Diary	Arras Ecole Normale	01/05/1917	01/05/1917
War Diary	Arras	02/05/1917	18/05/1917
War Diary	Sombrin	18/03/1917	22/05/1917
War Diary	Wail	22/05/1917	31/05/1917
Heading	B.E.F. Summary of Medical War Diaries of 47th F.A. 15th Div. 6th Corps. 3rd Army. 18th Corps from May 6th 19th Corps From 22nd May.		
Miscellaneous	B.E.F. 47th F.A. 15th Div. 6th Corps. 3rd Army. Officer Commanding-Lt. Col. J.F. Ritchie. May 1917	00/05/1917	00/05/1917
Miscellaneous	B.E.F. 47th F.A. 15th Div. 18th Corps. 3rd Army. Officer Commanding-Lt. Col. J.F. Ritchie. May 1917	00/05/1917	00/05/1917
Miscellaneous	B.E.F. 47th F.A. 15th Div. 19th Corps. 3rd Army. Officer Commanding-Lt. Col. J.F. Ritchie. Western Front May 1917	00/05/1917	00/05/1917
Miscellaneous	B.E.F. 47th F.A. 15th Div. 6th Corps. 3rd Army. Officer Commanding-Lt. Col. J.F. Ritchie. Western Front May 1917	00/05/1917	00/05/1917
Miscellaneous	B.E.F. 47th F.A. 15th Div. 18th Corps. 3rd Army. Officer Commanding-Lt. Col. J.F. Ritchie. May 1917	00/05/1917	00/05/1917
Miscellaneous	B.E.F. 47th F.A. 15th Div. 19th Corps. 3rd Army. Officer Commanding-Lt. Col. J.F. Ritchie. May 1917	00/05/1917	00/05/1917
Heading	War Diary For June 1917 by Lt Colonel H.G. Monteith. RAMC. O.C Infy 47th Fd Ambulance. Vol 23		
War Diary	Wail	01/06/1917	20/06/1917
War Diary	Gauchin	21/06/1917	21/06/1917
War Diary	Marest	22/06/1917	22/06/1917
War Diary	Norrent Fontes	23/06/1917	24/06/1917
War Diary	Thiennes	25/06/1917	25/06/1917
War Diary	Caestre	26/01/1917	26/01/1917
War Diary	Vlamertinghe Mill	27/06/1917	30/06/1917

Miscellaneous	B.E.F. Summary of Medical War Diaries of 47th Field Ambulance. 15th Div., 19th Corps, 5th Army. From 18/6/17	18/06/1917	18/06/1917
Miscellaneous	B.E.F. 47th Field Ambulance, 15th Div. 19th Corps, 5th Army. O.C. Lieutenant-Colonel H.G. Monteith Western Front, June 1917	00/06/1917	00/06/1917
Miscellaneous	B.E.F. Summary of Medical War Diaries of 47th Field Ambulance, 15th Div., 19th Corps, 5th Army. from 18/6/17	18/06/1917	18/06/1917
Miscellaneous	B.E.F. 47th Field Ambulance, 15th Div 19th Corps, 5th Army. Western Front, June 1917	00/06/1917	00/06/1917
Heading	47th Field Ambulance War Diary For July 1917 By Lt Colonel H.G Monteith RAMC O.C 47th Field Ambulance. Volume 25		
War Diary	Vlamertinghe Mill	01/07/1917	31/07/1917
Heading	War Diary For August 1917 of 47th Field Ambulance by Lt Colonel H.G. Monteith RAMC 47th Field Ambulance. Vol 25		
War Diary	Vlamertinghe Mill	01/08/1917	03/08/1917
War Diary	Luna Park L9 b 2.3 Sheet 27	04/08/1917	05/08/1917
War Diary	Luna Park	06/08/1917	20/08/1917
War Diary	Red Farm G 5D 25 (Sheet 28)	21/08/1917	28/08/1917
War Diary	Brandhoek	29/08/1917	30/08/1917
War Diary	L 19 B 63	31/08/1917	31/08/1917
Heading	War Diary For September 1917 of 47th Field Ambulance by O.C. Casually. Lt Colonel H.G Monteith RAMC Vol 26		
War Diary	Watou Area L 9 B 6.3 Sheet 27	01/09/1917	01/09/1917
War Diary	Agnez K17A Sheet 51C.	02/09/1917	05/09/1917
War Diary	Agnez	06/09/1917	06/09/1917
War Diary	Blangy G 23 D. 0.5 Sheet 51B	07/09/1917	23/09/1917
War Diary	Blangy	24/09/1917	30/09/1917
Heading	War Diary of 47th Field Ambulance for October 1917 By Lt Colonel H.G Monteith RAMC 47th Fd Amb. Vol 27		
War Diary	Blangy G 23 D 2.5 Sheet 51B	01/10/1917	03/10/1917
War Diary	Blangy	04/10/1917	31/10/1917
Heading	War Diary of 47th Field Ambulance for November 1917 by Lt Colonel H.G Monteith RAMC OC 47th Fd Amb. Vol 28		
War Diary	Blangy	01/11/1917	30/11/1917
Heading	War Diary of 47th Field Ambulance for December 1917 By Capt HM Vickers RAMC A/OC 47th Fd Ambulance. Vol 29		
War Diary	Blangy	01/12/1917	31/12/1917
War Diary	War Diary For January 1918 of 47th Field Ambulance by Lt Colonel HG Monteith RAMC OC 47th Field Ambulance. Vol. 30		
War Diary	Blangy	01/01/1918	01/01/1918
War Diary	Blangy to Avesnes-Le-Comte & J 26. D. 34 Sheet 51C.	02/01/1918	02/01/1918
War Diary	Avesnes Le-Comte.	03/01/1918	31/01/1918
Heading	War Diary of 47th Field Ambulance for February 1918 by Lt Col H.G Monteith D.S.O. RAMC Commdg. 47th Fd Amb. Vol 31		
War Diary	Avesnes Le Comte 926 d 3.4 Sheet 51C	01/02/1918	05/02/1918
War Diary	Hospital St Jean Arras	06/02/1918	28/02/1918

Heading	War Diary of 47th Field Ambulance for March 1918 By Lt Colonel H.G. Monteith D.S.O. RAMC 47th Fd. Amb. Vol 32		
War Diary	Hosp St Jean Arras	01/03/1918	06/03/1918
War Diary	Ecole Normal Arras.	07/03/1918	28/03/1918
War Diary	Ecole Normal	29/03/1918	31/03/1918
Heading	War Diary Of 47th Field Ambulance For April 1918 By Lt Colonel H.G Monteith D.S.O. RAMC 47th Fd Amb. Vol 33		
War Diary	Warlus 51C K36 d	01/04/1918	05/04/1918
War Diary	Warlus	06/04/1918	06/04/1918
War Diary	Agnez Les Duisans 51C LIC 55	07/04/1918	12/04/1918
War Diary	Agnes Les Duissans	13/04/1918	20/04/1918
War Diary	LIC 55 Sheet 51C.	20/04/1918	22/04/1918
War Diary	Auchel	23/04/1918	30/04/1918
Heading	War Diary For May 1918 Of 47 Field Ambulance By Lt Colonel H.G. Monteith D.S.O. RAMC Commdg. 47th Fd Amb. Vol 34		
War Diary	Auchel	01/05/1918	02/05/1918
War Diary	Hosp St Jean Arras	03/05/1918	31/05/1918
Heading	War Diary Of 47 Field Ambulance For June 1918 By Lieut Colonel H.G. Monteith D.S.O. RAMC Commdg. 47th Vol 35		
War Diary	Hosp St Jean Arras	01/06/1918	30/06/1918
Heading	War Diary Of 47 Field Ambulance For July 1918 By Lieut Colonel H.G Monteith D.S.O. RAMC Commdg 47th Fd Amb. Major T.M. Vickers RAMC Vol 36		
War Diary	Hosp St Jean Arras.	01/07/1918	04/07/1918
War Diary	St-Catherine G15a 3.3	05/07/1918	09/07/1918
War Diary	St Catherine	10/07/1918	11/07/1918
War Diary	St. Catherine Agnez. L.I.C. 55	11/07/1918	11/07/1918
War Diary	Gouy-Servins	12/07/1918	16/07/1918
War Diary	Aubigny	17/07/1918	17/07/1918
War Diary	Liancourt Beauvais District	18/07/1918	18/07/1918
War Diary	Liancourt	19/07/1918	19/07/1918
War Diary	Haute Fontaine (Wood Soissons District)	20/07/1918	21/07/1918
War Diary	Bivouacs 1/2 Kilo South "b" in Montgobert (Soissons Map)	22/07/1918	22/07/1918
War Diary	Bivouac 1/2 a Kilo South of "b" in Montgobert	23/07/1918	25/07/1918
War Diary	Bivouac 1/2 a Kilo South of the "b" Montgobert (Soissons district)	26/07/1918	31/07/1918
War Diary	Confidential War Diary Of Lt Colonel HG Monteith DSO RAMC O.C 47th Field Ambulance August 1st To 31st 1918. Volume 38		
War Diary	Bivouac In Wood 1/2a Kilometer South of "b" in Montgobert. (Soissons Area)	01/08/1918	04/08/1918
War Diary	Sacy-Le-Grand (Beauvais Area)	04/08/1918	06/08/1918
War Diary	Houvin Inft Lanc	07/08/1918	07/08/1918
War Diary	Houvin	08/08/1918	16/08/1918
War Diary	Briqueterie Wanquetin K 28 D. 5.3. 51 C	17/08/1918	17/08/1918
War Diary	Wanquentin	18/08/1918	21/08/1918
War Diary	St Sauveur Arras G 29 C. 88	22/08/1918	22/08/1918
War Diary	Hosp St Jean Arras	23/08/1918	23/08/1918
War Diary	Gouy-Servins	24/08/1918	24/08/1918
War Diary	K 20 A 58 44b	25/08/1918	26/08/1918
War Diary	Ruitz K 20 A 58	27/08/1918	31/08/1918

Heading	War Diary of 47th Field Ambulance for September 1918 by Lieut Colonel H.G. Monteith D.S.O. RAMC Colonel 47th Field Ambulance. Vol 38		
War Diary	Ruitz K20 A 5.8	01/09/1918	05/09/1918
War Diary	K 20 A 5.8	06/09/1918	14/09/1918
War Diary	Bracquemont L 25b. 33	15/09/1918	16/09/1918
War Diary	L 25 B 53	17/09/1918	30/09/1918
Heading	War Diary of 47th Field Ambulance for October 1918 By Lieut Colonel. H.G. Monteith DSO RAMC Commdg. F.A. Vol 39		
War Diary	Bracquemont L 25b. 33	01/10/1918	01/10/1918
War Diary	L 25 B 33	02/10/1918	08/10/1918
War Diary	Bracquemont	08/10/1918	16/10/1918
War Diary	I. 9 a 28	17/10/1918	17/10/1918
War Diary	La Rosiere K 12 a 44 A N.E.	18/10/1918	18/10/1918
War Diary	Cappelle F 29 A 7.4	19/10/1918	20/10/1918
War Diary	Berlu	21/10/1918	21/10/1918
War Diary	B 21 C 88 (Sheet 44)	22/10/1918	24/10/1918
War Diary	Bercu B. 21. C.8.8 (Sheet 44)	25/10/1918	31/10/1918
Heading	War Diary of 47th Field And By Lieut Colonel HG Monteith DSO RAMC For November 1918 Vol 40		
War Diary	Mouchin B 21C 88	01/11/1918	08/11/1918
War Diary	Petit Rumes B 21 G	09/11/1918	09/11/1918
War Diary	Washes W 28D Sheet 37	10/11/1918	10/11/1918
War Diary	Willaupuis X 22 a. Sheet 37	11/11/1918	13/11/1918
War Diary	Willaupuis	14/11/1918	23/11/1918
War Diary	Autreppe	24/11/1918	30/11/1918
Heading	War Diary By 47th Fd Ambulance for December 1918 By Lieut Colonel H.G. Monteith DSO RAMC OC 47th Fd Amb. Vol 41		
War Diary	Autreppe T1d.99. Map 38	01/12/1918	08/12/1918
War Diary	Autreppe	09/12/1918	17/12/1918
War Diary	Chievres	18/12/1918	18/12/1918
War Diary	Braine Le Comte	19/12/1918	31/12/1918
Heading	15 Div Box 1624 No. 47 Field Ambulance.		
War Diary	Braine Le Comte	01/01/1919	31/01/1919
Heading	No. 47 Field Ambulance		
War Diary	Braine-Le Comte	01/02/1919	28/02/1919
Heading	Confidential. War Diary. 47th Field Ambulance. March. 1919 Vol 44		
War Diary	Braine-Le Comte	01/03/1919	31/03/1919
Heading	Confidential War Diary 47 Field Ambulance April 1919 Vol. 45		
War Diary		01/04/1919	13/04/1919
War Diary	Braine Le Comte	14/04/1919	30/04/1919
Heading	Confidential. War Diary of 47th Field Ambulance Vol. May 1919		
War Diary	Braine-Le Comte	01/05/1919	31/05/1919
Heading	47th F.A. June 1919		
War Diary	Blaine Le Comte	01/06/1919	16/06/1919
War Diary	Antwerp	24/06/1917	30/06/1917
Heading	47th F.A. July 1919 160/3585 Issued.		
War Diary	Antwerp	01/07/1919	07/07/1919
War Diary	Boulogne	08/07/1919	09/07/1919

WO95/1932/1

15TH DIVISION

47TH FIELD AMBULANCE
JLY 1915-DEC 1918
1919 JLY

121/6607

15th Division

47th Field Ambulance
Vol I.

From 9 July to 31 Aug. 15

July 1915
August "

WAR DIARY or INTELLIGENCE SUMMARY

Army Form C. 2118

47th FIELD AMBULANCE
XV DIVISION.

(Erase heading not required.)

Instructions regarding War Diaries and Intelligence Summaries are contained in F.S. Regs., Part II. and the Staff Manual respectively. Title Pages will be prepared in manuscript.

Place	Date	Hour	Summary of Events and Information	Remarks and references to Appendices
Marlborough	9.7.15	10 a.m. 2.30 a.m.	Moved from MARLBOROUGH to SOUTHAMPTON in two train loads arriving 12.30 p.m. & 2.30 p.m. respectively	PPR.
Southampton	9.7.15	5 p.m.	168 Officers & men embarked at 6 p.m. in LA MARGUERITE. Sailed at 7.30 p.m. Arrived at HAVRE 5 a.m. 10.7.15	PPR.
			46 Officers & men with all transport embarked at 1 p.m. on BLACKWALL. Sailed 5 p.m. Arrived HAVRE 9 a.m. 10.7.15	PPR.
HAVRE	10.7.15	1 p.m.	Complete unit left HAVRE for Restcamp SANVIC 2 & 2. Arriving at 3.30 p.m.	PPR.
SANVIC	11.7.15	8.16 p.m.	Left SANVIC Restcamp for HAVRE Gare Maritime. Point 6. Arrived 10 p.m. Entrained 11.45 p.m. Left 1 a.m.	PPR.
ST OMER	12.7.15	9 a.m.	Arrived ST OMER 9 p.m. Detrained & marched to MOULLE arriving 2 a.m. 13.7.15	PPR.
MOULLE	13.7.15	12 noon	Remained at MOULLE in billets	PPR.
MOULLE	14.7.15	12 noon	Remained at MOULLE	PPR.
MOULLE	15.7.15	7.30 a.m.	Left MOULLE at 7.30 a.m. with 44th Inf Bde for ACQUIN & HAZEBROUCK arriving at 4 p.m.	PPR.
HAZEBROUCK	16.7.15	8.30 a.m.	Left HAZEBROUCK at 8.30 a.m. for CONNEHEM arriving at 6 p.m.	PPR.
CONNEHEM	17.7.15	6 p.m.	Left CONNEHEM at 6.30 p.m. marched to HOUCHIN arriving 3 a.m. 18.7.15	PPR.
HOUCHIN	18.7.15	12 noon	Remained at HOUCHIN in Divmac. A School taken over as a small reception hospital	PPR.
HOUCHIN	19.7.15	12 noon	Remained at HOUCHIN in billets	PPR.
HOUCHIN	20.7.15	12 noon	Remained at HOUCHIN Private houses inspected & kits disinfected	PPR.
HOUCHIN	21.7.15	12 noon	Remained at HOUCHIN	PPR.
HOUCHIN	22.7.15	6 a.m.	A Section less ½ Bearer Subdivision (Lt. J.E.L. KEYES, Lt. G.V. BROWN & Lt. W.S. WALLACE) proceeded to NOEUX-LES-MINES for attachment to 2/6 (LONDON) Field Ambulance	PPR.

WAR DIARY or INTELLIGENCE SUMMARY

Army Form C. 2118

(Erase heading not required.)

Instructions regarding War Diaries and Intelligence Summaries are contained in F. S. Regs., Part II. and the Staff Manual respectively. Title Pages will be prepared in manuscript.

Place	Date	Hour	Summary of Events and Information	Remarks and references to Appendices
HOUCHIN	23.7.15	12 noon	Reconnaissance of HOUCHIN. Wiring GHQ line from 44th & 2nd Divs.	92R.
HOUCHIN	24.7.15	12 noon	Remained at HOUCHIN	92R.
HOUCHIN	25.7.15	12 noon	A Section returned (Lt KEYES WALLACE and BROWN) B. Section 3 Officers & 30 men (Lt OZANNE STEVEN & McLEAN) to NOEUX-LES-MINES for attachment to R.E. 6 (LONDON) Full Ambulance	92R. 92R.
HOUCHIN	26.7.15	12 noon	Remained at HOUCHIN. Small numbers of Sick went in.	92R.
HOUCHIN	27.7.15	12 noon	M.T. drivers & vehicles attached to B.Sec R.E. 6 (London) F. A. to Sevenadain for Catanuel Dressing Stations.	92R.
HOUCHIN	28.7.15	12 noon	C Section with 2 G.S. Wagons & 1 Limber Vehicle proceeded to NOEUX-LES-MINES Filling for attachment to R.E. 6 (LONDON) F.A. (Lt G.F. CLIFTON & Lt R. H. BONNYCASTLE) B. Section returned (Lt OZANNE STEVEN & McLEAN) Following Limits to Captains G.F.CLIFTON R.C.OZANNE W.S.WALLACE (London Gazette)	92R.
HOUCHIN	29.7.15	12 noon	Remained at HOUCHIN. 6 Benzol cases in Hospital.	92R.
HOUCHIN	30.7.15	12 noon	Remained at HOUCHIN.	92R.
HOUCHIN	31.7.15	12 noon	Remained at HOUCHIN. A few slight cases admitted.	

Army Form C. 2118

WAR DIARY
or
INTELLIGENCE SUMMARY

(Erase heading not required.)

Instructions regarding War Diaries and Intelligence Summaries are contained in F. S. Regs., Part II. and the Staff Manual respectively. Title Pages will be prepared in manuscript.

Place	Date	Hour	Summary of Events and Information	Remarks and references to Appendices
H.Q. 13/PPR HOUCHIN	1.8.15	12 noon	Remained at HOUCHIN. about 10 Stg't cases of Sickness from the R/5 Sech.	PPR
HOUCHIN	2.8.15	9 a.m.	A Section plus 20 men of C Sech proceeded to NOEUX-LES-MINES to take over positions occupied by 2/6 (County of LONDON) Field Ambulance. Transport & horses also sent.	PPR
		2 p.m.	Section C Sech is now complete at Advanced Dressing Station LES BREBIS and MAZINGARBE. B Sech relieves	
		10 p.m.	at HOUCHIN huts relieved by a detachment from 2/4 S.F.A. Troops of A Section arrived 10 p.m. Personnel accommodated in billets. 2 lorry drivers taken ill as a hospital and discharged.	
HOUCHIN	3.8.15	8.30 a.m.	B Section left HOUCHIN. Lt McLean and 2 men remain here attached to O.C. 4/5 F.A.	
NOEUX-LES-MINES	3.8.15	10 a.m.	On the departure of 2/6 (County of LONDON F.A.) 47th Field Gen. is distributed as follows: A+B Sections at Main Dressing Station in NOEUX-LES-MINES. C Sech at Advanced Dressing Stations at LES BREBIS and MAZINGARBE Capt. C.F. CLIFTON & Lt. J.V. BROWN at LES BREBIS A.D.S. Sech. Lieut P. Rush-Dunne at MAZINGARBE Lt. J.F.L. KEYES & LT. R. H. BONNYCASTLE with 19 men are at MAZINGARBE. All in billets	98 R
		4 p.m.	Adv. unmounted det. to Divisions. All sick are to be sent to No 45 F.A. at HESDIGNEUL. Sick to 47th Sanitation	98 R
		6 p.m.	All sick of 47 Division that have been sent to 5th (LONDON) F.G.	98 R
NOEUX-LES-MINES	5.8.15	12 noon	Remained at NOEUX-LES-MINES.	98 R
NOEUX-LES-MINES	6.8.15	2 p.m.	Dismounted arrived from MAZINGARBE. The O.C. of Mr Scarlet Fever 11 cadets from 10/Ser. Bn	98 R
		6 p.m.	Sent Pte Cuthbert to BOUVIGNY to Queens ARR SUR from R.M.A. 1 Reinforcement arrived STAR.	
NOEUX-LES-MINES	7.8.15	12 noon	Received a small amount of canned unused. Removed all sick to H.S. DIENEUL (45 F.G.)	PPR
NOEUX-LES-MINES	8.8.15	12 noon	Small number of command Returned to Evacuated	PPR

1875 Wt. W593/826 1,000,000 4/15 J.B.C. & A. A.D.S.S./Forms/C. 2118.

Army Form C. 2118

WAR DIARY
or
INTELLIGENCE SUMMARY
(Erase heading not required.)

Instructions regarding War Diaries and Intelligence Summaries are contained in F. S. Regs., Part II. and the Staff Manual respectively. Title Pages will be prepared in manuscript.

Place	Date	Hour	Summary of Events and Information	Remarks and references to Appendices
NOEUX-LES-MINES	9.8.15	12 noon	Joined up HQ	
NOEUX-LES-MINES	10.8.15	9.30 am	Proceeded with A.D.M.S. to examine next-up stations Bn 1st & 2nd Bdes and intended st̄ations by 45th Bn J 4.30 pm D.D.M.S. IV Corps visited Dressing station & Noeux-les-Mines Mazimgarbe & at Les Brebis. Signed & report.	
NOEUX-LES-MINES	11.8.15	12 noon		
NOEUX-LES-MINES	12.8.15	12.30 nn	Professor Leishman & Capt. Austin (Inoculation Commission) accompanied by D.D.M.S. IV Corps visited Noeux-Les-Mines, Mazimgarbe and Les Brebis hospl.	
NOEUX-LES-MINES	13.8.15	4.30 pm	Lt. Inspector Hosp. Commanding 10 Armee inspected Bn & 1st Hosp.	
NOEUX-LES-MINES	14.8.15	11.30 am	Colonel Bellew A.M.S. visited the 2 new Dressing Station hosps.	
NOEUX-LES-MINES	15.8.15	9.15 am	Proceeded with A.D.M.S. IV Division to Area about Grenay and Maroc. In his absence proceeded to Mazimgarbe and Le Philosophe & found further arrangements for sick command.	
MIEUX-LES-MINES	16.8.15	12 noon	Very heavy rain & storm broken. This has considerably damaged the huts in our command billets.	
NOEUX-LES-MINES	17.8.15	12 noon	Only small number of admissions to Bn each with mainly accidental. Col. Dickson 10/ Gurkhas attained Warrant Pvt & Cholera.	
NOEUX-LES-MINES	18.8.15	6 pm	A supply of kettles for unit otomitis received & issued for lord and depot.	
NOEUX-LES-MINES	19.8.15	5 pm	Instr̄n in Stretchers from A.D.M.S. XII division. Lieut. J.E.L.Keyes had been detailed for duty with 203 Field Ambulance	
NOEUX-LES-MINES	20.8.15	9 am	L. J.E.L.Keyes proceeded for duty with 203 Field Ambulance B Section relieves C Section hosps. at Les Brebis and Mazimgarbe.	
		8 pm		
NOEUX-LES-MINES	21.8.15	24	Huts at B Section at Les Brebis and Mazimgarbe completed. Lieut R.A.T. Capts. Ozanne & Lt. McLean and at Les Brebis and Capt. Wallace and Lt. Steven C Section. To the road. Capt. W.H. Forsyth R.A.M.C. arrived & joined for duty from 2.1.F.E.	

Army Form C. 2118

WAR DIARY
or
INTELLIGENCE SUMMARY
(Erase heading not required.)

Instructions regarding War Diaries and Intelligence Summaries are contained in F. S. Regs., Part II. and the Staff Manual respectively. Title Pages will be prepared in manuscript.

Place	Date	Hour	Summary of Events and Information	Remarks and references to Appendices
NOEUX-LES-MINES	23.8.15	9 am	Nothing of note passing.	92R.
NOEUX-LES-MINES	24.8.15	10 am	Nothing of importance to note.	92R.
NOEUX-L-M.	25.8.15	10 am	Capt. W.S. WALLACE returns from MAZINGARBE to NOEUX-LES-MINES for duty as Transport Officer.	92R.
NOEUX-L-M.	26.8.15	2 pm	B. Sect. Encounter Entrance Dressing Station at LES BREBIS now returns to NOEUX-LES-MINES. Capt. R.C. OZANNE returns to NOEUX-LES-MINES. Lt McLEAN to MAZINGARBE.	92R.
NOEUX-LES-MINES	27.8.15	12 noon	B. Section in List: in a field near Hospital. Another game known.	92R.
NOEUX-LES-MINES	28.8.15	12 noon	Nothing of note of importance. Amal. Inauguration of ? attended.	92R.
NOEUX-LES-MINES	29.8.15	12 noon	Visited A station in rear of MAZINGARBE with A.D.M.S. with a view to forming a Collecting Station. Capt. CLIFTON and Lt BROWN on duty at same (beginning.)	92R.
NOEUX-LES-MINES	30.8.15	6 am	Visited Bde Hospitals with Bde Insp. Gen. Arrangements for evacuation of wounded.	92R.
NOEUX-L-M.	31.8.15	12 noon	Nothing of importance to note.	92R.

J.F. Rutter Major.
O.C. 49th Field Ambulance

121/7/53.

15th Division

Summarised

47th Field Ambulance
Vol 2

Sept. 15.

Sept. 15.

WAR DIARY or INTELLIGENCE SUMMARY

Army Form C. 2118

47th Field Ambulance

Place	Date	Hour	Summary of Events and Information	Remarks and references to Appendices
NOEUX-LES-MINES	1.9.15	12 noon	Only a few cases without warning.	PAR
NOEUX-LES-MINES	2.9.15	12 noon	Visited PHILOSOPHE QUALITY STREET and Regimental Aid Posts.	PAR
NOEUX-LES-MINES	3.9.15	12 noon	Nothing of importance to note.	PAR
NOEUX-L-M	4.9.15	12 noon	Capt. R.C. OZANNE proceeded to MAZINGARBE today for duty as Advanced Dressing Station	PAR
NOEUX-L-M	5.9.15	12 noon	Catholic Chaplain Stewart held a service at Divisional Dressing Station today.	PAR
NOEUX-L-M	6.9.15	12 noon	Inspected Billet. Case to be admitted to this F.C. and cases hence sent to 45 F.C.	PAR
NOEUX-L-M	7.9.15	12 noon	Have now accumulated a great number of dressings and stretchers. Plenty H₂	PAR
NOEUX-L-M	8.9.15	12 noon	3 Wheeled Stretchers received today from 2/1 C.C.S.	PAR
NOEUX-L-M	9.9.15	12 noon	Fine warm weather. Small number of Sick attended. Nothing unusual	PAR
NOEUX-L-M	10.9.15	12 noon		
NOEUX-L-M	11.9.15	3 p.m.	D.M.S. 1st Army inspected dressing Station today.	PAR
NOEUX-L-M	12.9.15	10.30 a.m.	Proceeded to conference with ADMS XI Division. 4 Motor Cook-up Cases received.	PAR
NOEUX-L-M	13.9.15	10 a.m.	Visited QUALITY STREET and Poste 207. One Motor Cook-up Car handed over to 46 F.C. 1 & A.D.M.S.	PAR
NOEUX-L-M	14.9.15	12 noon	Nothing of importance to note	PAR
NOEUX-L-M	15.9.15	12 noon	Nothing of importance to note	PAR
NOEUX-L-M	16.9.15	12 noon	Completed arrangements for Bearer division from advanced Dressing Station at Rear Post.	PAR
NOEUX-L-M	17.9.15	12 noon	Nothing of importance to note. Another Ambulance Cars has arrived.	PAR

1875 Wt. W593/826 1,000,000 4/15 J.B.C. & A. A.D S./Forms/C. 2118.

WAR DIARY or INTELLIGENCE SUMMARY

Army Form C. 2118

(Erase heading not required.)

Place	Date	Hour	Summary of Events and Information	Remarks and references to Appendices
	18.9.15		9/R	
NOEUX-L-M.	18.9.16	10.30 a.m.	Proceeded to Conference with A.D.M.S. XI Division. A wire party detailed to improve tramway from QUALITY STREET.	9.9.R.
NOEUX-L-M.	19.9.15	6 p.m.	Proceeded to MAZINGARBE and FOSSE N°7 to arrange bearer details as to their advanced dressing station.	9.9.R.
NOEUX-L-M.	20.9.15	6 p.m.	Capt. R.C. OZANNE LT. J.F. STEVEN and LT R. McLEAN with B Sect. Bearers proceeded to FOSSE N°7 de BETHUNE for duty at advanced dressing station. Billeted in Bulletin. 2 Buses leave at MAZINGARBE. Rev. A.H. BROUGHTON C.F. reported his disposition for duty at N°3 Stationary Hospital for duty.	9.9.R.
NOEUX-L-M.	21.9.15	10.30 a.m.	Proceeded to FOSSE N°7 and inspected arrangements made by Capt. R.C. OZANNE. On additional nurse to MAZINGARBE.	9.9.R.
NOEUX-L-M.	22.9.15	6 p.m.	3 new wheeled stretchers sent up to FOSSE 7. Nothing else in all.	9.9.R.
NOEUX-L-M.	23.9.15	12 noon	Ammunition wagon used to bring wounded in addition to present arrangements.	9.9.R.
NOEUX-L-M.	24.9.15	7 p.m.	Heavy gun firing. 2 wheeled stretchers with personnel on attack from B.R.C. Society Point Type 70517 (2 in all) Remainder of Bearers proceed to FOSSE N°7 at 7 p.m. From N°32 Stn. section attached to 63 for details from Infantry. D.D.M.S. to carpt docks the Atchurg Station Abby. 3 motor posts at ABBATOIR MAZINGARBE to present.	9.9.R.
NOEUX-L-M.	25.9.15	5 a.m.	Intense bombt Advance Proceeded to FOSSE N°7 and Saw Bearer Division at work. Wounded Stretchered ... by tramline. Motor ambulance to take wounded from PHILOSOPHE.	9.9.R.
		12 noon	Returned to advanced dressing Station. From Party at walking cases at MAZINGARBE placed under command. N.C. Dennis R.C.O. and directed them to the tramp station. A.S. Admissions from 9 a.m. to 12 noon. 145 (24 lying cases 121 sitting)	
		2 p.m.	Returned to FOSSE 7 found train under instruction to autour and ordered evacuation from FOSSE 7 to British Ambulance Train up additional stretchers.	
		9 p.m.	Re. 9 p.m. dut. from 12 noon to 9 p.m. 485 (89 lying & 396 sitting).	

1875 Wt. W593/826 1,000,000 4/15 J.B.C. & A. A.D.S.S./Forms/C. 2118.

WAR DIARY or INTELLIGENCE SUMMARY

Army Form C. 2118

Place	Date	Hour	Summary of Events and Information	Remarks and references to Appendices
NOEUX-L-M.	26.9.15	6 a.m.	Informed O. Comdg of all ArRT Sund cases of our patients RT Bornes and cases Received from 8 p.m. 1548. A.O.C. Arrived for Evacuation.	99R.
do.	do.	10 a.m.	Capt W.H. FORSYTH RAMC Became involved and required a change of under garment & warmed accommodation. Dut up BIGGINS AND Additional Blankets & found Rents.	99R.
do.	do.	12 noon	227 wounded received from 6 a.m. Rents are blanket with transport and hotpots & oxygen of inhalers & Blan. Evacuated Remaining 27 lying and 456 sitting. All available accommodation used up. Evacuation trains (8AII) Cap. emptied.	99R.
do.	do.	9 p.m.	488 received from 12 noon. Remaining 294 (lying 150 sitting 744) Evacuated. Cap. 7 O.I.E. 17 (ambulance Collected wounded Post A & B (London Field Ambulance.	99R.
NOEUX-L-M.	27.9.15	6 a.m.	Lying by all night. 367 received from 9 p.m. Remaining ((1031 i.e. lying 180 sitting 851) 116 lying Evacuated in Hospital Train. Married Bclin patients and have been kit. As officially is supplying troops to evacuate.	99R.
do.	do.	12 noon	298 received from 6 a.m. Have been able to evacuate 70 lying cases. Remaining lying 16 sitting 1056.	98R.
do.	do.	9 p.m.	Sir John French C in C Visited the Dressing Station and was pleased & express his approval.	
do.	do.		Evacuation to HDS CHAVRE and ambulance trains that afternoon. 285 evacuated. Remaining 771 (2 lying 769 sitting) Josse R. 17 ans Allarai wounded D. Burton. Right duty Taken on by C Section 58th Field Amb. (Capt. E.G.H. COWEN LT F.W. OVERHOLT LT W.A.H. BIRREL)	99R.
NOEUX-L-M	28.9.15	6 a.m.	No wounded Received during the night. 766 Remaining all sitting cases. Remov. & get the wounded evacuated by MAC and ambulance Train. AMA 819 Hr. Special goods up train.	
		3 pm	Firing Station clear of all wounded 36 Gas cases Remain for further treatment. Been Visited (Capt R.C. OZANNE LT J.F. STEVEN and LT R. McLEAN) rejoin. Us. TOPd admitted from 26.9.15 & 9 p.m. 27.9.15 2325	
		4 p.m.	C Section 58th Field Ambulance (Capt E.G.H. COWEN 2nd F.W. OVERHOLT LT W.A.H. BIRREL) rejoined their unit.	99R.
NOEUX-L-M	29.9.15	3.30 p.m	Remanent Non-Commissioned Officers and men Goe and Serve 11N in Hospital. Bore an Serve. Submitted list of names of officers N.C.O's and men to A.D.M.S. who deformed acts of gallantry and Devoted stout service during the Recent operations, list of names in appendix.	99R. Apps 1

WAR DIARY
or
INTELLIGENCE SUMMARY

Army Form C. 2118

Place	Date	Hour	Summary of Events and Information	Remarks and references to Appendices
NOEUX-L-M	30.9.15	10.30 pm	Orders received from A.D.M.S. to hand over buildings at A.D.M.S. 1st Division, 1st Field Ambulance held present Quarters (Oct 1st) to bivouac at HALLICOURT. Any sick remaining in Hospital to be transferred to 46th F.A.	J.A.R.
			To C.O. Bau.	

J.A. Ritchie Major
Commdg 47th Field Ambulance

WAR DIARY 47th Field Ambulance
or
INTELLIGENCE SUMMARY

Army Form C. 2118

Appendix I

Names of Officers, N.C.O.'s and men of 47th Field Ambulance brought to notice for gallantry and good service during the operations of Sept 25-27th

Captain WILLIAM HENRY FORSYTH R.A.M.C.
Captain RONALD CATHCART OZANNE R.A.M.C.
Lieut JOHN FRASER STEVEN R.A.M.C. (for gallantry near Loos & capturing 22 Germans)
Lieut. FRED DAVIS R.A.M.C.

No. 36299 Lancecorporal Serg.t McDOWAL J.
No. 30907 Staff Serg.t MARTIN R.R.
No. 31306. Sergeant LITTLEWOOD R.
No. 38867 Sergeant MONCRIEFF S.
No. 35903 Corporal LINDSAY W.J.
No. 52396 L/Corporal SMALL S.C.
No. 40218 L/Corporal SHEPHERD E. (for gallantry in LOOS on 26.9.15)
No. 32172 Pte BUTCHER E.G. (for gallantry near HILL 70 on 25.9.15)

A.S.C. M.T.
    No. M/2 27701 Sergeant BOWLER A.E.
A.S.C. H.T.
    No. T 17100 Acting S.S.M. COULSON A.

P.J. Austin Major.
Comdt. 47th Field Amb.

121/7517

15th Division

47th Field Amb:
Vol 3

Oct 15.

Oct 15

Army Form C. 2118

WAR DIARY
or
INTELLIGENCE SUMMARY 47th Field Ambulance.
(Erase heading not required.)

Instructions regarding War Diaries and Intelligence Summaries are contained in F. S. Regs., Part II. and the Staff Manual respectively. Title Pages will be prepared in manuscript.

Place	Date	Hour	Summary of Events and Information	Remarks and references to Appendices
NOEUX-L-M	1.10.15	10.30 a.m	Left NOEUX-LES-MINES and marched to HAILLICOURT arriving 11.40. Bivouacked in a field.	
HAILLICOURT	2.10.15	12 a.m.	Remained in bivouac. Weather fine. Tents drilled for reception of sick at the Sanitate buildings acquired	
HAILLICOURT	3.10.15	10.20 a.m.	Received orders to proceed with 46th & 48th Fd Ambces to LILLERS. Left at 12.10 p.m. and arrived at LILLERS 4.30 p.m. B I C Sections in billets. A Section in bivouac.	
LILLERS	4.10.15	12 noon	Remained in LILLERS. A few sick sent to C. C. S.	
LILLERS	5.10.15	12 noon	Further arrangements made from Army LILLERS to take on the form of Plan 9 Vs H727 An officer as a Admin Road.	
LILLERS	6.10.15	12 noon	Since arrival the men have been pranced and before breakfast a route march after, and protection drill in the afternoon. A few men of B Section influenza & diarrhoea (mild cases) have remained in billets	
LILLERS	7.10.15	12 noon	AMS the Division R A have placed in charge of Allentown Staned. Capt. H. the litter bearer to begin training has been handed into Advanced Dressing St. 51/87	
LILLERS	8.10.15	12 noon	Remained at LILLERS. Lt. J.F. STEVEN attached Reserve dressing station 61.7/camion 16 February during the absence of Lt. POWELL on leave.	
LILLERS	9.10.15	12 noon	Section funds rate a funeral awake of sick all day T.	
LILLERS	10.10.15	6 p.m.	Lt. R.H. BONNYCASTLE attached Company Field care of 8th K.O.S.B during the absence of Lt. JACKSON on leave. Submitted confidential report on Q. M. S. McDONALD for promotion to Warrant Rank and upon in test of Sgt Pestrange being acted Revision form of litter bearers.	
LILLERS	11.10.15	12 noon	A.D.M.S. XV Division inspected our Camp Billets and Expense Motor-Rd Stace.	

Army Form C. 2118

47th Field Ambulance

WAR DIARY
or
INTELLIGENCE SUMMARY
(Erase heading not required.)

Instructions regarding War Diaries and Intelligence Summaries are contained in F. S. Regs., Part II. and the Staff Manual respectively. Title Pages will be prepared in manuscript.

Place	Date	Hour	Summary of Events and Information	Remarks and references to Appendices
LILLERS	12.10.15	11.45 a.m.	Orders received for Brigade to billet in MARLES-LES-MINES the ALLOUAGNE and LOZINGHEM. Ambulance to be in Readiness to move forward to LOZINGHEM at 5.30 p.m.	
	do.	2 p.m.	Left LILLERS and billets at LOZINGHEM	
LOZINGHEM	13.10.15	12 noon	Remained in billets at LOZINGHEM	
LOZINGHEM	14.10.15	12 noon	Remained at LOZINGHEM	
LOZINGHEM	15.10.15	10 a.m.	Marched from LOZINGHEM to LABEUVRIERE and left one officer and Ptr non Officer bearers for sick N.C.Os & men as billets for Ambulance	
LABEUVRIERE	16.10.15	11.45 p.m.	Orders received from A.D.M.S. to proceed to HAILLICOURT. N Sec & Billets	
LABEUVRIERE	16.10.15	12 p.m.	Left LABEUVRIERE and Arrived at HAILLICOURT	
HAILLICOURT	16.10.15	10.30 p.m.	Arrived at HAILLICOURT. R & in billets. R.A.M.C. personnel in tents.	
HAILLICOURT	17.10.15	12 noon	Remained at HAILLICOURT. In field ambulance as before. Rear Section in billets/tent/ownership	
HAILLICOURT	18.10.15	12 noon	Remained at HAILLICOURT	
HAILLICOURT	19.10.15	12 noon	Remained at HAILLICOURT	
HAILLICOURT	20.10.15	12 noon	Remained at HAILLICOURT	
HAILLICOURT	21.10.15	8.30 a.m.	Received orders from A.D.M.S. to proceed to NOEUX-LES-MINES. 1 Section to proceed to NUNNERY PHILOSOPHE	
			Left HAILLICOURT at 1 p.m.	
NOEUX-LES-MINES	21.10.15	2.15 p.m.	Arrived at NOEUX-LES-MINES and left one Section which we had previously occupied from 6th (LONDON) Field Ambulance. A.T.C. Received the Convoy in train destined Station. 1 B Section (Capt R.C. OZANNE Lt J.R. STEVEN and Lt R. M'LEAN) Take on at PHILOSOPHE from 6th Field Ambulance. R.G.A.C. personnel / A.S.C. M.T. at train destined Station and in billets. A.S.C. M.T. Car broken down 4. All personnel of B. Sectn. in billets at PHILOSOPHE	

WAR DIARY 47th Field Ambulance

Army Form C. 2118

Place	Date	Hour	Summary of Events and Information	Remarks and references to Appendices
NOEUX-LES-MINES	22.10.15	11 a.m.	Proceeded to NUNNERY PHILOSOPHE and inspected arrangements made by O.C. B Section. Good accommodation, patients few, and all apparently cheerful.	
NOEUX-L-M	23.10.15	12 noon	Men had hearty repast. Cleaned out and billeting is being well carried on by Patients. Reps and temp taken of returns of wounded at Nunnery and B Section	
NOEUX-L-M	24.10.15	12 noon	Weather very cold and wet. This venue in respect was returned by French authorities at school quarters.	
NOEUX-L-M	25.10.15	12 noon	Instrument van taken to Tatinghem ... Hall for greater comfort of patients. Lt. will accommodate 100 being carried. Lt. R. H. BONNYCASTLE returned from duty with 2nd B.Q. RY. 13. Lt. R. MCLEAN to leave, returned to camp aide	
NOEUX-L-M	26.10.15	12 noon	British convoy all good and met. Visited PHILOSOPHE and submitted dispatches for same	
			Lt. Col: P Adjutant's Main Dressing Stations to A.D.M.S.	
NOEUX-L-M	27.10.15	12 noon	Title van Chap. 9. Prisoners Ball Mountebay.	
NOEUX-L-M	28.10.15	12.15 am	1 Officer & 20 men proceeded to Tatinghem in Royal Rovers (Lt J.V.BROWN in Command). Capt. G.F. CLIFTON assumed command and acted of 11th A.V.S. posts from today.	
NOEUX-L-M	29.10.15	12 noon	A number of accidental & self-inflicted wounds in Hospital. Operation unit of A.D.M.S. Lt A.R. ROCHE Royal. Attached temporarily and posted to B Section.	
NOEUX-L-M	30.10.15	12 noon	Few cases treated but cases seen.	
NOEUX-L-M	31.10.15	12 noon	Few cases and not	

To A.G.
Base.

J.J. Ritchie, Major.
Comdg. 47th Field Ambulance.

WAR DIARY
INTELLIGENCE SUMMARY

Army Form C. 2118

47th Field Ambulance

Place	Date	Hour	Summary of Events and Information	Remarks and references to Appendices
NOEUX-LES-MINES	1.11.15	10 a.m.	Colonel Wallace A.M.S. inspected the Main Dressing Station & Relief being met.	
NOEUX-L-M	2.11.15/12 a.m.		Had not arrived. Officer on leave to England from 3.11.15 to 11.11.15	
NOEUX-L-M	3.11.15		Handed over command to Capt W.H. FORSYTH RAMC. J.P. Ritz—	
do	4.11.15		Took over from Major Ritzla. Argument between ADMS & Divisional Armoury Station truce. Lancing Regt Col Ramsay —	
do			Colonel Ramsay postus & 25th Division noticed by Col. C.E. Pollock as ADMS. Great increase in the number of sick admitted — chiefly rheumatism & catarrhs. Weather cold but fine.	
do	5.11.15	11 a.m.	The new ADMS (Lt Col C.E. POLLOCK) inspected the hospital. A few cases of Trench feet — these are the first we have had this winter.	
do	6.11.15		Weather most mild but fine.	
do	7.11.15	2.45pm	The O/C XV Div Train inspected the horse lines today, found everything satisfactory.	
do	8.11.15	4.45pm	Sgt Major ARUNDEL transferred to ETAPLES for duty. Many cases of Trench feet admitted — most of a slight nature	
do	9.11.15	12.30pm	D.D.M.S. div Corps visited the hospital. A few cases of Trench Feet. Re orders about attending the men's feet prior to going to the trenches are not being carried out. He is going to report this to the Corps Commander. I reported it to A.D.M.S. The nearest and at present is at ARQUES Divisional Baths — There is a great scarcity of Dentists. There is one at present in at ARQUES about 35 kilometres from us. Divisional Baths have taken over from us by the 46th Field Ambulance.	

Army Form C. 2118

47th Field Ambulance

WAR DIARY
or
INTELLIGENCE SUMMARY
(Erase heading not required.)

Instructions regarding War Diaries and Intelligence Summaries are contained in F. S. Regs., Part II. and the Staff Manual respectively. Title Pages will be prepared in manuscript.

Place	Date	Hour	Summary of Events and Information	Remarks and references to Appendices
NOEUX-LES-MINES	10.11.15		Lt. R. McLean assumed medical charge of the 72nd Bde R.F.A. during the absence of Lt. Proctor on leave.	
do	11.11.15		Weather very wet. Pouring most of the day	
do	12.11.15		Cold & wet & dull	
do	13.11.15		Captain D.J. Wallace assumed medical charge of the 7th K.S.L.R. during absence of Lieut M.O. on leave. Transfer on ambulance to charge in T.T. Ritchie. Visiting K. Cpt Lame	
do	15.11.15	9 am	Returned from leave 163my and BSR men from Capt W.H. FORSYTH.	
NIEUX-L-M.	14.11.15	12 noon	Cases of trench feet Continue to arrive. Weather damp cold and wet.	
NOEUX-LES-MINES	15.11.15	12 noon	Strength & report. Cases of trench feet still coming in.	
do	16.11.15	12 noon	Duke B.O.R. from Windles and from NOEUX & be admitted All command M to be sent to 46th Field Ambulance (A.D.M.S. XI Division)	
do	17.11.15	12 noon	Proceeded to PHILOSOPHE to inspect Advanced Dressing Station.	
do	18.11.15	12 noon	Capt W.H. FORSYTH R.A.M.C. proceeded on leave to UK.	
do	19.11.15	12 noon	Strength & report. Weather cold but no rain.	
do	20.11.15	12 noon	Cases of 'trench feet' continue to arrive. Chain Park. Trenches of Johns etc (being M) now being attended to	
do	21.11.15	12 noon	Weather still comparatively dry but very cold.	

WAR DIARY
or
INTELLIGENCE SUMMARY

Army Form C. 2118

47th Field Ambulance

(Erase heading not required.)

Place	Date	Hour	Summary of Events and Information	Remarks and references to Appendices
NOEUX-LES-MINES	22.11.15	11 a.m.	Orders received from A.D.M.S. to send Subaltern & Orderly VERMELLES to take over from 37th Field Ambulance	
do.	23.11.15	11 a.m.	2 Officers (Capts. R.O. OZANNE & 2nd Lt. R.P. McLEAN) & 8 O.R's to relieve VERMELLES to see arrangements of 37th Field Ambulance for evacuation	
do.	24.11.15	9 a.m.	2 Person establishment in an command of Capt. R.O. OZANNE posted to BREWERY VERMELLES. Nunnery Philosophe have been a portion of 45th Field Ambulance. 1st Lieut 2 Aid Posts with a Dressing only in each Hq. at QUARRY CHARING CROSS and EARTH. Wounded evacuated to Brewery at VERMELLES. Lt. J.F. STEVEN joined on loan to Scotland today	
do.	25.11.15		Capt. G.F. CLIFTON returned from leave today	
do.	26.11.15		QUARRY dug out has been sandbagged & all girders are now Supported to Charing Cross of Post.	
do.	27.11.15		Lieut SMITH to Capt. W.H. FORSYTH has been detached to 11.12.15	
do.	28.11.15		In morning duties of Trench feet lately briefly treated & trench feet. Clean footgear	
do.	29.11.15		Very heavy rain today. 2 unit to R.S.L. Lamp at thirty wheelworks on not coming in.	
do.	30.11.15		2 units of importance to R.S.L. One has wounded coming in.	

J.F. Peters Major.
Comdg. 47th Field Ambulance

47th Fa.
fol: 4

121/7678

15th Division

Nov 15.

Nov 1915

47th R.F.A.
Vol: 5

121/7231

1/5th R.E.

Dec. 1915

WAR DIARY or INTELLIGENCE SUMMARY

Army Form C. 2118

47th Field Ambulance

(Erase heading not required.)

Instructions regarding War Diaries and Intelligence Summaries are contained in F.S. Regs., Part II. and the Staff Manual respectively. Title Pages will be prepared in manuscript.

Place	Date	Hour	Summary of Events and Information	Remarks and references to Appendices
NOEUX-LES-MINES	1.12.15	12 noon	Weather much colder.	
do.	2.12.15	12 noon	Nothing of importance to note.	
do.	3.12.15	12 noon	Weather very wet	
do.	4.12.15	12 noon	Two motor ambulance Staff Cars & then carriages received one for 46th F.A. & one for an advanced dressing station	
do.	5.12.15	12 noon	An H.E. Shell burst in yard of Advanced Dressing Station Estaires. 2 men M.T. & S.C. & 1 horse but fortunately principal	
do.	6.12.15	12 noon	[illegible] Did not not [illegible] cases 9 hands feet our Chemin Rugg in Smithers & officer. 1. A bullets effect	
do.	7.12.15	12 noon	Nothing of importance.	
do.	8.12.15	12 noon	Nothing of importance.	
do.	9.12.15	12.15 p.m.	D.D.M.S. IIe Corps & Officer Admin Dressing Station.	
do.	10.12.15		Orders received from A.D.M.S. IIe Corps that Ambulance will proceed at an early date to AUCHEL.	
do.	11.12.15	10.30 a.m.	O.C. 5th London Field Ambulance visited the dressing station with a view to taking over. Proceeded to VERMELLES with him & Captain Preston of dressing station with an view & officer of R.A.P. Aid Posts. 1 Officer & 3 N.C.O. of 5th (LONDON) Field Ambulance attached to Advanced Dressing Station	
do.	do.	2 p.m.	Proceeded to AUCHEL for the MAIRIE and saw billets.	
do.	12.12.15	4 p.m.	C Section Bearers with drawn from VERMELLES on relief by bearers of 5th (LONDON) F.A.	

Army Form C. 2118

47th Field Amb Balance

WAR DIARY
or
INTELLIGENCE SUMMARY
(Erase heading not required.)

Instructions regarding War Diaries and Intelligence Summaries are contained in F. S. Regs, Part II. and the Staff Manual respectively. Title Pages will be prepared in manuscript.

Place	Date	Hour	Summary of Events and Information	Remarks and references to Appendices
NOEUX-L-M	13.12.15	8.20 a.m.	Transport left for AUCHEL under command of Capt. G.F. CLIFTON via VAUDRICOURT PLACE BRUAY-MARLES	
"	"	9.30	Remainder of personnel (Capt. R.C. OZANNE Lt. J.F. STEVEN and Lt. R. McLEAN) evacuated from VERMELLES	
"	"	12 n.n.	All Rank & personal baggage entrained at NOEUX (m LILLERS (arriving at 1.15 pm.) train is in charge Quarter Bearers of AUCHEL. Handed over Bell Scharf to O.C. 6th LONDON Field Ambulance.	
AUCHEL	"	2.45 pm	Arrived at AUCHEL. Took over Le MAIRIE as a hospital. B. VC section billeted in the MAIRIE. A Section in Lowes Leon, G.S.C. M.T. in Lowes. H.T. A.S.C. also billeted. All horses in stable. Took over 20 beds from 5th (LONDON) F.A. but little else on hand both as from NOEUX. breakfast, fires.	
AUCHEL	14.12.15	12 n.n.	1st of 5 Horse Lines at RAIMBERT and AUCHEL. Training classes starting from Divisional Laundry inspected beds which are fitted up. No Divisional known receipts. Sure are Shower baths in Auberge 42 at Raimbert	
AUCHEL	15.12.15	9 a.m.	Ambulance at RAIMBERT arranged with 46th Div. yes as to hours & allotment of baths.	
AUCHEL	16.12.15	12 n.n.	Shower Branches of block admitted. Breakfast first Flag.	
AUCHEL	17.12.15	12 n.n.	Findings a working shaft for R.E. B Section detailed for this.	
AUCHEL	18.12.15	9 a.m.	Commenced billeting at RAIMBERT	
AUCHEL	19.12.15	8 p.m.	Sure few billets Sand brethren Broad Brelean.	
AUCHEL	20.12.15	12 n.n.	Seinal cases of Pre MeV admitted today. One Orderly O fficious but duties formed to be Reglebet.	
AUCHEL	21.12.15	12 n.n.	All Camps & arteries are fee punctuated & Recovery Return Carried out.	
AUCHEL	22.12.15	12 n.n.	Nothing of importance to note. Capt. R.C. OZANNE granted leave to England.	

Army Form C. 2118

WAR DIARY
or
INTELLIGENCE SUMMARY

47th Field Ambulance

(Erase heading not required.)

Instructions regarding War Diaries and Intelligence Summaries are contained in F. S. Regs., Part II. and the Staff Manual respectively. Title Pages will be prepared in manuscript.

Place	Date	Hour	Summary of Events and Information	Remarks and references to Appendices
AUCHEL	23.12.15	12 noon	Weather continues cold and wet.	
AUCHEL	24.12.15	12 noon	Small numbers of sick mostly slight. Night 7 slight & return.	
AUCHEL	25.12.15	12 noon	Xmas Day.	
AUCHEL	26.12.15	12 noon	Sick up of no importance to W.L.I.	
AUCHEL	27.12.15	12 noon	Sick up of no importance to unit.	
AUCHEL	28.12.15	12 noon	Sick etc. being met and cold.	
AUCHEL	29.12.15	11 a.m.	All lines inspected by A.D.M.S. and inspected will Mattein.	
AUCHEL	30.12.15	12 noon	27 pairs of boots handed into stores in our dresser. All sent forward.	
AUCHEL	31.12.15	9 a.m. 12 noon	Strained small parts & Tuka front in Westrip scheme with A.D.M.S. Mules and wagons inspected by O.C. Train. All in good condition.	

J.J. Rutter Major.
O.C. 47th Field Ambulance

15

47th F.A.
Vol. 6

15th Div
F/114/11

Jan 1916

Army Form C. 2118

WAR DIARY
or
INTELLIGENCE SUMMARY

47th Field Ambulance

(Erase heading not required.)

Instructions regarding War Diaries and Intelligence Summaries are contained in F.S. Regs, Part II. and the Staff Manual respectively. Title Pages will be prepared in manuscript.

Place	Date	Hour	Summary of Events and Information	Remarks and references to Appendices
AUCHEL	1.1.16	12 noon	Lt. R.H. BONNYCASTLE and J.V. BROWN proceeded on leave to UK.	
AUCHEL	2.1.16	12 noon	D.D.M.S. 4th Corps inspected Hospital Filter.	
AUCHEL	3.1.16	12 noon	A.D.M.S. IV Division inspected the Hospital Filter.	
AUCHEL	4.1.16		Completed arrangements for postponing the Divisional Baths. 1 Officer, 15 men and 2 Motor Ambulances will remain at AUCHEL.	
AUCHEL	5.1.16	9.20 a.m.	The AUCHEL Div. Bn. marched to FERFAY—AMES—LIERES—AUCHY AU BOIS—COHEM & FLECHINELLE from D pt to 46th and 13th Amb. Locale fine and roads good. Trans. font great well.	
FLECHINELLE	do.	7 pm	Arrived in FLECHINELLE. All ranks treated in Baths. All very comfortable.	
FLECHINELLE	6.1.16	9 am	Proceeded on Divisional Route Marching w/ 141st Bde & 1st Div Engrst. Rain falling. Picadilly. Returned to billets 2 pm.	
FLECHINELLE	7.1.16	10.20	Marched to CUHEM—LIGNY-LES-AIRE—AUCHY-AU-BOIS—CAUCHY-A-LA-TOUR & Heads of AUCHEL.	
AUCHEL	8.1.16	12 noon	A. Bn. 9 other 8 other ranks in Hospital. Camp D. Scabies appeared to be due to trip to Divisional.	
AUCHEL	9.1.16		Lt. R.H. BONNYCASTLE and J.V. BROWN returned from leave to UK. Ordinance work carried out. Offices to follow up about 9.15 Division	
AUCHEL	10.1.16	2 pm	Proceeded to NOEUX-LES-MINES to arrange with O.C. 141st Fld Ambulance as to Taking over billeting their hatching staff and to be in MAIRIE and 2 cots. Old Filter. Commenced clothing station at PHILOSOPHE and LOOS. 1 Private to the Production at QUALITY STREET	
AUCHEL	11.1.16	2.0 p.m.	Lt. R. McLEAN with 3 N.C.O's proceeded to PHILOSOPHE to Take over Sanitary duties	
AUCHEL	12.1.16 9 a.m.		2 Mtr. Ambulance 1 officer 1 G.S. Wagon 1 Interior and 8 men to PHILOSOPHE	
do		2 pm	Capt. G.F. CLIFTON and 25 other ranks proceeded to PHILOSOPHE. 2 men to Commercen there for duty	

1875 Wt. W593/826 1,000,000 4/15 J.B.C. & A. A.D.S.S./Forms/C. 2118.

WAR DIARY or INTELLIGENCE SUMMARY

Army Form C. 2118

47th Field Ambulance

Place	Date	Hour	Summary of Events and Information	Remarks and references to Appendices
ABEELE	13.1.16	7.30 a.m.	Remainder of Unit (3 Officers & 103 Other Ranks) proceeded to LILLERS by route march & entrained for B. & Maine Gavaere. Regiment his Officers & the first contingent of the ambulance which is composed of Hotel-Dieu-Vierge. Transport proceeded by road NOEUX-LES-MINES via MARLES and LE TOUCHIN	
NOEUX-LES-MINES	do	6 a.m. do 11 a.m.	Arrived at NOEUX and took over the MAIRIE and the Soeur des Ecoles from No 10 Field Ambulance. Also Accommodation in billets. Horses in temporary stables. About 50 sick taken over from 141st F.A. All our patient's were carried with us. Just our food building and south Accommodate about 200. Visited advanced dressing station at BREWERY PHILOSOPHE, our hour detachments have had Accommodation line & cellars for about 200. Our liaison with infantry supports in keep at artillery and Post QUALITY STREET and 1 RCO and six hrs at LOOS Water factor. Are relieved every 24 hours.	
NOEUX-LES-MINES	14.1.16	5 p.m.	Visited LOOS to see method of evacuation. Good relays have been established and are attended at all events. 2nd Car & horse wagons are used to evacuate. Roads very bad. Can evacuate wounded at FORT GLATZ. Visited Depot Central aid Posts	
"	"	10 p.m.		
NIEUX-LES-MINES	15.1.16	12 Noon	Following knowns and certain of have been posted to effect: - LT J.F. STEVEN R.A.M.C. T.C. To be a lieutenant of the. Steven per Promotion :— LT J.F. STEVEN R.A.M.C. T.C. To receive Lt Rank from 16.6.9 per of list :— LT& Qr.Mr F. DAVIS R.A.M.C. To receive Lt from 15.6.9 per :— Hon. Lieut Ramc Hon. Lt/Captain Ramc E. SHEPHERD Ramc. Pte E. G. BUTCHER Ramc (promoted) Sgt has served with unit	

1875 Wt. W593/826 1,000,000 4/15 J.B.C. & A. A.D.S.S./Forms/C. 2118.

Army Form C. 2118

WAR DIARY
or
INTELLIGENCE SUMMARY 47th Field Ambulance
(Erase heading not required.)

Instructions regarding War Diaries and Intelligence Summaries are contained in F. S. Regs., Part II. and the Staff Manual respectively. Title Pages will be prepared in manuscript.

Place	Date	Hour	Summary of Events and Information	Remarks and references to Appendices
NOEUX-LES-MINES	16.1.16	12 noon	1st and 2nd receiving huts ready & started but later received an order all sections C. Smith & cases of scabies until further orders	
NOEUX-LES-MINES	17.1.16		Proceeded at Advanced Dressing Station at PHILOSOPHE Lieut. L. MASSIAH RENNIE. Opened May for Company duty.	
NOEUX-LES-MINES	18.1.16		Capt. & B[revet]-Major R.C. OZANNE relieves LT J.F. STEVEN D.S.O. in Medical Charge of School GOSNAY	
NOEUX-LES-MINES	19.1.16		1 Officer & 6 Other Ranks 111th Field Ambulance attached for instruction at A.D.S. PHILOSOPHE	
NOEUX-LES-MINES	20.1.16		1 Officer to remain at LOOS for 24 hours.	
NOEUX-LES-MINES	21.1.16		Nothing of importance to report	
NOEUX-LES-MINES	22.1.16		Nothing of importance to report	
NOEUX-LES-MINES	23.1.16	4 hrs	C. Pectral (Bронскi Fibrillation) Relieved B Section. Bennis at PHILOSOPHE Goal.	

Army Form C. 2118

WAR DIARY
or
INTELLIGENCE SUMMARY

(Erase heading not required.)

47th Field Ambulance

Instructions regarding War Diaries and Intelligence Summaries are contained in F. S. Regs., Part II. and the Staff Manual respectively. Title Pages will be prepared in manuscript.

Place	Date	Hour	Summary of Events and Information	Remarks and references to Appendices
NOEUX LES MINES	24.1.16		Lieut R. McLEAN proceeds on leave to England.	
NOEUX-LES -MINES	25.1.16		1 Officer & 12 Other Ranks 111th Field Ambce attached for instruction at Advanced Dressing Station	
NOEUX-LES -MINES	26.1.16		Visited LOOS and interviewed with Capt Rose R.A.M.C. R.M.O. D.A.D.M.S. and Capt Sams scavenging.	
NOEUX-LES -MINES	27.1.16	7.30p.m	Large draft of wounded in LOOS. Proceeded to LOOS to supervise clearing of same. Sent up additional bearer party of two additional bearers. Received a draft of 1 Sergt & 9 men. And linen wagons.	
NOEUX-LES -MINES	28.1.16	12 a.m	Visited a Gas Casualties number of wounded from LOOS, all probably intoxicated. A.M.S received from A.D.M.S. 15th Division to vacate MAIRIE and take over STATE SCHOOL from 111th F.A.	
NOEUX-LES MINES	29.1.16	9a.m	Appointed Temporary Lt Stuart Stiles in command of 47th Field Ambulance. Moved into STATE SCHOOL today.	
NOEUX-LES -MINES	30.1.16		Inspection & maintenance of Motor Ambulances	
NOEUX-LES -MINES	31.1.16		Instructions to Lieut. Pte F.J. DAVIES R.A.M.C. detailed to proceed to G.H.Q. for duty in office of D.G. M.S.	

J.E. Ritchie Lt Colonel
Commdg 47th Field Ambulance

Feb. } 1916.
Mar } 41st Field Ambulance

Programme of Training — Tent Division — Rest Period

Hour	1st day	2nd day	3rd day	4th day	5th day	6th day	7th day	8th day	9th day
11am to 12noon	Lecture on Fractures with brief anatomical details. Signs & appearance.	2nd Lecture on Fractures.	3rd Lecture on Fractures.	Arrest of Haemorrhage. Treatment of wounds.	2nd Lecture on Treatment of wounds. Field treatment of Abdomen.	Lecture on the Care of Surgical instruments, their sterilization & preservation.	2nd Lecture on preceding subject.	Treatment of Gas poisoning and shock.	Lecture on Treatment of Scabies & Pediculosi.
2–4pm	Regional revision of bandaging. Preparation of splints.	Preparation and application of various splints. Moving & carrying injured. Stretcher dept. retained members.	Continuation of preceding. Demonstration of Field fractures.	Application of Tourniquets. Bandaging. Description of common wound antiseptics.	Fomentation. Sterilization of hands, Instruments and dressings.	Demonstration of Field Medical & Surgical Panniers.	Lidocaine an improvised "Theatre" — lay out equipment etc.	Demonstration of Oxygen Cylinders. Artificial respiration.	Case of wounds, observation & records of pulse, temperature & administration of medicines.
	×		×	×			×	×	
2–4 from to	Squad & stretcher drill	Moving & carrying injured, stretcher dept. retained members	Wagon drill	Wagon drill	Loading and unloading e.g. wagons Hundreds	Care and use of field & lantern.	First Field Dressings & shell dressings & management of clothes.	Artificial Respiration & use of oxygen.	Improvising splints. Emergency arrest of Haemorrhage.

Sanitary Orderlies will be trained in the construction of Latrines, Urinals, Incinerators, Greasetraps, Water Orderlies in the care & management of Water cart.
Physical drill from 6.30 to 7am daily
Route march for bearers as frequently as possible (10 to 12 daily)
× Bearers will also attend these lectures.
Instruction to 6 Officers on hilling hour & Hospital administration.

47ᵗʰ F. a.
vol: 7

Army Form C. 2118

WAR DIARY
or
INTELLIGENCE SUMMARY
(Erase heading not required.)

47th Field Ambulance

Instructions regarding War Diaries and Intelligence Summaries are contained in F. S. Regs., Part II. and the Staff Manual respectively. Title Pages will be prepared in manuscript.

Place	Date	Hour	Summary of Events and Information	Remarks and references to Appendices
NOEUX-LES- MINES	1.2.16		Weather cold and wet. Only small numbers of sick + wounded being dealt with	
NOEUX-LES- MINES	2.2.16		Weather continues to be very inclement. Dressing of importance to note.	
NOEUX-LES- MINES	3.2.16		Orders received at 10.30 to proceed with Operations to New Railway line into LOOS.	
NOEUX-LES- MINES	4.2.16		Received reinforcements (7 men)/Military. Lieut. Rev. Watkins C.F. proceeds to duty with 9/B'LackWatch. Capt. R. Silcock R.AM.C. appointed to duty for day.	
NOEUX-LES- MINES	5.2.16	10 a.m	Lieut. G. F. STEVEN R.A.M.C. assumed temporary medical charge of 71st Bde R.F.A. Our patient sick is being cared for.	
NOEUX-LES- MINES	6.2.16		Nothing of importance to note. Because we being stationed in huts proper careful inspection and defence against gas & enemy attack.	
NUEUX-LES- MINES	7.2.16		Styles number on and being received. Inspection of Royal Aid Posts proceeded on attack.	
NOEUX-LES- MINES	8.2.16		Capt W. S. WALLACE RAMC on Ammunition Store and Capt. CLIFTON proceeded on leave. Lieut. S.C. MANSHAM proceeds to BOULOGNE for duty.	
NOEUX-LES- MINES	9.2.16		Nothing of importance to note. Capt CLIFTON + Capt SILCOCK proceeded on leave	

Army Form C. 2118

WAR DIARY
or
INTELLIGENCE SUMMARY 47 in Field Ambulance
(Erase heading not required.)

Instructions regarding War Diaries and Intelligence Summaries are contained in F. S. Regs, Part II. and the Staff Manual respectively. Title Pages will be prepared in manuscript.

Place	Date	Hour	Summary of Events and Information	Remarks and references to Appendices
NOEUX-LES-MINES	10.2.16		Capt. W.H. FORSYTH R.A.M.C. rejoined from leave France.	
NOEUX-LES-MINES	11.2.16		Lecture of importance to R.M.O. Requested A.D.M.S. PHILOSOPHE with reference to Deficiencies in Field Ambulance Equipment at Front.	
NOEUX-LES-MINES	12.2.16		The motor Reserve Personnel is transferred from unit. 1914 Infantry Equipment. 1882 (Indian Equipment) returned to R.T.O.	
NOEUX-LES-MINES	13.2.16		2 Lieut of R.A.C. Army Service Corps retd. from L.O.S.	
NOEUX-LES-MINES	14.2.16		3 men admitted to Hospital. No case of slow returned for more than seven days.	
NOEUX-LES-MINES	15.2.16		Group of R.A.T.C. field Amb and arranged to hand in Extensive Allocation Posn at FORT GLATZ included 9. At Quatorze N.-N.E. comm of L.O.S. This will be more convenient as old Comm.'d Postured beyond transport.	
NOEUX-LES-MINES	16.2.16		Weather being hot and roads very muddy.	
NOEUX-LES-MINES	17.2.16		Lt. J.F. STEVEN D.S.O. proceeds on a fortnight's leave today (Received 17 inst.) Capt. CLIFTON and Capt. SILCOCK returned from leave.	
NOEUX-LES-MINES	18.2.16		Capt. R. SILCOCK transferred permanently to 1/15 F.A. for duty (A.D.M.S. 15th Divn) Capt. E.A. LUMLEY reported for duty having exchanged with Lt. McLEAN from ETAPLES	
NOEUX-LES-MINES	19.2.16		Lieut. J.F. RYAN reported for duty having exchanged with Lt. J.F. STEVEN Lieut. J.F. RYAN has come from 9th London C.C. Sta. Lieut. R. McLEAN posted at ETAPLES 26th Reserve Park A.S.C.	

Army Form C. 2118

WAR DIARY
or
INTELLIGENCE SUMMARY 47 in Field Ambulance
(Erase heading not required.)

Instructions regarding War Diaries and Intelligence Summaries are contained in F. S. Regs., Part II. and the Staff Manual respectively. Title Pages will be prepared in manuscript.

Place	Date	Hour	Summary of Events and Information	Remarks and references to Appendices
	20.2.16			
NOEUX-LES-MINES	20.2.16		Weather fine & cold & pleasant. Pte NEWMAN Reuben sentenced to 60 days F.P.R. 80 by F.G.C.M. Insubordinate language to an N.C.O.	
NOEUX-LES-MINES	21.2.16		Routine to date	
NOEUX-LES-MINES	22.2.16		Lieut. J.F. RYAN proceeds to GUISNAY to attend temporary Medical Camp of 15th Division School. D.D.M.S. conferred with A.D.M.S. 15th Division Field Train dressing Station.	
NOEUX-LES-MINES	23.2.16		Weather very wet snow and sleet first. Six admissions to hospital in Rate Beng tour.	
NOEUX-LES-MINES	24.2.16		Weather continues very wet snow storm continues with wind & frost.	
NOEUX-LES-MINES	25.2.16		Still very cold weather. Snow for back and deep. Rev P Winterbourne to H.Q. United PHILOSOPHE to inspect Bearer Sub division.	
NOEUX-LES-MINES	26.2.16		Lieut. A.C. STURDY R.A.M.C. attached this arrival today from No. 22 C.C.S. in relief of Capt. B. Urwyn R.C. OZANNE British Adamant No. Paris Station & Reg'l And Posts hobbs with A.D.M.S. 15th Division	
NOEUX-LES-MINES	27.2.16		Capt. + B' Major R.C. OZANNE is still doing temporary duty with 70th B.H.R.F.A. he will remain under his return to Lieut TAYLOR R.A.M.C when he proceeds to No. 22 C.C.S. for duty.	

1875 Wt. W593/886 1,000,000 4/15 J.B.C. & A. A.D.S.S./Forms/C. 2118.

WAR DIARY
or
INTELLIGENCE SUMMARY 47th Field Ambulance

Army Form C. 2118

(Erase heading not required.)

Instructions regarding War Diaries and Intelligence Summaries are contained in F. S. Regs., Part II. and the Staff Manual respectively. Title Pages will be prepared in manuscript.

Place	Date	Hour	Summary of Events and Information	Remarks and references to Appendices
NOEUX-LES-MINES	28.2.16		Section has been instructed & a return in progress.	
NOEUX-LES-MINES	29.2.16		Present distribution of the unit is:- 1 Bearer Subdivision at PHILOSOPHE relieved every 10 days. 6 men with 1 R.C.O. at LOOS relieved every 24 hours. 1 Officer with LOOS relieved every 24 hours. 2 Officers at PHILOSOPHE. There are permanent Bearer Officers. Remainder of unit at NOEUX-LES-MINES. Less 1 Officer at COSNAY and 1 Officer in late 70th B4R 2 G. N.22 C.C.S. Capt. 13th Major R.C. OZANNE proceeded to late for duty with 70th B4R #2 G. One is present in details see appendix	

P.P. Roche Lt.C.
O.C. 47th Field Ambulance

47 Field
amb
Vol 8

Army Form C. 2118

47th Field Ambulance

WAR DIARY
or
INTELLIGENCE SUMMARY

(Erase heading not required.)

Instructions regarding War Diaries and Intelligence Summaries are contained in F. S. Regs., Part II. and the Staff Manual respectively. Title Pages will be prepared in manuscript.

Place	Date	Hour	Summary of Events and Information	Remarks and references to Appendices
NOEUX-LES-MINES	1.3.16.		Weather very cold. Capt. WALLACE is commandt. B. Station vice Busti Major OZANNE	
NOEUX-L-M.	2.3.16.		Two hours in hospital of 1st Army Corps from Ethane.	
NOEUX-L-M.	3.3.16.		D.D.M.S. 1st Corps inspected Rum + Adjutanas Meeting of Lins Officer	
NOEUX-L-M.	4.3.16.		Cold windy weather. Will huns and front. Sure cases of Trench Feet. Capt. J.F. STEVEN D.S.O. returned from leave today appointed to 1/2 London C.C.S. for duty.	
NOEUX-L-M	5.3.16.		Two Puxer weather continues. 5 ck in Hosp.l. 3D. 1 evacuated.	
NOEUX-L-M.	6.3.16.		Weather very cold. 3 cases of Trench Feet. 40 in Hospital. On arrival French Publicists reports his departure. Lieut. 45 in R.G. interpretar will be available of Reformed. Captain Brifford D.C.M. promoted Captain for gallantry in the field (Reasons retired) 50 remain in Hops.	
NOEUX-L-M.	7.3.16.		66 in Hospital this morning. One suspected Cases of Cereb Sprinal Fever discovered & isolation.	
NOEUX-L-M.	9.3.16.		77 in Hospital. Weather very cold. Lieut. J.T. GRIFFITHS Reserve reported his arrival yesterday. He will be attached to Unit until fit for training troops. Lieut. ADMOND Medical Charge 8. 10/Gordons. Capt. LUMLEY will return his former Medical Charge & 10/Gordons vice Capt. COAD who will be temporarily attached to this unit spending decision of Board as to his disposal.	
NOEUX-L-M	10.3.16.		86 in Hospital today. A hard month due influenza & suspectia. 3 new Trench Feet. Capt. COAD reported his departure for ETAPLES today. Capt. W.H.FORSYTH has been nominated for command of 7. R? 3D Field Ambulance.	
NOEUX-L-M	11.3.16.		71 sick remain. 10 Trench Feet admitted. Weather very cold. Capt. W.H. FORSYTH ALSO M. Enspath on attempt orders and 7. R? 3D Field Amb. Lt. R.H. BONNYCASTLE posted on duty in return.	

1875 Wt. W 593/826 1,000,000 4/15 J.B.C. & A. A.D.S.S./Forms/C. 2118.

Army Form C. 2118

47th Field Ambulance

WAR DIARY
or
INTELLIGENCE SUMMARY

(Erase heading not required.)

Instructions regarding War Diaries and Intelligence Summaries are contained in F. S. Regs., Part II. and the Staff Manual respectively. Title Pages will be prepared in manuscript.

Place	Date	Hour	Summary of Events and Information	Remarks and references to Appendices
NOEUX-L-M	12.3.16		62 sick remain Fitpc. Weather has changed & is now much colder. Influenza & Bronchitis are still prevailing epidemics.	
NOEUX-L-M	13.3.16		Commenced Inoculation of unit with New Mixture Typhoid Prophylactic Serum. Given to 74 N.C.O's and Men. 51 sick remain hospital. 6 Tunnel feet.	
NOEUX-L-M	14.3.16		59 sick hospital. D.D.M.S. Inspec. Inspected Main Dressing Station.	
NOEUX-L-M	15.3.16		51 sick hospital. Lt. R.H. BONNYCASTLE Taken off duty & in hospital.	
NOEUX-L-M	16.3.16	2 p.m.	Brought MARLES-LES-MINES to find Hospitals a site for Field Ambulance. In and reports are in A.H. and not available. only a small village but Available which is suitable. Reported accordingly to DMS. 53 in hospital hosp. 179 Men are Influenza cases. Capt. E.A. LUMLEY assumed permanent Medical charge 9/10/Indian Fitpc.	
NOEUX-L-M	17.3.16		46 Remain Hospital. 17 Influenza.	
NOEUX-L-M	18.3.16		47 Sick Remain Hospital. In Ambulance with Suppr. to MAIRIE AUCHEL Stables.	
NOEUX-L-M	19.3.16		44 sick remain hospital. Lecture Venereal Disease. Capt: G.F. CLIFTON address troops. Breakfast Camp of 9/R H-LI Ry. BEUVRY.	
NOEUX-L-M	20.3.16		41 sick remain hospital.	
NOEUX-L-M	21.3.16		42 sick remain hospital.	
NOEUX-L-M	22.3.16		35 sick remain hospl. Major H. RAWNSLEY admitted to 6 Canadian hosp. H.E. the F.G.C.M. Inquiring on the G.O.C. 4/6 in Inf. Bde. for arrest of the prospective N. (Refusing a trust). Orders Postponed.	

1875 Wt. W593/826 1,000,000 4/15 J.B.C. & A. A.D.S.S./Forms/C. 2118.

WAR DIARY
or
INTELLIGENCE SUMMARY

(Erase heading not required.)

Army Form C. 2118

47th Field Ambulance

Place	Date	Hour	Summary of Events and Information	Remarks and references to Appendices
2 NOEUX -L-M	28.3.16		Visited AUCHEL to make arrangements for Taking over the MAIRIE	
			2 Officers & 20 O.R. 113th F.A. to A.D.S. PHILOSOPHE	
			32 sick. 18 g. water and exchanges	
NOEUX-L-M	24.3.16		23 sick in Hosp. 1 Officer and 35 O.R. 113th F.A. to PHILOSOPHE to complete Relief	
			Weather becoming worse.	
			Lt. A. C. STURDY admitted into Infantry Medical Comp. of 71st Bde R.F.A.	
			Capt. W.S. WALLACE placed on the List Sitting.	
NOEUX-L-M	25.3.16		All personnel and transport had been withdrawn from PHILOSOPHE and LOOS.	
			31 sick in Hospital.	
NOEUX-L-M	26.3.16	8.30 a.m	Units moves to AUCHEL today. Transport left NOEUX at 8.30 a.m. Arriving AUCHEL 12.30 p.m.	
		11.30	2 Officers and 10 O.R. by train to LAPUGNOY thence by Motor Buses to AUCHEL.	
			33 sick in Hosp. Weather very bad.	
AUCHEL	27.3.16	1 p.m.	Took over HOTEL DE VILLE on arriving today. Personnel in billets (Cinema Hall) Stores in billets.	
			30 sick transferred to 113th F.A. Taken over duties at AUCHEL and RAIMBERT.	
AUCHEL	27.3.16		17 sick. Weather very cold. 6th M.A.C. Drew Situations New hand-institued by 125th M.A.C.	
AUCHEL	28.3.16		18 sick. Weather very cold. Lt. J.R. MAGEE Returned Reported for duty.	
AUCHEL	29.3.16		29 sick. Serving R report.. A.D.M.S. 15th Division inspected during Station Stores.	
AUCHEL	30.3.16		41 sick. 20 Exchanges. 7 Scabies. Capt. WALLACE off sick list Still.	
AUCHEL	31.3.16		52 sick in Hosp. 23 Exchanges. D.D.M.S. 1st Army inspected Bathing Station Stores	
			Conference N.O.C. of Field Ambulances with A.D.M.S.	
			J.F. Ritchie Lt Col.	
			OC. 47th Field Ambulance.	

April 1915.

15th May.

No. 47 F. Amb.

COMMITTEE FOR THE
MEDICAL HISTORY OF THE WAR
Date 9 – JUN. 1915

Army Form C. 2118

WAR DIARY or **INTELLIGENCE SUMMARY**

(Erase heading not required.)

47th Field Ambulance

Vol 9

Instructions regarding War Diaries and Intelligence Summaries are contained in F.S. Regs., Part II and the Staff Manual respectively. Title Pages will be prepared in manuscript.

Place	Date	Hour	Summary of Events and Information	Remarks and references to Appendices
AUCHEL	1.4.16		Fine warm weather. Future. Attended a Staff ride with 45th Inf. Bde.	
AUCHEL	2.4.16		Visited ECOLE DES GARCONS with A.D.M.S. 15th Division re Take over Ecole as a Hospital. Proceeded on leave today. Capt. W.S. WALLACE takes over command & hands camp by dinner.	27 Oct 25 Oct 27 Rum at 4pm Q.G.
AUCHEL	3.4.16			
AUCHEL	3.4.16		Took over command from Lt Col Ritchie. 67 patients in hospital.	
AUCHEL	4.4.16		66 in hospital. Capt N. BLACK reported his arrival for duty. D.D.M.S. 1st Corps visited ECOLE DES GARCONS.	
AUCHEL	5.4.16		70 in hospital. Lt J.R. MAGEE reported his departure for 12th Division. Received orders to prepare ECOLE DES GARCONS for Corps Ital Hospital. A.D.M.S. 15th Division visited dressing station. Weather very cold.	
AUCHEL	6.4.16		68 in hospital. Went with Capt. N. BLACK to AIRE for gents gas lecture. Received instructions re 15th Divisional exercise. Lt J.V. BROWN returned to duty from CIMIEZ convalescent home for officers.	
AUCHEL	7.4.16		Went with Capt BLACK to AIRE for 2nd Anti Gas Lecture. Unit under Lt. BROWN marched out with XV Division for divisional exercise. Unit took up billets at RELY where Capt BLACK & I joined it.	

1875 W¹: W593/826 1,000,000 4/15 J.B.C. & A. A.D.S.S./Forms/C. 2118.

Army Form C. 2118

47th Field Ambulance

WAR DIARY or INTELLIGENCE SUMMARY

(Erase heading not required.)

Instructions regarding War Diaries and Intelligence Summaries are contained in F. S. Regs., Part II. and the Staff Manual respectively. Title Pages will be prepared in manuscript.

Place	Date	Hour	Summary of Events and Information	Remarks and references to Appendices
RELY	8.4.16		Unit did training from billets at RELY. Weather very fine.	
RELY	9.4.16	12 PM	Unit marched behind 46th Inf. Bgde. Divisional Service finished at BELLERY	
		3 PM	Returned to billets at AUCHEL & formed D.D.M.S. 1st Corps inspecting Hospital	
AUCHEL	10/4/16	10 AM	Wanted D.A.D.M.S. XV Division returned with him to inspect new Corps Vtd Hospital. Received orders to have Vtd hospital ready to receive patients on 11.4.16. Lt STURDY relinquished temporary medical command 71st Bgde R.F.A. returned to Unit.	
AUCHEL	11.4.16		46 in hospital. New Corps Scabies station opened.	
AUCHEL	12.4.16		56 in hospital. Lt R.H. BONNYCASTLE granted leave to England.	
AUCHEL	13.4.16		59 in hospital. Lt. Col. RITCHIE returned from leave & resumed command.	
AUCHEL	13.4.16		Returned from leave F/Lieut. J.F. Ritchie Lt Col Reeve	
			Wm S Wallace Capt R.A.M.C.	
AUCHEL	14.4.16		54 in Hospital F/Lieut. Lt. R.H. BONNYCASTLE returned from leave from BOULOGNE Lt. J.V. BROWN (in Command) and Lt. A.C. STURDY are detached for duty with I Corps Scabies Station	

1875 Wt. W593/826 1,000,000 4/15 J.B.C. & A. A.D.S.S./Forms/C. 2118.

Army Form C. 2118

WAR DIARY
47th Field Ambulance

INTELLIGENCE SUMMARY

(Erase heading not required.)

Place	Date	Hour	Summary of Events and Information	Remarks and references to Appendices
AUCHEL	15.4.16.		Submitted arrangements for laundry as I Corps Scabies Station to D.D.M.S. through A.D.M.S. for approval. 60 Sick remaining under treatment 22 of which are influenza.	
AUCHEL	16.4.16.		43 Sick remaining. Lt. S.A.W. MUNRO RAMC reported his arrival taking on duty in place of Lt. A.C. STURDY RAMC who proceeds to No 43 C.C.S. as Surgical Specialist.	
AUCHEL	17.4.16		35 Sick remaining. Very cold and wet. Lt. A.C. STURDY left for No 43 C.C.S. FOLQUE. 40 N.C.O's and men have been at GOSNAY in a working party unloading stone. O.C. 91st Field Coy R.E. has written to say that they have worked exceedingly well.	
AUCHEL	18.4.16		38 remaining. Weather bitter. Snow in Fields.	
AUCHEL	19.4.16.		43 Sick remain. 4 accidentally wounded at Band School FERFAY	
AUCHEL	20.4.16		41 Sick remaining	
AUCHEL	21.4.16.		38 Sick remaining. Proceeded to VERQUIGNEUL with a view to taking over work as a Field Ambulance also at the request of A.D. Kemp LeedS as a Bathing Station. 1 Capt and 4 men No 38 F.A. are in possession.	
AUCHEL	22.4.16		45 Sick remaining. Very wet day. No orders to finish forward and equipment for Divisional Laundry ALLOUAGNE. Also remain at AUCHEL. Lt Sturge Ca 1/2 men for Divisional Laundry ALLOUAGNE.	
AUCHEL	23.4.16		No 1 on. MAIRIE AUCHEL Lt No 37 Field Ambulance re 24.4.16. The 33rd/34 Lt SINCLAIR R. Parkinson to 2 Fd I.H.C. for posting & seeing with the property of the Batt. 45 Sick remaining. Capt. M. BLACK & 5 Personnel No 37 F.A. arrived to 2 at 2.45 F.A. Dr. was shown in complete. 2 Officers & 36 men of No 37 F.A. arrived taking on a charge of property & took over MAIRIE. Weather very fine. A.D.M.S. inspected Hospital taking also D.D.M.S. I Corps.	

Army Form C. 2118

47th Field Ambulance

WAR DIARY
or
INTELLIGENCE SUMMARY

(Erase heading not required.)

Instructions regarding War Diaries and Intelligence Summaries are contained in F. S. Regs., Part II. and the Staff Manual respectively. Title Pages will be prepared in manuscript.

Place	Date	Hour	Summary of Events and Information	Remarks and references to Appendices
AUCHEL	24.4.16	P.20.	Aero.ntcl portion under Capt. N. BLACK by road march to LILLERS thence by road to BETHUNE and by road march to VERQUIGNEUL arriving 11.30 a.m.	
		8.35 a.m	Transport leaves under Capt. WALLACE via LOZINGHEM – MARLES – HESDIGNEUL – VAUDRICOURT arriving 12 noon	
			25 sick transferred to No. 87 Field Ambulance.	
VERQUIGNEUL	24 & 25.4.16	11.30.	Arrived and billeted in ECOLE DES FILLES. Accommodation 150. Lt. A.H.O. ARTHUR & Lake in sick, working party of 40 men in Pits attached to 12 Div Signal Co. B Section in Camp A. I Capt Senior Station (2 officers) I officer and 12 men at ALLOUAGNE (Div Laundry) Stretcher Bearer fins, Reserve and A.S.C. M.T. to billets, A.S.C. H.T. to cts.	
VERQUIGNEUL	25.4.16		Sick Remaining Nil. Weather fine. All personnel working w. Cleaning up & holding kit etc. Capt. N. BLACK proceeded to No. 45 Field Ambs for duty. Col. MACHIN to 45 Field Ambulance as L. to Brigadier to DEPUTATION.	

Army Form C. 2118

WAR DIARY 47th Field Ambulance
or
INTELLIGENCE SUMMARY

Instructions regarding War Diaries and Intelligence
Summaries are contained in F. S. Regs., Part II.
and the Staff Manual respectively. Title Pages
will be prepared in manuscript.

(Erase heading not required.)

Place	Date	Hour	Summary of Events and Information	Remarks and references to Appendices
VERQUINEUL	26.4.16		Sick Remaining NIL. Health very Good. All Vehicles including Motors are being repainted. Kitchen and Latrine incinerators are being built	
VERQUINEUL	27.4.16		No sick being admitted. Relief to R.A.M.C. Slight Frost. 9 Cars were removed at about 7.30 a.m.	
VERQUINEUL	28.4.16		Estab: Duty Officer to cover field Ambulance of 1st Div. R.S.K.p. to R.A.M.C.	
VERQUINEUL	29.4.16		Capt. W. S. WALLACE proceeds on leave 5 days	
VERQUINEUL	30.4.16		R.A.M.p. to R.A.G. Present distribution of Unit Head Quarters & A Sect. at VERQUIGNEUL B Sect at I Corps Scabies Station (25 Strong) 50 men attached to I Corps R.E. as working party 14 men at Divisional Laundry (1 Officer)	

J.J. Rutter Lt. Col.
O.C. 47th Field Ambulance.

May 1916.

No. H] 7. Amb.

Army Form C. 2118

Vol. 10

47th Field Ambulance

WAR DIARY or INTELLIGENCE SUMMARY

(Erase heading not required.)

Instructions regarding War Diaries and Intelligence Summaries are contained in F. S. Regs., Part II. and the Staff Manual respectively. Title Pages will be prepared in manuscript.

Place	Date	Hour	Summary of Events and Information	Remarks and references to Appendices
VERQUIGNEUL	1.5.16		Routine to date.	
VERQUIGNEUL	2.5.16		Capt. G.F. CLIFTON returned Sick from Medical charge 11th A. and S. HQrs.	
VERQUIGNEUL	3.5.16		Weather cold and wet	
VERQUIGNEUL	4.5.16		Lt. S.A.W. MUNRO Talkd on temporary Medical charge of 180th Coy R.E. Surg. Major McDOWALL proceeds on leave to U.K. H.Q.nr	
VERQUIGNEUL	5.5.16		Weather still cold. Routine to date.	
VERQUIGNEUL	6.5.16		Lt. MUNRO Relinquishes temporary Medical charge of 180th Coy R.E.	
VERQUIGNEUL	7.5.16		Lt. R.H. BONNYCASTLE proceeds to U.K. H.Q.nr on expiring of contract. Lt. J.T. GRIFFITHS proceeds on leave to U.K. H.Q.nr Capt. G.F. CLIFTON attaining charge of Divisional Sanitary Section from Lt. J.T. GRIFFITHS.	
VERQUIGNEUL	8.5.16		Routine to date.	
VERQUIGNEUL	9.5.16		Visited I Corps Scabies Station at AUCHEL and Divisional Laundry at ALLOUAGNE	
VERQUIGNEUL	10.5.16		Lt. & QM. F. DAVIS returned leave to Scotland from Folane. Capt. W.S. WALLACE returned from leave France.	
VERQUIGNEUL	11.5.16		Routine to date.	

WAR DIARY or INTELLIGENCE SUMMARY

Army Form C. 2118

47th Field Ambulance

Place	Date	Hour	Summary of Events and Information	Remarks and references to Appendices
	1916			
VERQUIGNEUL	12.5.16		Weather very warm. Nothing of importance to note.	
VERQUIGNEUL	13.5.16		Sheet ropes have been provided for Kitchen Lieutenant's Store and Mess.	
VERQUIGNEUL	14.5.16		Nothing to note.	
VERQUIGNEUL	15.5.16		Sergeant Major McDOWALL returns & Lieut J. McGORTY R.A.M.C. reports his arrival & taking for duty. Reporting to note. Nº GRIFFITHS returned from leave.	
VERQUIGNEUL	16.5.16		Proceeded to Divisional Laundry ALLOUAGNE & held Stand for Examination of underclothing & nothing. Lt. H.M. VICKERS R.A.M.C reports his arrival & taking for duty.	
VERQUIGNEUL	17.5.16		Lt GRIFFITHS attained change of I. Corps School. Returns via Capt. J.V. BROWN Battery & returned to England on 5th March & on Outbreak of contract Lt M° R.A.M.C Sent to England on 15th instant & taking for duty.	
VERQUIGNEUL	19.5.16		Capt W.S. WALLACE sent to report on Relief for All Ranks in Trenches.	
VERQUIGNEUL	20.5.16		Visited I Corps School & Division AUCHEL and Divisional Laundry ALLOUAGNE.	
VERQUIGNEUL	21.5.16		1 Private reported for duty on Completion of W.E. on late Depot returned to 15th Div Supply Column.	
VERQUIGNEUL	22.5.16		1 Private 1 N.C.O. and 1 L.D. N.C.O returned on reduction of W.E.	
VERQUIGNEUL	23.5.16		Lt H.M VICKERS attained Medical Charge of 15th Divisional Train for this date. Weather warm and heavy rain Thunder.	

Army Form C. 2118

47th Field Ambulance

WAR DIARY
or
INTELLIGENCE SUMMARY

(Erase heading not required.)

Instructions regarding War Diaries and Intelligence Summaries are contained in F. S. Regs., Part II. and the Staff Manual respectively. Title Pages will be prepared in manuscript.

Place	Date	Hour	Summary of Events and Information	Remarks and references to Appendices
VERQUIGNEUL	24.5.16		Posting to Duty.	
VERQUIGNEUL	25.5.16		Visited ALLOUAGNE and AUCHEL.	
VERQUIGNEUL	26.5.16		Conference w. O.i.C. Field Ambulances with A.D.M.S. Submitted scheme for opening up. Received a draft of 4 men.	
VERQUIGNEUL	27.5.16		Working party (50 men) rejoined on completion of duty with I Corps Signals.	
VERQUIGNEUL	28.5.16		Weather very warm.	
VERQUIGNEUL	29.5.16		Capt. W.S. WALLACE left 20 L.C.C.T. and been posted at VERMELLES to an advanced Field Ambulance Dug outs.	
VERQUIGNEUL	30.5.16		Raining at intervals, weather very fine.	
VERQUIGNEUL	31.5.16		Present distribution of unit: Working party VERMELLES 1 offr 20 O.R. 1 Corps Sanitary Station AUCHEL 1 offr 25 O.R. 15th Sqn Rendezvous ALLOUAGNE 1 offr 14 O.R. 15th Div. Training School GOSNAY 1 offr 3 O.R. H.Q. "A" Sect. 1 Open Motor Transit VERQUIGNEUL	

J.F. Ritchie Lt Col
OC 47th Field Ambulance

COMMITTEE FOR THE
MEDICAL HISTORY OF THE [?]
Date   5 AUG. 1916

CB. 47 J.A.

June 1916.
5

Army Form C. 2118

WAR DIARY
or
INTELLIGENCE SUMMARY
(Erase heading not required.)

47th Field Ambulance

Vol 11

Instructions regarding War Diaries and Intelligence Summaries are contained in F.S. Regs., Part II. and the Staff Manual respectively. Title Pages will be prepared in manuscript.

June

Place	Date	Hour	Summary of Events and Information	Remarks and references to Appendices
VERQUIGNEUL	1.6.16.		Nothing of importance to note.	
VERQUIGNEUL	2.6.16.		Captain J.V. BROWN returned from leave England. A.D.M.S. inspected I Corps scabies station Labeuvrière	
VERQUIGNEUL	3.6.16.		Visited I Corps Scabies Station and dispersion at Labeuvrière	
VERQUIGNEUL	4.6.16.		Nothing to note. Weather unsettled	
VERQUIGNEUL	5.6.16.		Capt. G.F. CLIFTON granted leave to England	
VERQUIGNEUL	6.6.16.		Nothing to note.	
VERQUIGNEUL	7.6.16.		Nothing to note.	
VERQUIGNEUL	8.6.16.		Weather broke, impelled with heavy rain. Received a draft of 7 Poor Rein. C.	
VERQUIGNEUL	9.6.16		Visited I Corps Scabies Station and Divisional Laundry	
VERQUIGNEUL	10.6.16.		Lt S.A.W. MUNRO returned from temporary duty with 10th Sco. Rifles.	
VERQUIGNEUL	11.6.16.		Two very heavy thunderstorms today. Weather broke. Parade hindered & wet	
VERQUIGNEUL	12.6.16.		Nothing to note	
VERQUIGNEUL	13.6.16.		Lt S.A.W. MUNRO granted leave to England from Tilbury.	
VERQUIGNEUL	14.6.16.		All weather advance I have at 11 p.m. tonight	
VERQUIGNEUL	15.6.16		3 Poor reinforcements received. Orders received to take over "B" Section I Corps Rest Station at FOUQUIERES from 38th Field Ambulance. 1 Officer & 20 O.R. sent over as advance party. 1st Aid Post & retain dressing station in No School at VERQUIGNEUL	

Army Form C. 2118

WAR DIARY
or
INTELLIGENCE SUMMARY — 47th Field Ambulance

(Erase heading not required.)

Instructions regarding War Diaries and Intelligence Summaries are contained in F.S. Regs., Part II. and the Staff Manual respectively. Title Pages will be prepared in manuscript.

Place	Date	Hour	Summary of Events and Information	Remarks and references to Appendices
VERQUIGNEUL	16.6.16.	10 p.m. 2 p.m.	Unit proceeds to FOUQUIERES arriving 2 p.m. A small detachment under an N.C.O. left at VERQUIGNEUL till A Sect. Detachment in care but hire to follow shortly. Taken over 58th Field Ambulance.	
VER FOUQUIERES	17.6.16.		136 in. I Inspt Rest Stn. Found boiler at Laundry FOUQUIERES in an unsatisfactory condition being old and inadequately filled. Asked for N.C.E. to inspect it. S.S.O. Sanitary Sect. is still kept used but it now in charge of (1) I.B. Section I Inspt Rest Station (2) I Inspt Scabies Station (3) 15th Divisional Laundry (4) Providing a working party of 86 men for Field Ambulance dugouts in front of Lone Farm in the new sector.	
FOUQUIERES	18.6.16		131 remaining. 2 Refp of importance to Rt.	
FOUQUIERES	19.6.16		128 remaining. D.P.M.S. I Inspt inspected Hospital Train.	
FOUQUIERES	20.6.16		122 remaining. Terminated Contract for Steam Engine.	
FOUQUIERES	21.6.16		116 remaining. I.O.M. Scabies section inspected & condemned Boiler at Laundry as being Absolutely unsafe to use.	
FOUQUIERES	22.6.16		Proceeded on leave. Transferred over charge to Capt. J V BROWN Rain C.	J R Rutter Lt Colonel

Army Form C. 2118

WAR DIARY or INTELLIGENCE SUMMARY

47th Field Ambulance

(Erase heading not required.)

Instructions regarding War Diaries and Intelligence Summaries are contained in F. S. Regs., Part II. and the Staff Manual respectively. Title Pages will be prepared in manuscript.

Place	Date	Hour	Summary of Events and Information	Remarks and references to Appendices
FOUQUIÈRES	22/9/16		Took over 47th Field Ambulance from Lt Col Ritchie - Lt Col Ritchie granted leave from 23/9/16 - 30/9/16.	
FOUQUIÈRES	23/9/16		Too down large marquee - priest bedior type morning stripping. Concert to Patients by Band of Lanc. Fus. No. of Patients remaining 104. Eight men returned from Camp.	
			1st Corps Scabies Station taken over by 111th Fd Ambulance. Lieut Griffith + 14 N.C.O.s men returned from AUCHEL. No. of Patients remaining 105 - Complimentary visit by Brig-Genl Skerdilands (late 2nd Cavalry).	
FOUQUIÈRES	24/9/16		Monthly O.D.R. attack remaining 102. Nothing of importance took	
FOUQUIÈRES	25/9/16		Visited A.D.M.S. re plans of 1st Corps Rest Station showing proposed improvements - Instructed by A.D.M.S. to go ahead & improvements. Patients remaining 93.	
FOUQUIÈRES	26/9/16		Visit by A.D.M.S. & D.A.D.M.S. New return started. Inspection of unit in full marching order - also of men returns return. Weekly scabies inspection no cases found. Lieut Munro Pratt on Sick list - Patients remaining 103.	
FOUQUIÈRES	27/9/16		Lieut McGarty sent to 46th Fd Ambulance for 1 months training Lieut O'Dell reported for duty from 46th Fd Ambulance. Inspection of section stores - Inspection in full marching order for clothing & sanitation unit at VERQUIGNEUL.	

1875 Wt. W593/826 1,000,000 4/15 J.B.C. & A. A.D.S.S./Forms/C. 2118.

WAR DIARY or INTELLIGENCE SUMMARY

Army Form C. 2118

47th Field Ambulance

(Erase heading not required.)

Place	Date	Hour	Summary of Events and Information	Remarks and references to Appendices
FOUQUIERES	27/9/16		Patients remaining 100	
FOUQUIERES	28/9/16		Patients remaining 112 – Nothing of importance to note.	
FOUQUIERES	29/9/16		Patients remaining 101. Inspection of Transport by A.S.C.	
FOUQUIERES	30/9/16		Patients remaining 86. Lieut. Col. Ritchie returned from leave and resumed command over him. Took over duty as Censor from leave. J.P. Ritchie Lt. Col. OC. 47th Field Amb. Strength of Unit on 30.9.16. 18 Offrs and 14 O.R. at Divisional Laundry ALLOUAGNE 1 Offr and 1 Pte at Divisional School GOSNAY 1 Offr (Capt WALLACE) in command of working party of 46th & 48th Field Amb. Remainder of Unit with I Corps Rest Station B Section FOUQUIERES IN.C.O and 3 P. at School VERQUIGNEUL J.P. Ritchie Lt Col OC. 47 F.A. A. Brown Capt R.A.M.C.	

Confidential. July/16

War Diary

of

47th Fld Ambce R.A.M.C

From 1st July 1916
To 31st July 1916

(Volume 12)

A.D.M.S.

15th Division

Herewith forward diary of this unit for the month of July 16.

J.F. Ritchie Lt Colonel
O.C. 47th Field Amb.

1.8.16.

Army Form C. 2118

WAR DIARY
or
INTELLIGENCE SUMMARY

47th Field Amb[ulance]

(Erase heading not required.)

Place	Date	Hour	Summary of Events and Information	Remarks and references to Appendices
FOUQUIERES	1.7.16		Returned from leave Today. Isolation still on. 9.9 Return 1st est. 82 in Hospital remaining.	
FOUQUIERES	2.7.16		84 in Hospital. Reconstruction of Rest Camp proceeding. In Kitchen longest closet up to dining place and attention given places in a more convenient bldg. Provisions were taken in at an investigate distance. 75 in Hospital.	
FOUQUIERES	3.7.16		Improved arrangements for baths & washing to be taken with us for the Great & an advance also supplies of fuel for potatoes. Arrangements made for storing surplus Equipment left behind. Medical Board inspection. 91 remaining in Hospital.	
FOUQUIERES	4.7.16		90 remaining in Hospital today. No incident in camp delay in construction of new kitchen.	
FOUQUIERES	5.7.16		98 remaining in Hospital. 1 Pte reinforcement received today. Clearing of all ranks ordered to Cambridge Reductions. Captain W.H. STEELE R.A.M.C. reported his arrival for duty from 15th D.A.C. and is posted to command C Section and Transport Officer during the absence of Capt. WALLACE	
FOUQUIERES	7.7.16		102 remain. Capt. G.F. CLIFTON R.A.M.C. having been appointed to permanent Medical Charge of 6/17 R. Scots Fusiliers in stock off the train 6th from Fauline (A.D.M.S. 15th Division) 2nd Q.M. E. DAVIS assumed charge of 15th Division laundry from Capt. G.F. CLIFTON	

Army Form C. 2118

47th Field Ambulance.

WAR DIARY
or INTELLIGENCE SUMMARY

(Erase heading not required.)

Instructions regarding War Diaries and Intelligence Summaries are contained in F.S. Regs., Part II. and the Staff Manual respectively. Title Pages will be prepared in manuscript.

Place	Date	Hour	Summary of Events and Information	Remarks and references to Appendices
FOUQUIERES	8.7.16		108 remain. Healthy save for 2 P.U.O. Reinforcements received today. Under orders in canvas strife communicated to all ranks.	
FOUQUIERES	9.7.16		102 remain today. Kit inspection. 12 months service in the Field today.	
FOUQUIERES	10.7.16		115 remain today. Captain F.M. ROBERTSON RAMC reported his arrival T.F. today for duty. 1 O.G.S.C. reinforcement received	
FOUQUIERES	11.7.16		121 remain today.	
FOUQUIERES	12.7.16		143 remain today. Health again very unsettled.	
FOUQUIERES	13.7.16		140 patients remaining. 3 P.U.O. Reinforcements arrived today	
FOUQUIERES	14.7.16		135 patients remaining. Lecture on importance of salute.	
FOUQUIERES	15.7.16		117 patients remaining. Corporals SHELLEY and JARVIS appointed acting Sergeants vice 2 Sergts evacuated sick to L.O.C. L/Cpls HENDERSON and MASSES appointed acting Corporals (DDMS I Appx 127/9)	
FOUQUIERES	16.7.16		138 patients remaining. Dressing shops packed at night to be under cover.	
FOUQUIERES	17.7.16		122 patients remaining. Capt F.M. ROBERTSON R.A.M.C. attached to duty to 45 2.C. as a temporary measure.	
FOUQUIERES	18.7.16		148 patients remain.	

Army Form C. 2118

47th Field Ambulance

WAR DIARY
or
INTELLIGENCE SUMMARY
(Erase heading not required.)

Instructions regarding War Diaries and Intelligence Summaries are contained in F. S. Regs., Part II. and the Staff Manual respectively. Title Pages will be prepared in manuscript.

Place	Date	Hour	Summary of Events and Information	Remarks and references to Appendices
FOUQUIERES	19.7.16		140 patients remain. Lt. G.J. McGORTY appointed to medical charge of 12th H.L.I. Battery and in rotation of its strength from this date. Lt. A.M. VICKERS reported his arrival for duty. Lt. J. O'DEA Returns medical charge of 15th additional School in relief of Lt. S.W. MUNRO who is posted to its strength having been appointed to medical charge of 7th 8/Seaforths.	
FOUQUIERES	20.7.16		132 patients remaining. 4 Pt'r Rank & reinforcements received, hut now completed & established. The remodelling of the B.S.P. Station is now practically completed. Separate athletic dressing rooms have been constructed for patients & personnel. Kitchen has been rebuilt in a convenient site. Running in fuel and in detriment has been already effected. A storage hut is in course of Construction and the wooden huts are being re-roofed with corrugated iron roofing felt. Quite a lot filling of unsuitable cases which have been sent to Light Rwn Station for Autowuck. G.A.D.M.S.	
FOUQUIERES	21.7.16		145 patients remain. Received orders to land men Light Rwn Station to FA Station. O.C. 25th Field Amb (Lt Guy) over a portion at 5 p.m. 6 To/CA men, Staff Suffr Tackman & Lister-Quartering Luts proceeded to LA PUGNOY Rwn men & join 46th Fd Bn.	
FOUQUIERES	22.7.16	6a.m. 2p.m.	145 remain. Orders handed over to 25th Field Amb & hut movements to HEUCHIN. Lt. FOUQUIERES via CASNAY - MARLES - CALONNE - PERMES to HEUCHIN. A trip that took any arrived at HEUCHIN and went into billets. Lieut. J. DICKSON Reported supporting his arrival for duty.	

Army Form C. 2118

WAR DIARY
or
INTELLIGENCE SUMMARY

(Erase heading not required.)

Instructions regarding War Diaries and Intelligence Summaries are contained in F. S. Regs., Part II. and the Staff Manual respectively. Title Pages will be prepared in manuscript.

Place	Date	Hour	Summary of Events and Information	Remarks and references to Appendices
HEUCHIN	23.7.16		Remained at HEUCHIN. Obtained a certain amount of accommodation stores. All ranks equipped with steel helmets. Rest commenced by men going to BRUAY. Personnel billeted in farms.	
HEUCHIN	24.7.16		Remained at HEUCHIN with 46th Inf. Bde.	
HEUCHIN	25.7.16		Still at HEUCHIN.	
HEUCHIN	26.7.16	9 a.m.	Marched with 46th Inf 15th Bde BERGUENEUSE – WAVRANS – SIRACOURT – CROISETTES	
WIGNACOURT	26.7.16	2 p.m.	WIGNACOURT. Personnel + horses accommodated in farms. SVR straight to ST POL. Motors proceeded to army portion there.	
WIGNACOURT	27.7.16	9 a.m.	Marched to VILLERS L'HOPITAL via BLANGERMONT – MONCHEL – VACQUERIE – LE – ROUCQ.	
VILLERS L'HOPITAL		2 p.m.	Personnel + horses in billets. Personnel + horses in billets. Lt. Auto in for farmout. SVR straight to DOULLENS.	
VILLERS L'HOPITAL	28.7.16	7.45 a.m.	Marched to ST HILAIRE via FROHEN-LE-GRAND and BERNAVILLE. A very hot day and many men fell out.	
ST HILAIRE		1 p.m.	Arrived at ST HILAIRE. Personnel in billets. SVR in a good position at farms. SVR extended to DOULLENS.	
ST. HILAIRE	29.7.16		Rested in billets.	
ST HILAIRE	30.7.16		Rested in billets.	
ST. HILAIRE	31.7.16	4.30 p.m.	Marched to FLESSELLES. An early start rendered + led burdened of troops	
FLESSELLES	31.7.16	8.50 a.m.	Arrived at FLESSELLES. Went into billets.	

G.G. Ridden Lt Colonel
O.C. 47th Battn Canadians

Confidential

War Diary

of

47. Fd. Ambulance R.A.M.C.

from 1/8/16
to 31/8/16.

(Volume)

Army Form C. 2118

August 1916.   47th Field Ambulance.

WAR DIARY
or
INTELLIGENCE SUMMARY
(Erase heading not required.)

Instructions regarding War Diaries and Intelligence Summaries are contained in F.S. Regs., Part II. and the Staff Manual respectively. Title Pages will be prepared in manuscript.

Place	Date	Hour	Summary of Events and Information	Remarks and references to Appendices
FLESSELLES	1.8.16		Remained in billets. Sick evacuated to No. 1 (NEW ZEALAND) Stationary Hospital 3 Officers 42 O.R. remain.	98R.
FLESSELLES	2.8.16		Remained in billets. Medical Insp. hut. 26 remaining sick.	98R.
FLESSELLES	3.8.16		Remained in billets. Sick evacuated to No. 4 C.C.S. 22 evacuated 13 remain.	98R.
FLESSELLES	4.8.16	5 a.m.	Marched with 145th Inf. Bde L. MOLLIENS-AU-BOIS. Capt. W.H. STEELE and 10 O.R. to LAVIEVILLE	98R.
MOLLIENS-AU-BOIS	4.8.16	7.30 p.m	Arrived and went into billets. Lt. GRIFFITHS posted 5 days grand leave to England.	98R.
MOLLIENS-AU-BOIS	5.8.16	6.30 a.m	Marched with 145 Inf. Bde to LAVIEVILLE	98R.
LAVIEVILLE	5.8.16	10.30 a.m	Arrived at LAVIEVILLE and took over from 58th Field Ambulance. Returned 1 sick in train.	98R.
LAVIEVILLE	6.8.16		Remained at LAVIEVILLE. Constructed a new kitchen and known improvements.	98R.
LAVIEVILLE	7.8.16		Remained at LAVIEVILLE.	98R.
LAVIEVILLE	8.8.16	4 a.m	Marched independently via DERNANCOURT - MEAULTE - BECORDEL & CHATEAU BECOURT.	98R.
BECOURT	8.8.16	10.30 a.m	Arr and took over from 71st Field Amb. Buildings close to LAVIEVILLE and evacuated in own cars to No.1 and No.2 main dressing stations to 69th Field Ambulance.	98R.
BECOURT	9.8.16		Remained at BECOURT. Returned in our own cars to Aug.T.S.	98R.
	9.8.16	7 p.m	Capt. W.S. WALLACE and R. Att. Buried Portuguese to FRICOURT. Kurf. from 115th Field Ambulance	98R.
BECOURT	10.8.16		Visited CONTALMAISON to interview O.C. 45th Field Amb. re arrang. details for accomp. him further if necessary.	98R.

Army Form C. 2118

August 1916.

47th Field Ambulance

WAR DIARY
or
INTELLIGENCE SUMMARY

(Erase heading not required.)

Instructions regarding War Diaries and Intelligence Summaries are contained in F.S. Regs., Part II. and the Staff Manual respectively. Title Pages will be prepared in manuscript.

Place	Date	Hour	Summary of Events and Information	Remarks and references to Appendices
BECOURT	11.8.16		Proceeded to CONTALMAISON to arrange details of reinforcements for 45th Field Amb. When relieved. Italian party had gone bathing. Lt. BRIFFITHS proceeded on distn. duty. I/leave to 14th Div Bn.	92R
BECOURT	12.8.16	10 a.m.	Men in Chatham from A.D.M.S. Again proceeded to CONTALMAISON for further conference with O.C. 45th F.A.	92R
	12.8.16	5.30 p.m.	C Section Bearer Subdivision took over duties of Lt. D'DEA sent to CONTALMAISON as relief.	
			Reinforcement to 45th F.A. 7 Nurses Platoons with them. 2 Motor Ambulances & F/L COURT/18p. a. relief.	
BECOURT	13.8.16		Lt. DICKSON & camp. proceed Camp N 11th Q. & S. Mess.	
			B. and C. Tent Subdivisions to H/I M.D.S. MILLENCOURT for duty. Capt. F. M. ROBERTSON Capt. W.M. STEELE and Lt. H.M. VICKERS Batt. to MILLENCOURT with tent party.	92R
BECOURT	14.8.16		Capt E. GORDON Ram: reported his arrival for duty.	92R
BECOURT	15.8.16		C Section Bearers returned from CONTALMAISON. Report to the Division of A.D.M.S. that good work and gallantry displayed by Capt. WALLACE and Surg. JACOBS on March of 12/13th R.O. DEA to MILLENCOURT	92R
BECOURT	16.8.16		Lt. GRIFFITHS returned from leave England. 1 Capt. and 10 Rs reinforcements arrived from Base.	92R, 92R
BECOURT	17.8.16		3 P.O. to ENGLAND for further training as Artillery Certificates. B Section Bearers returned Today from CONTALMAISON.	92R

WAR DIARY or INTELLIGENCE SUMMARY

Army Form C. 2118

III Aug 1916.   47th/2nd Field Ambulance

Place	Date	Hour	Summary of Events and Information	Remarks and references to Appendices
BECOURT	18.8.16		Routine report.	97 R.
BECOURT	19.8.16		C. Section Bearers returned from CONTALMAISON Vy.	97 R.
BECOURT	20.8.16		Arranged with O.C. 45th Field Ambulance to loan a German Detachment, always ready to burn at Pont Noyelle.	
BECOURT	21.8.16		Returning to Unit. 2/Lt. MORTIMER appointed acting Reg'l Gas Officer. (D.D.M.S. III Corps)	97 R.
BECOURT	22.8.16		Lt. S.A. McCLINTOCK Reserve Reported his arrival for duty. Gas.	97 R.
BECOURT	23.8.16		Lt. S.A. McCLINTOCK posted to 1st Div. (No.27 G.) and reports his departure.	10 R.
BECOURT	24.8.16		Returned to Unit.	97 R.
BECOURT	25.8.16		Returned to Unit.	97 R.
BECOURT	26.8.16		Motor Ambulance Cars inspected today by Inspector of Army Cars & formed in very good order. Surgeon General W.G. MACPHERSON inspected the evening Station Group.	97 R.
BECOURT	27.8.16		Took over A.D.S. at FLATIRON COPSE at 8 p.m. today, so from the Unit 201 Field Amb. Capt. WALLACE with Capt. GORDON to R. Sect. Bearer personnel etc. for duty & the ADS ADS and appointed aid posts and arranged details of evacuation. Wheeled Stretcher has been from Reg. aid posts to A.D.S. Motors by Cars & from ADS to Main Dressing Station via BOTTOM WOOD 3 Cars on Duty at BOTTOMWOOD till the United Amb. dugouts relieved army 24 Lorries. Beaumé also relieved army the hmE. 2 Beaumé Stretchers of 5th LONDON Field Amb. attached for duty to the Armament R. Capt. CALDER and Capt. NESBIT	93 R.

WAR DIARY or INTELLIGENCE SUMMARY

Army Form C. 2118

IV August 1916.   47th Field Ambulance

Place	Date	Hour	Summary of Events and Information	Remarks and references to Appendices
BECOURT	28.8.16		Visited A.D.S. and Regtl Aid posts. Final Evacuation arrangements working smoothly. Q.M.S. WILSON proceeded to dump at CORBIE for drugs etc. Weather still bad — heavy rain and roads very bad for cars.	92R
BECOURT	29.8.16		Capt. F.M. ROBERTSON and Lt. VICKERS with B. Tent Subdivision returned Ealing on completion of duty with 9.1 Train Dressing Station. Weather still very bad. Lt. VICKERS attached temporary Medical Charge of 71st Bde R.F.A. Relieving Capt. S.C. DYKE sick & sent to Adv. Rest Station.	92R
BECOURT	30.8.16		Heavy continuous rain all day. Horse Ambulance Wagons are now being used to clear from FLATIRON A.D.S. to BOTTOM WOOD as road being practically impassable for motors. D.D.M.S. III Corps inspected Dressing Station at 3 p.m. afterwards.	79R
BECOURT	31.8.16		Weather improved today. Visited A.D.S. and Regimental aid posts. Present distribution of units: HQrs and at BECOURT. Rest are T.R.T. subdivision at 2.1 Main Dressing Stn. 2 Bearer Subdivisions 6th (London) 3rd C.&.E. attached.	92R

92.Rilton 2nd Lieut
O.C. 47th Field Ambulance

CONFIDENTIAL

WAR DIARY

of

Lt. Col. T. F. RITCHIE. RAMC
O.C. 1/M. Field Amb"
from 1st Sept 1916 to 30 Sept 1916

Army Form C. 2118

47th Field Ambulance

WAR DIARY
or
INTELLIGENCE SUMMARY
(Erase heading not required.)

Instructions regarding War Diaries and Intelligence Summaries are contained in F.S. Regs., Part II. and the Staff Manual respectively. Title Pages will be prepared in manuscript.

Place	Date	Hour	Summary of Events and Information	Remarks and references to Appendices
BECOURT	1.9.16		Capt W. S. WALLACE evacuated to Hospital. Lieuts and Sergt JACOBS Lieut St.C. Mn. (G.O.C. in C.)	98 R.
BECOURT	2.9.16		Visited A.D.S. and Regimental Aid Posts today. Shell arrangements for dental work and travel in conjunction with O.C. 8/1 Field Ambulance.	98 R.
BECOURT	3.9.16		Walked the Wet Weather Bivouacs to water.	98 R.
BECOURT	4.9.16		2/Lt O'DEA attached temporary practical charge of 26/ Infantry Battalion Field Ambulance following. 2/Lt VICKERS returned from 7 Gen 13th R.F.A. and proceeded to R.A. 1 Reserve Dressing Station for duty.	98 R.
BECOURT	5.9.16		Visited upper Aid Posts and A.D.S. Different arrangements to be put in effect for the Q.U.A.R.R.Y. at BAZENTIN-LE-PETIT and public dressing accommodation at BOTTOM WOOD and reinforced duty with A.D.M.S. New appointee. 2/Lt O'DEA returned from 26/ N.F. Capt CALDER and his team attached Relay Posts to & Sin LONDON F.A. following evacuated duty ADVANCED DRESSING POST at BOTTOM WOOD and visited A.D.S. Kitchen. Public Accommodation.	98 R.
BECOURT	7.9.16		Visited Front letter. 9 Pte R.A.M.C. received as reinforcement and 1 C.S.G. H.T. 2/Lt GRIFFITHS SARAH H. T. 29 c Ferry in the Rear. O/C and Pte at the Picture. Visited R.O.'s and upper Aid Posts in front lines supplied public improvement at FLATIRON COPSE	98 R.
BECOURT	8.9.16		Capt. SPARROW and 30.O.R. from 48 O.R. attached for duty following. Lieut Col. SLOGGETT D.G.M.S. in Bécourt.	98 R. 97 R.
BECOURT	9.9.16		9 Pte Return to reinforcement to 9/17 Field Ambulance for duty and Pte H. T. the Principle.	98 R.

WAR DIARY
INTELLIGENCE SUMMARY

(Erase heading not required.)

Army Form C. 2118

47th Field Ambulance

Place	Date	Hour	Summary of Events and Information	Remarks and references to Appendices
BECOURT	10.9.16		Took over duties from FLATIRON COPSE to Field Amb. 1st 50th Div.n. Extra transport sent up to No 17.G.C.	22R.
BECOURT	11.9.16		Capt. GORDON Capt. SPARROW and one bearer subdivision 46th 2.C. Witchaw from FLATIRON COPSE and rejoined headquarters today. The unit of [...] has been subdivision remains at BECOURT and will assist if necessary. 2/2 Proththeland F.C. to clear front line divisional D.C. 2/2 Northumberland Field Ambulance and arrange details Lt. J.S. DICKSON appointed to Advanced Medical Store OC of 11/6. & S.M. and in charge 877 on return from 9.9.16	22R. 22R.
BECOURT	12.9.16		Capt. SPARROW and one bearer subdivision to remain attached to Infantry brig. A.D.M.S. 15th and 50th Div. to arrange details of future evening operation. Received orders to take over CHATEAU CONTALMAISON from 2nd Bgd. ambulance 2.C. Forwarded lorries to Brigade Amm Reserve IS. Took on clearing of 15th Divn Aid Posts and aid post 15th Durham L. I. & 150th brigade.	22R.
BECOURT	13.9.16	10am	Took on CHATEAU CONTALMAISON with no bearer subdivision Capt. WALLACE Capt. GORDON and RIBERTON.	22R.
		4pm	Sent up bearer div. of 4 teams (4 subdivisions) at intervals during the day with Capt. SPARROW.	
		11pm	Received at CHATEAU with 2 lorries established Capt. BROWN 2/L & W. DAVIS 2/L LEAMAN (45th Field Ambulance)	
BECOURT	14.9.16		Made preliminary arrangements as to disposal of wounded. 6 cars of 45th F.C. 3 horse am.co. wagons 1/45th 146th 2.C. L. G.S. wagons 1 Heavy spring cart attached from transport total transport 13 cars 8 horse wagons, 16 G.S. wagons, 1 & tray	

Army Form C. 2118

47th Field Ambulance

WAR DIARY
or
INTELLIGENCE SUMMARY
(Erase heading not required.)

Instructions regarding War Diaries and Intelligence Summaries are contained in F.S. Regs., Part II. and the Staff Manual respectively. Title Pages will be prepared in manuscript.

Place	Date	Hour	Summary of Events and Information	Remarks and references to Appendices
CONTAL MAISON	14.9.16		In addition to transport of 2/ Northern Inland F.A. am now attached a considerable number of wounded during the night. 70 men of Salvage by lorry as trans- arrived. Left L/O'DEA and a small detachment at BECOURT.	B.R.
CONTAL MAISON	15.9.16	7 a.m.	Immediate began to arrive and from a Battery Position Cheifly SW. Between Guns prowlers under Captain WALLACE. 3 Officers and 90 O.R. in reserve and posts the QUARRY in VILLA WOOD. And in a dressing post in O.G.I. 90 men in reserve in O.G.I. Received 100 infantry from 44th bn R.W.F. as carrying stretcher bearers	
		10 a.m.	First 9 horse Amb. Wagons up to O.G.I. to fly from there to the dressing station at CONTALMAISON. Cars coming up regularly and Stretcher forwarding well. Walking cases and directed to ROSE COTTAGE FRICOURT. With both repairs at Tramp Cleared first: The both of the dressing station photos applied by Officer Kinderman/mafrhen wounded German prisoners are being used as Stretcher B.C.B. Received wire at 1:30 pm Capt STEELE L'VILLERS	P.R.
		8 p.m.	Situation progressing well. Number of wounded evacuated from 6 a.m. to 6 p.m. Lying 503 Sitting 273	
			L/C STEVENS Cashier of Prior Priest Journal Brevet ATS A.D.S. Wounded Still arriving in large numbers but circulation is satisfactory and no congestion. 1 Sitting Other a man reported sick in most useful. Injuries go by car to R.D.1. Main dressing station Setting / Walking by Lotr wagon. G.S. cars and horse whom available to ROSE COTTAGE	

WAR DIARY

INTELLIGENCE SUMMARY

Place	Date	Hour	Summary of Events and Information	Remarks and references to Appendices
CONTALMAISON	16.9.16	2.15 am	The flow of wounded lessening. Further reinforcement of ORs that the trains enough for the A.D.S. is now been of wounded & evacuation has been very good. During the night the CHATEAU had been shelled but no damage has been caused from men being rapidly handled by splinters.	Q.Q.R.
		6 a.m.	Number of wounded evacuated: Lying 138, from 1 a.m. Sitting 150. Total number of wounded in previous 24 hours. About 100 German wounded have passed through C.M.	
		10.30 a.m.	A.D.M.S. and A.A. & Q.M.G. 15th Division visited A.D.S. Wounded are still coming in but in smaller numbers & less frequently.	
		6 p.m.	Evacuated from 6 a.m. Lying 128, Sitting 199.	
CONTAL-MAISON	17.9.16	1 a.m.	23 Lying and 39 Sitting evacuated during the night. Shells have been falling round CHATEAU all morning.	G.Q.R.
		3.30 pm	Lt. Colonel Sir HANBURY WILLIAMS and C. Russell Pencoed visited the A.D.S.	
		4.30 p.m.	6 shells burst which came into being from a Rum and knocking 5 Tents.	
		6 p.m.	40 Lying 61 Sitting evacuated.	

Army Form C. 2118

27th Field Ambulance

WAR DIARY
or
INTELLIGENCE SUMMARY
(Erase heading not required.)

Instructions regarding War Diaries and Intelligence Summaries are contained in F.S. Regs., Part II. and the Staff Manual respectively. Title Pages will be prepared in manuscript.

Place	Date	Hour	Summary of Events and Information	Remarks and references to Appendices
CONTALMAISON	18.9.16	6 a.m.	85 lying and 146 sitting evacuated during night	
			Captains WALLACE and BROWN R/field MARTIN PUICH in charge of Rw. and posts	
			Weather very wet and cold. Evacuation proceeding well.	
		6 p.m.	26 lying and a 84 sitting evacuated during last hour.	
			O.C. 69th Field Ambulance with an advanced party arrived Fricourt to take over.	9.R.
CONTALMAISON	19.9.16	6 a.m.	20 lying and 37 sitting evacuated during the night	
			Handed over at CONTALMAISON to 69th Field Ambulance and handed over BECOURT	
			to 71st Field Ambulance.	
		10 a.m.	Proceeded into BECOURT and ALBERT. E.7.A. 8 up also ALBERT Ambrine Road	9.R.R.
			wet weather very wet. took with us 1 Grittage Gun Common arms.	
			Total Wounded evacuated from CONTALMAISON 962 lying and 1624 sitting. Total 2586.	
			Casualties in the unit 1 killed and 8 wounded	
			45th F.A. others 1 killed and 1 wounded	
			46th F.A. others 1 killed and 2 wounded.	
~~Albert~~				
E.7.A. ALBERT (Ambrine Road)	20.9.16 12 p.m.		Arrived and bivouacked. Lt. B. IDEN is temp. in Mess Officer 10/11 A.F.S.	9.R.R.
E.7.A.	20.9.16		Remained in bivouac. Weather hot and wet. Capt. STEELE sick to A.D.R.S.	
E.7.A.	21.9.16		2 Tent subdivisions Lieut WALLACE GORDON and ROBERTSON and 21 VICKERS attached for duty to 3rd/1st Anzac Lt Prov. R.H.Am.	9.R.R.

Army Form C. 2118

WAR DIARY
or
INTELLIGENCE SUMMARY
(Erase heading not required.)

47th Field Ambulance

Instructions regarding War Diaries and Intelligence Summaries are contained in F.S. Regs., Part II. and the Staff Manual respectively. Title Pages will be prepared in manuscript.

Place	Date	Hour	Summary of Events and Information	Remarks and references to Appendices
E.7.A	22.9.16		Remained in bivouacs. Nothing to report. 1 Cpl. Rank T.E. arrived as reinforcement	97R.
E.7.A	23.9.16		Captain A.M. MATTHEW R.A.M.C. reported his arrival for duty from Brocklin Base AMB.	98R.
E.7.A.	24.9.16		Captain A.M. MATTHEW assumed temporary medical charge of 11th A. & S. H'lders	98R.
E.7.A	25.9.16		P. 40547 Pte W. DAVIES proceeded to England being released for Munitions Work	99R.
E.7 A	26.9.16		Carried out reinstatement of A & T.S. H. with T.A.V.	99R.
E.7.A.	27.9.16		Nothing to report.	97R.
E.7.A.	28.9.16		Nothing to report.	92R.
E.7.A.	29.9.16		Capt WALLACE and Lt. JEEVES attached for instruction in motor tox reffn duties at Tara	92R.
E.7.A	30.9.16		Nothing to H.E. on the build. of tent subdivisions for R.'1 Main Dressing Station (n'27.G.) knap ALBERT situated sheet	99R.
E.7.A			Remainder of unit in bivouacs at E.7.A. knap ALBERT situated sheet	

J.F. Arthur Lt. Colonel
O.C. 47 Field Amb.C.

J.F. Arthur Lt. Colonel
O.C. 47 Field Amb.C.

WAR DIARY
Lt Col J.E. RITCHIE RAMC
O.C. of 1/M FA. from 1st Sept 1916 to 30th Sept 1916

Volume XV

140/1811

Oct. 1916
Evidence

15th Divn.

Medical Service

Var Iran
of
Lt Colonel T. F. RITCHIE R.A.M.C.
O.C. 47th Field Ambulance

from 1-10-16 to 31-10-16.

Volume XVI

COMMITTEE FOR THE
MEDICAL HISTORY OF THE WAR
Date -9 DEC. 1916

Army Form C. 2118

WAR DIARY
or
INTELLIGENCE SUMMARY 47th Field Ambulance
(Erase heading not required.)

Instructions regarding War Diaries and Intelligence Summaries are contained in F.S. Regs., Part II. and the Staff Manual respectively. Title Pages will be prepared in manuscript.

Place	Date	Hour	Summary of Events and Information	Remarks and references to Appendices
E.T.A. Rawlinson's Hut	1.10.16	11 a.m.	Attended a conference at HQrs 9 A.D.M.S. 15th Division. Capt. E. GORDON to Corp. Rest Camp 9/13.W.	9 A.R.
		2.30 p.m.	Received orders to take over R.C. Station HENENCOURT WOOD from 141st Field Amb.	
HENENCOURT WOOD		6 p.m.	Unit arrived at HENENCOURT WOOD. Cmd. HTR over. Patients & equipment accommodated in huts in the wood. On relief had to clear out the R.C. Station on the departure of 141st F.C. No further admissions to be made.	9 A.R.
1=7A HENENCOURT WOOD D-	2.10.16		213 patients remain. Lectures but Transport of 141st Field Ambulance left Etaing by Road.	9 A.R.
HENEN-COURT WOOD	3.10.16		150 patients remain. Personnel of 141st Field Ambulance left Etaing by bus. Promotions received from ADMS & Order Lt. J. O'DEA OBE to Eton S.M. from 25.9.16 Has been appointed to permanent Medical Charge of 11th A + S. H. C.A.S.	9 A.R.
HENENCOURT WOOD	4.10.16		94 remain. Weather very hot. Huts and dark Dugout huts winter quarters. This is an unsuitable place for a Div. Rest Station. Sgt. E.H. JONES proceeded to Eton on 4 day leave. Camp been granted a committee.	9 A.R.
HENENCOURT WOOD	5.10.16		20 remain.	
HENENCOURT	6.10.16		6 remain. See return and letter. Capt WALLACE & Capt BROWN visit 8 Reserve Substations proceeded at 2 p.m. to III Corps Beam Camp to Insp. D.D.M.S. Arrgt visited the Field Amb & Letting and from in the actions & had all equipment sent to be sent to III Corps R.C. Station.	9 A.R.

WAR DIARY or INTELLIGENCE SUMMARY

Army Form C. 2118

47th Field Ambulance

Place	Date	Hour	Summary of Events and Information	Remarks and references to Appendices
HENENCOURT WOD.	7.10.16		Snow remain and Rest Station. Snow Horse at Advanced Bathing Establishment to III Corps Rest Station. Received orders to take over III Corps Main Dressing Station R.O.1 from R.2.2 Field Amb.? Work to be completed on 9th by 9 a.m.	R.R.R.
HENENCOURT WOD	8.10.16	8 a.m.	Left for BECOURT CHATEAU R.O.1 Main Dressing Station. Capt. MATTHEW outposted from 11th A+ S.W.	R.R.R.
BECOURT	8.10.16	9 a.m.	Commenced Taking over R.O.1 Main Dressing Station. Capt. MATTHEW taking on charge of Sick Hospital ALBERT Park.	R.R.R.
BECOURT	9.10.16		Took on Ro2 F.A. R.O.R. wounded. Only lying cases to be admitted. All walking Sick & Slightly Wounded. B.8.O.R. Evacuated every 70 Evacuated to C.C.S. EDGEHILL and 6 remain. 2 Tent Division 710th F.A. left Camp. 1 Tent Subdivision 2/2 Northumberland F.A. arrived for duty.	R.R.R.
BECOURT	10.10.16		Sgt. JACOBS D.C.M. and 3 O.R. Wounded. Eating Rich with Grease. 144 admitted. 133 Evacuated. 3 and 7 wounds 14 remain. The following have been Granted a field. Cleanly duties Authority G.O.C. III Corps. 39762 Cpl. HENDERSON 9970 Cpl MEERTEN 36811 P.O. Branch 32265 Pte McDONNELL 36949 Pte HOWELLS T35092 Sgt. NEWMAN H.T.A.S.C. 2229701 Lieut. A.E. BOWLER M.T.A.S.C. Bivon are being put into use all Tents. Capt. & Knight of all times from HENENCOURT WOD to III Cpl Rest Station.	R.R.R.
BECOURT	11.10.16		63 admitted 2 and 7 wounds. 74 evacuated. 2 stretcher cases. 2 sick branches (Pupils wds.) and 1 remain. Lt. H.F. BELLAMY and Lt. W.S.T. CONNELL Reported for duty. 2 stretcher Cases 1 (General) returned. Capt. MATTHEW proceeded from Div Hospital ALBERT to III Cpl Rest Camp and is relieved by Lt. CONNELL. Capt. BROWN joined W.Q. from III Cpl Beam Camp	R.R.R.

WAR DIARY or INTELLIGENCE SUMMARY

Army Form C. 2118

47th Field Ambulance

Place	Date	Hour	Summary of Events and Information	Remarks and references to Appendices
BECOURT	12.10.16		2 Officers admitted + transferred. 6 ␣ O.R. admitted 2 died 59 transferred and 1 remain.	99R.
BECOURT	13.10.16		1 Officer admitted and transferred. 134 O.R. admitted 130 transferred and 5 remain.	98 R.
BECOURT	14.10.16		3 Officers admitted + transferred. 121 O.R. admitted 2 died 115 transferred and 9 remain.	70 R. 99R.
BECOURT	15.10.16		4 Officers admitted 3 transferred and 1 remained. 70 O.R. admitted 73 transferred and 6 remain. Following letter from A.D.M.S. 23rd Divn. :- "A.D.M.S 15th Divn has been instructed that you kindly arrange for the Bearer subdivision of 45th & 47th Field Ambulances are Appreciative of their excellent services during the last 5 weeks under arrangement of L.F. SARL. 2 Officers and other ranks looked up hurriedly and 9 O.R. for and obtain any bodies left to be taken behind of offensive."	99R
BECOURT	16.10.16		3 Officers admitted 2 transferred and 2 remain. 45 O.R. admitted 1 died 46 transferred and 4 remain.	99R
BECOURT	17.10.16		2 Officers admitted 1 died 1 transferred 2 remained. 31 O.R. admitted 1 died 9 died 32 transferred and 9 remain.	99R. 99R.

Army Form C. 2118

WAR DIARY
or
INTELLIGENCE SUMMARY 47th Field Ambulance

(Erase heading not required.)

Place	Date	Hour	Summary of Events and Information	Remarks and references to Appendices
BECOURT	18.10.16		1 Offr admitted and nil evacuated and remains.	
			36 O.R. admitted 30 evacuated and 6 remain.	9AR.
			1 NCO received return of 1 Serge & 8 Pts Rank	
BECOURT	19.10.16		81 O.R. admitted and 87 evacuated and 9 remain. Western Rwy attd and lost.	9AR
BECOURT	20.10.16		2 Offrs admitted and 9 evacuated. 1 remains.	
			74 O.R. admitted 3 and 7 inmates 69 evacuated and 4 remain.	9AR
BECOURT	21.10.16		Capt. F.M. ROBERTSON evacuated to Base sick and joined off Strength from 18.10.16	
			1 Offr admitted and remains	9AR
			70 O.R. admitted 67 evacuated and 7 remain	
			Capt. T.P. SEYMOUR RAMC posted to this unit for duty from 2/2 Northumbrian Field Ambulance.	9AR
BECOURT	22.10.16		4 Offrs admitted 2 evacuated and 3 remain.	
			40 O.R. admitted 42 evacuated and 5 remain	9AR
			D.M.S. 4th Army inspected Main Dressing Station Evac.	
			2 Offrs admitted and 5 evacuated, nil remain	
BECOURT	23.10.16		66 O.R. admitted 1 and 1 inmates 66 evacuated and 6 remain	9AR.
			Capt E. GORDON transferred & Permanent charge of 9th Black Watch and is struck off strength	9AR
BECOURT	24.10.16		1 Offr admitted & evacuated nil remain.	
			27 O.R. admitted 28 evacuated and 1 remains.	9AR.

Army Form C. 2118

WAR DIARY
or
INTELLIGENCE SUMMARY 47th Field Ambulance
(Erase heading not required.)

Place	Date	Hour	Summary of Events and Information	Remarks and references to Appendices
BECOURT	25.10.16		2 Officers admitted and 2 Evacuated. None remain. 14 O.R. admitted 2 died of wounds 14 Evacuated and 8 Remain. Two Tent Subdivisions 2/2 Northumbrian Field Amb 6th Division HQ of Unit (Capt CROWLEY Capt DICKIE Capt G.A. GREAVES) reported his arrived from 20th Reserve Park for temporary duty. Rev. KEYMER C.F. 3rd class reported his arrived for temporary duty. Capt. T.P. SEYMOUR Evacuated Sick to No 20 & 21 C.C.S.	P.P.R.
BECOURT	26.10.16		Nil Officers admitted. 27 O.R. admitted 3 died of wounds 28 Evacuated and 4 remain. 2 Tent Subdivisions 1/1 S. MIDLAND Field Ambulance arrived for duty (Major BUEDICKER Capt HARRISON Capt FERGUSON) G.O.C. 15th Division inspected Main Dressing Station Lottie. 35903 Sergt LINDSAY and 32016 Pte J.W. FRY awarded Meritorious Service Medals (London Gazette 18.10.16)	P.P.R.
BECOURT	27.10.16		Officer admitted Nil. 24 O.R. admitted 1 died of wounds 24 Evacuated and 3 remain. Capt. T.P. SEYMOUR Evacuated to C.C.S. sick P.U.O. and attack of Phlebitis Left Leg	P.P.R.
BECOURT	28.10.16		3 Officers admitted 1 died of wounds 1 Evacuated and 1 remains. 35 O.R. admitted 3 died of wounds 32 Evacuated and 3 remain.	P.P.R.

Army Form C. 2118

WAR DIARY
or
INTELLIGENCE SUMMARY 47th Field Ambulance

(Erase heading not required.)

Instructions regarding War Diaries and Intelligence Summaries are contained in F. S. Regs., Part II. and the Staff Manual respectively. Title Pages will be prepared in manuscript.

Place	Date	Hour	Summary of Events and Information	Remarks and references to Appendices
BECOURT	29.10.16		1 Officer admitted 2 evacuated and 1 died of wounds. 2 1.O.R. admitted	98R.
BECOURT	30.10.16		2 Officers admitted. 22 evacuated and 2 remain (2 self inflicted wounds admitted) 20 O.R. admitted 16 evacuated and 4 remain. One Officer & O.R died of wounds during rain	9RR.
BECOURT	31.10.16		2 Officers admitted 2 evacuated 15 O.R. admitted 1 died of wounds 16 evacuated and 1 remained. Leader with 1 N.C.O. all personnel in Camp. Present distribution of units 2 horse ambulances at III Corps Beever Camp. Remainder of Units at III Corps 2 1/1 train dressing Station 2 T&T Battalion 1/1 S. Mid. Field Ambulance attached	9RR.

J.F. Restris 2/L Colonel
OC 47th Field Ambulance

CONFIDENTIAL

15th Div
140/903

War Diary
of
Lt Col T.F. Ritchie RAMC
& K Field Ambulance
from 1st Nov to 30th Nov 1916

Vol 16

Volume No. 17.

Nov 1916

COMMITTEE FOR THE
MEDICAL HISTORY OF THE WAR
Date 31 JAN. 1917

Army Form C. 2118

WAR DIARY
or
INTELLIGENCE SUMMARY
(Erase heading not required.)

Instructions regarding War Diaries and Intelligence Summaries are contained in F. S. Regs., Part II. and the Staff Manual respectively. Title Pages will be prepared in manuscript.

Place	Date	Hour	Summary of Events and Information	Remarks and references to Appendices
BECOURT	1.11.16		1 Officer admitted and 1 evacuated. 1 now remain. 10 O.R. admitted 4 died 9 wounds 7 evacuated and now remain. (1 Remained from 31.10.16)	PAR
BECOURT	2.11.16		No Officers admitted. 12 O.R. admitted 9 evacuated and 3 remain. Lt. W.S.T. CONNELL reported his departure to H.Q. for duty at ABBEVILLE. Lt. C. MACDONALD A.M.S. RTR on as D.D.M.S. III Army from Col. B.M. SKINNER and inspected Brown Seating Station Hutton.	PAR. PAR.
BECOURT	3.11.16		No Officers admitted. 20 O.R. admitted 20 evacuated and 3 remain. Capt. WALLACE and Capt. MATTHEW rejoined unit "B" & "C" Bearers from III Corps Bearer Camp. Major BOEDICKER Capt. HARRISON & Capt. FERGUSON met 2 Tent subdivisions 11/ Scotland Field Ambulance reported motor Ambulance to rejoin HQ' 9 dets met.	PAR
BECOURT	4.11.16		No Officers admitted. 7 O.R. admitted 5 evacuated and 2 remain.	PAR.
BECOURT	5.11.16		1 Officer admitted and 1 evacuated. None remain. 18 O.R. admitted 12 evacuated and 8 remain.	PAR
BECOURT	6.11.16		8 Officers admitted 7 evacuated and 1 remain. 67 O.R. admitted 1 died 9 wounded 47 evacuated and 17 remain.	PAR.

1875 Wt. W593/826 1,000,000 4/15 J.B.C. & A. A.D.S.S./Forms/C. 2118.

Army Form C. 2118

WAR DIARY
or
INTELLIGENCE SUMMARY
(Erase heading not required.)

Instructions regarding War Diaries and Intelligence Summaries are contained in F.S. Regs., Part II. and the Staff Manual respectively. Title Pages will be prepared in manuscript.

Place	Date	Hour	Summary of Events and Information	Remarks and references to Appendices
BECOURT	7/11/16		4 Officers admitted 2 Evacuated and 3 Remain. 89 O.R. admitted 1 died 9 wounds 89 Evacuated and 16 Remain.	P.R.
BECOURT	8.11.16		3 Officers admitted 3 Evacuated and 3 Remain. 29 O.R. admitted 1 died 9 wounds 40 Evacuated and 4 Remain. G.O.C. III Corps inspected Main Dressing Station Billet. Two Lorries Pm. O/C M.A.C. Main Dressing Station Billet.	P.R.
BECOURT	9.11.16		4 Officers admitted 5 Evacuated and 2 Remain. 31 O.R. admitted 2 died of wounds 26 Evacuated and 5 Remain. Capt. W.S. WALLACE M.C. posted Leave to Scotland from 11th to 16th inst. And post-leave leave from 10th.	P.R.
BECOURT	10.11.16		3 Officers admitted 1 died of wounds 4 Evacuated none Remain. 33 O.R. admitted 1 died of wounds 1 to duty 26 Evacuated and 10 Remain.	P.R.
BECOURT	11.11.16		1 Officer admitted and 1 died of wounds. None remain. 25 O.R. admitted 27 Evacuated and 8 Remain. 1 Tent Subdivision sent to III Corps P&RS Station for Temporary duty.	P.R.
BECOURT	12.11.16		1 Officer admitted and 1 Evacuated. None Remain. 21 O.R. admitted 28 Evacuated and 1 Remaining.	P.R.

Army Form C. 2118

WAR DIARY
or
INTELLIGENCE SUMMARY
(Erase heading not required.)

Place	Date	Hour	Summary of Events and Information	Remarks and references to Appendices
BECOURT	13.11.16		2 BSras admitted 1 evacuated and 1 remaining. 33 O.R. 32 admitted 32 evacuated and 2 remaining. Capt E. ROBINSON S.R. MC rejoined his Unit from Temporary duty Estbn.	AAR
BECOURT	14.11.16		1 Officer admitted and 2 evacuated. None remain. 15 O.R. admitted and 17 evacuated and remain.	AAR
BECOURT	15.11.16		4 Officers admitted 1 died of wounds 3 evacuated. None remain. 53 O.R. admitted 2 died of wounds 43 evacuated 8 remain.	AAR
BECOURT	16.11.16		1 Officer admitted 1 evacuated and none remain. 31 O.R. admitted 2 died of wounds 28 evacuated and 9 remain. Capt E. ROBINSON proceeds Estbn to 46th Field Ambulance in Exch Capt GREAVES to 20th Res Park CCS	AAR
BECOURT	17.		None of 14 O.R. Reinforcements join 1st Bttn.	AAR
BECOURT	17.11.16		1 Officer admitted 1 evacuated. None remain. 24 O.R. admitted 27 evacuated and 6 remain.	AAR
BECOURT	18.11.16		1 Officer admitted 1 evacuated. None remain. 54 O.R. admitted 2 died of wounds 1 to III Corps Bor. Station 53 evacuated and 2 remain.	AAR

Army Form C. 2118

WAR DIARY
or
INTELLIGENCE SUMMARY
(Erase heading not required.)

Instructions regarding War Diaries and Intelligence Summaries are contained in F.S. Regs., Part II. and the Staff Manual respectively. Title Pages will be prepared in manuscript.

Place	Date	Hour	Summary of Events and Information	Remarks and references to Appendices
BECOURT	19/11		2 Officers admitted 1 evacuated and 1 returned.	
			26 O.R. admitted 2 and 17 wounds 23 evacuated and 11 remain	
			from Tio Bav + Sutland from 20th inst. Capt J.V. BROWN assumed the duties in	P.P.R.
			my absence. 9.9 Ritchie Lt. Stand.	
BECOURT	20/11		Assumed temporary charge of 47th Field ambulance — Vice Lt Col Ritchie	JMS
			on leave from 25th inst	
			Opened extra accommodation for remnants pro from III Corps Rest Station	
			30 cases admitted p.u.c. — aduff. P.w.O.— duespatch. — Invalids — (2 Officers)	
			admitted wounded 52 — including 4 officers.	
			D.D.M.S. visited at 12 noon.	
BECOURT	21/11		one Officer + 10 O.R. admitted sick — one Officer + 23 O.R. admitted wounded OTS	
	,,		5 Walseley cars sent to Army H.Q. in exchange for 5 Siemens —	
	,,		D.A.M.S. III Corps visited	JMS
	,,		Huts (annexe) commenced in woods back of Hospital.	
	,,		Kitchens for personnel moved from front yard to woods about mid garden.	
	,,		Supervised in same lines from the Continuation	
BECOURT	22/11		1 Officer + 9 O.R. sick — 1 Officer + 21 O.R. wounded to Hospital.	
			D.D.M.S. visited with A.D.M.S. 50th Div.	
	,,		3 Officers + 15 O.R. sick + 1 Officer + 2 O.R. wounded admitted.	
BECOURT	23/11	4:30p	Conference convened by A.D.M.S. 10th Div — from senior M.O. retreshing Pd. Case.	JMS

1875 Wt. W593/826 1,000,000 4/15 J.B.C. & A. A.D.S.S./Forms/C. 2118.

Army Form C. 2118

WAR DIARY
or
INTELLIGENCE SUMMARY
(Erase heading not required.)

Instructions regarding War Diaries and Intelligence Summaries are contained in F. S. Regs., Part II. and the Staff Manual respectively. Title Pages will be prepared in manuscript.

Place	Date	Hour	Summary of Events and Information	Remarks and references to Appendices
BECOURT	24th		3 Officers & 14 O.R. admitted wounded - (1 Officer & 2 Officers wounded at DS) 1 Officer & 21 O.R. admitted sick - D.D.M.S. & DADMS. Hilsborg visited.	JB
BECOURT	25th		6 Officers & 28 O.R. admitted wounded - 3 Officers & 15 O.R. admitted sick M.A.C. Officer visited CLAPPERTON RMMC - order list not available.	JB
BECOURT	26th		6 Officers Nil & 12 O.R. admitted wounded - 1 died of wounds. One Officer & 25 O.R. admitted sick - 17 evacuated B.E.S. 50 Running. 1 O.R. DIED from wounds	JB
BECOURT	27th		0 Officers & 15 O.R. admitted wounded - 1 O.R. admitted sick - 99 Remaining. 1 Officer Nil & 78 O.R. admitted sick - Capt W.S. WALLACE returned from leave.	JB
BECOURT	28th		3 Officers & 21 O.R. admitted wounded. 7 Officers Nil & 61 O.R. admitted sick - Remaining 106 O.R.	JB
BECOURT	29th		0 Officers Nil & 21 O.R. admitted wounded & 1 O.R. self inflicted - 2 died of wounds - Officers - Officers 3 & 68 O.R. admitted sick - Remaining 2 Officers 126 O.R. - 3 AMIENS huts erected. DADMS visited.	JB
BECOURT	30th	11 AM	4 Officers & 17 O.R. admitted wounded - 1 died of wounds - 1 Officer Running & 30 O.R. sick admitted - 105 Remaining. Kitchen for priests completed. Road into these huts completed. D.D.M.S. III Corp visited.	JB

J Brown Capt RAMC
OC 47th Field Ambulance

140/903

15th Div.

Medical Services

Vol 17

War Diary
of
Lt Colonel T F Roche
OC 47th Field Ambulance
from 1-12-16 to 31-12-16
Volume 19

CONFIDENTIAL
Dec 1916

COMMITTEE FOR THE
MEDICAL HISTORY OF THE WAR
Date 31 JAN. 1917

Army Form C. 2118

47th Field Ambulance
December 1916

WAR DIARY
or
INTELLIGENCE SUMMARY
(Erase heading not required.)

Place	Date	Hour	Summary of Events and Information	Remarks and references to Appendices
BECOURT	1/12/16		1 Officer + 61 O.R. admitted Sick — 7 evacuated — 87 remaining. 1 Officer + 27 O.R. admitted wounded — 1 O.R. died of wounds. Capt NALLACE & Capt WSRAME assumed temporary charge of 45th Res Ambulance Advancing at ECOLE SUPERIEUR ALBERT.	Syd
BECOURT	2/12/16	10 AM	A.D.M.S. 13th Div'n visited — 1 Officer + 66 O.R. admitted Sick — 117 remaining. Officers nil + 14 O.R. admitted wounded — D.D.M.S. III Corps visited. Lt Col RITCHIE J.F. R.A.M.C. returned from leave + assumed Command of unit. J. Brown Capt R.A.M.C.	Syd
BECOURT	2.12.16	7.30pm	Returned from leave hosptd. 2 Lt Ritchie 21 Lt.	88R
BECOURT	3.12.16		Admission N. Sick to III Corps Aux. Post Station 980.R. transferred to 1/1 N.F.A. 8. 13 k 44 — 99 2+R 95 evacuated. and remain. 950 R. Admissions to 47 in 2 field Amb (local) Sick 28R. 29 Transferred from 47 Field Amb to III Corps R.S. 9 Admitted to 47 in 2 field Amb 6. 10 Back Cut Stretchers to C.C.S. 10. Admitted to 20 / Armin Motor Station III Corps 1 Officer out Evacuated Lying Remain 6 Admitted 2 O.R. 28 admitted 20 Evacuated 10 Remain Wounded OR. OR. 28 admitted fr Wdg 183 evacuated 12 remain.	82.R.

1875 Wt. W593/826 1,000,000 4/15 J.B.C. & A. A.D.S.S./Forms/C. 2118.

WAR DIARY or INTELLIGENCE SUMMARY

Army Form C. 2118

47th Field Ambulance Dec 1916

Place	Date	Hour	Summary of Events and Information	Remarks and references to Appendices
BECOURT	4.12.16		Capts Eatock III Cops Auxiliary Rest Station #97 was remained 1 admitted and 1 evacuated 1 remain. S.R. 85 admitted 145 W/N.F.A. 26 duty 90 evacuated 74 remain. Admitted to R.I M.D.S. Brace Bet Remaining 1. O.R. 20; Adm December 4. 24 evacuated & 0 remain Admitted to 47th F Amb 6a Officers 6 evacuated 1 1 remain. O.R. 4; evacuated 4. None remain Captain P.S. BLAKER Reinf. reported his arrival for duty from Lt. H. E. BELLAMY proceeded for duty with 15th D.A. Bde Capt S.C. DYKE Reinf. Is on his proceeded to Base. III Cops Auxiliary Rest Station admitted Officers Ret. 1 Open Remains.	99R
RECOURT	5.12.16		R.1 Main AR&Ship Station III Cops admitted Officers Ret. 1 Open Remains. S.R. 52; 134 duty 23 evacuated 90 remain O.R. 24; 3 died 9 arrivals 20 evacuated 3 remain 47th Field Ambulance admitted Officers Ret. U.R. 10; Evacuated to C.C.S. 10	99R

Army Form C. 2118

WAR DIARY
or
INTELLIGENCE SUMMARY
(Erase heading not required.)

47th Field Ambulance

December 1916.

Instructions regarding War Diaries and Intelligence Summaries are contained in F. S. Regs., Part II. and the Staff Manual respectively. Title Pages will be prepared in manuscript.

Place	Date	Hour	Summary of Events and Information	Remarks and references to Appendices
BECOURT	5.12.16	6.30pm	At 6.30 p.m. Enemy Shelled Point Dressing Station Arriving at about 20 minutes High Velocity H.E. Shells & Long Calibre were used & having fell in a lean to to the hut being destroyed by a direct hit. About 1.30 A.M. the wounded in Hospital at this Time all walking cases were at once directed to the cellars and lying down wounded were carried in - a dug out & dressing tents as shelling was being persistent Shell after Shell fell into & in a small area. All cars at once turned out and after rapid clearing all wounded & staff were immediately evacuated. Shelling ceased at about 6.40 p.m. but recommenced at about 7.15 p.m. and lasted 15 to 20 minutes. Shells falling in roughly the same area. As soon as the second bombardment ceased Evacuation recommenced and all patients were evacuated by 8.15 p.m. 129 were evacuated to C.C.S. in this time. Casualties amounted were 5 killed & 33 wounded. 7 whom 2 died & wounds and 7 belonged to this unit. Capt J.V. BROWN & Revd. Revd. McDOWALL and Indians Ambulance in clearing work. All Sick were received during the night were sent to III Corps Rest Station and wounded sent on to C.C.S. Informed D.D.M.S. and A.D.M.S. at Authuille. Motor cars for Evacuation were borrowed from III Corps Rest Station.	99R. 99R.

1875 Wt. W593/826 1,000,000 4/15 J.B.C. & A. A.D.S.S./Forms/C. 2118.

IV

Army Form C. 2118

47th Field Ambulance
1st December 1916

WAR DIARY
or
INTELLIGENCE SUMMARY
(Erase heading not required.)

Instructions regarding War Diaries and Intelligence Summaries are contained in F. S. Regs., Part II. and the Staff Manual respectively. Title Pages will be prepared in manuscript.

Place	Date	Hour	Summary of Events and Information	Remarks and references to Appendices
BECOURT	6.12.16		Admittant to 47th Field Ambulance Officers 2 admitted v 2 evacuated. None remain. O.R. 4 admitted v 4 evacuated. None remain.	
			R.1 Main Dressing Station and IV Corps (nursing) Rest Station are provisionally closed. A.D.M.S. & D.D.M.S. inspected the damage caused last night by H.T. S.L.T.S. are damaged beyond total repair and a large number can be repaired locally by unit but are at present unserviceable. Grenwalks from ALBERT & ESBARTS FARM are being Corps Commander also visited main dressing Station today.	JPR.
BECOURT	7.12.16		In futher bombardment has taken place. Knocked over again & to received hit. On both. Serious cases and formation cases are kept in huts nearest shelter. Have opened an RSA with 26 beds leading from huts & access into cellars and have also shifted drain car leading to collars for 3 down cases. About 15 by up down cases can be accommodated in this way which seems ample. Instructions given R.D. to retain cases but to evacuate at once to C.C.S. 1 accidental case admitted and 1 evacuated. None remain. Infant Outfield D.C.M. wounded on 5.12.16 expired died T. wounds last night at C.C.S.	JPR.
BECOURT	8.12.16		Admittedto to 47th Field Ambulance Officers 1; evacuated 1. None remain. O.R. 6; Evacuated to C.R.S. 6. None remain. Officers Nil. O.R. 1 admitted 1 evacuated. None remain.	JPR.

1875 Wt: W593/826 1,000,000 4/15 J.B.C. & A. A.D.S.S./Forms/C. 2118.

Army Form C. 2118

WAR DIARY
or
INTELLIGENCE SUMMARY

(Erase heading not required.)

Instructions regarding War Diaries and Intelligence Summaries are contained in F.S. Regs, Part II. and the Staff Manual respectively. Title Pages will be prepared in manuscript.

47th Field Ambulance
December 1916

Place	Date	Hour	Summary of Events and Information	Remarks and references to Appendices
BECOURT	8.12.16		Received warning return from A.D.M.S. to exchange duties with 46th Field Ambulance his at ESBART's FARM, and 46th Field Ambulance takes over 2.0/1 M.D.S. III Corps and our Take over Div. Rest Station, Scabies Hospital and Mens Hospital	9.A.R.
BECOURT	9.12.16		Admitted to 47th Field Ambulance from Rel. O.R. 13. 12 Evacuated and 1 Remained. Admitted to 2.0/1 M.D.S. From Rel. O.R. 1. And 1 Evacuated and remain. Relieve ESBART's FARM. Relief takes place by sections of section left Ecoivre at 9 a.m. 2 Vickers in Command.	9.A.R.
		10h.	One section 46th Field Ambulance	9.A.R.
BECOURT	10.12.16	9 a.m.	B Section left Ecoivre for ES BART's FARM. 1 Section 46th Field Ambulance arrived 12 hrs. Admitted to 2.0/1 M.D.S. From hit O.R. 2 Sick, 13 Evacuated, 9 Remained and 6 Remain. Admitted to 47th F.A. 3 officers. 81 to III Corps Rest Station. 2 to 46th Field Ambulance ESBARTS. O.R. 10. 1 Evacuated to C.C.S. 10 Transferred to III Corps Rest Station	9.A.R.
BECOURT	11.12.16		Admitted 2.0/1 M.D.S. Officers Rel. O.R. 11. 1 Sick 9 Evacuate. 14 Evacuated and 2 transferred to 46th F.A. Admitted to 47th F.A. From Rel. O.R. 7. 6 to III Corps Rest Station. 1 to 46th F.A.	9.A.R.
		9.6.h.	A section left Ecoivre for ESBARTS FARM. Relief was effected of 2.0/1 M.D.S. landed nun to 46th F.A. L' BELLAMY handed over charge of Mons hier R.F.A. to Capt. DAY 46th Field Amb.	
ESBART		10h.	Arrived at ESBART's FARM and Left on Motor Speed Sector 15th Australian Rest Station in III Corps Scabies Station.	9.A.R.

1875 W. W593/826 1,000,000 4/15. J.B.C. & A. A.D.S.S./Forms/C. 2118.

WAR DIARY or INTELLIGENCE SUMMARY

Army Form C. 2118

47th Field Ambulance
December 1916

Place	Date	Hour	Summary of Events and Information	Remarks and references to Appendices
EBART	12.12.16		TM1 Undergoing III Cops Scabies StatN. 88 O.R. on tour Jan. 46,26. 15th D.R.S. 95 D.R. 88 Fant 16. Admitted to III Cops Scabies O.R. 8. T. Andy 5. K.C.C.S. 28. Evacuated 63 to 15th D.R.S. 8 ECW admitted Rel. to Andy 1. 15 remain. O.R. admitted 10. to Andy 16; K.C.C.S. 16. 73 remain to 47th 2nd Camb. Offices Rel. D.R. 4. transferred to 15th D.R.S. 4. Personnel 9 went Relieved as ammunition carried in NSPFP from A.S.C. 17th Essex horsed infantry trains. Lt VICKERS forwarded on leave tonight (on account of contract)	PR.
ECBART	13.12.16		Admitted to III Cops Scabies statN. "B" O.R. 10. to Andy 5. 68 remain. 15th D.R.S. 17 Gree 1. A.N.Z. B.T.Hosp 1. to Andy 2, K.C.C.S. 2. 11 remain. O.R. 12. to Andy 11, to C.C.S. 2. 72 remain. to 47th 2.C. O.R. 10; 1st Scabies Station 2 to N.Z. Stat7Hosp 7 to 15th D.R.S. Offices 1. to 15th D.R.S. 1.	PR.
ESBART	14.12.16		Admitted to TMI Cops Scabies Stat.N. Gorm O.R. 18; K Andy 3, K C.C.S. 18; 65 remain. 15th D.R.S. 7 Gree 4. and 15 remain. O.R. 7217, to Andy 11 K.C.C.S 9; 69 remain. 47th Field Amb. Officer 1 transferred to 15th D.R.S. 1. D.R. 12 transferred to Scabies Stat.N. 2; to 15th D.R.S 10. Weather very wet and wet.	PR.

WAR DIARY or INTELLIGENCE SUMMARY

Army Form C. 2118

47th Field Ambulance
December 1916

Place	Date	Hour	Summary of Events and Information	Remarks and references to Appendices
ESBART	15.12.16		Capt. WALLACE attended a course at Anti Gas School of that. Capt WALLACE and C Section teams 3rd proceeded to CONTALMAISON to help out 2.R. Admitted to III Corps Scabies Station O.R. 8; to duty 6; K C C S 9; 6 Remain 15th D. R. S. Mines Rids to duty 4; K C C S 1; 10 Remain O.R. 9; 13; to duty 22. 60 Remain 1st 47th Field Amb. O.R. 15"; to Scabies Station 6; to D.R.S. 9	98 R.
ESBART	16.12.16		Admitted to III Corps Scabies Station O.R. 7; to duty 3; to C C S 1; 9. Remain 15th D.R.S. Mines Rids. 10 Remain O.R. 22; to duty 7; K C C S 1; 74 Remain 47th Field Amb. O.R. 24; to Scabies Station 6; to D.R.S 17; K C C S 1	98 R.
ESBART	17.12.16		Admitted to III Corps Scabies Station O.R.6 J to duty 2; to C.C.S.10; 46 Remain 15th D. R. S. Mines Rids, to duty 1; 9 Remain D.R. Rest to duty 14; K C C S 8; 57 Remain 47th Field Amb. O.R. 11; to Scabies Station 5; to D.R. C.C.S 6. Attended conference 11.6 hr at A.D.M.S office Ribemont	98 R.

VIII

WAR DIARY
or
INTELLIGENCE SUMMARY

Army Form C. 2118

47th Field Ambulance
December 1916

(Erase heading not required.)

Instructions regarding War Diaries and Intelligence Summaries are contained in F.S. Regs., Part II. and the Staff Manual respectively. Title Pages will be prepared in manuscript.

Place	Date	Hour	Summary of Events and Information	Remarks and references to Appendices
ESBARTS	18.12.16		Admitted to III bays Sentries Station O.R. 7; to C.C.S 4; 49 Remain. to 15th D.R.S. Officers 2; to Duty 1; to C.C.S. 2; 8 Remain. O.R. 53; to Duty 5; to C.C.S 2; 53 Remain. to 47th Field Amb.ce O.R. 11; to Stations Station 7, to 15th D.R.S. Lt + O'h? F. DAVIS Rn.T.M. Learnt to England from 17th to 27th December.	98AP.
ESBARTS	19.12.16		Admitted to 47th Field Ambulance Officer 2, to C.C.S 1; to 15th D.R.S. 1. O.R. 14; to C.C.S 3; Admitted 4, to 15th D.R.S. to 15th D.R.S. Officers 3; to C.C.S. 1; 10 Remain. O.R. 8; to Duty 2; 61 Remain. to III bays Sentries Station O.R. 4; to C.C.S 4; 49 Remain. Captain J.V. BROWN proceeded on leave to England.	98AP
ESBARTS	20.12.16		Admitted to 47th Field Amb.ce Officers Nil. O.R. 15; to III bays Sentries 7; to 15th D.R.S. 8. to 15th D.R.S. Officers 1; to Duty 1; to C.C.S. 1; Remaining 9. O.R. 9; to Duty 4; Remaining 66. to III bays Station Note O.R. 7; to Duty 1; to C.C.S 4; 51 Remain. Capt. W.S. WALLACE M.C. rejoined from Temporary duty with 46th Field Ambulance.	9AP.

1875 Wt. W 593/826 1,000,000 4/15 J.B.C. & A. A.D.S.S./Forms/C.2118.

WAR DIARY or INTELLIGENCE SUMMARY

Army Form C. 2118

47th Field Ambulance
December 1916

Place	Date	Hour	Summary of Events and Information	Remarks and references to Appendices
E.BART	21.12.16		Admitted to 47th Field Ambulance Officer Sick. O.R. 17; to C.C.S. 1; to Scabies Station 2; to 15th D.R.S. 14.	
			to 15th D.R.S. Officer Out; to C.C.S. 1; 8 Remain. O.R. 16; to Amby 8; to C.C.S. 2; 77 Remain	P.R.
			to Major Scabies Station O.R. 3; to Amby 5; to C.C.S. 2; Remaining 47.	
E.BART	22.12.16		Admitted to 47th Field Ambulance Officer Sick 1; to Amby 1; to C.C.S. 1; Remaining 6. O.R. 16; to Amby 3; to C.C.S. 2; Remaining 77	
			to 15th D.R.S. Officer 1; to 15th D.R.S. 1. O.R. 23; to 15th D.R.S. 12; to Scabies 11.	
			to III hyp Scabies Station. O.R. 15; to Amby 2; to C.C.S. 2; 58 Remain.	P.R.

Army Form C. 2118

47th Field Ambulance
December 1916

WAR DIARY
or
INTELLIGENCE SUMMARY
(Erase heading not required.)

Instructions regarding War Diaries and Intelligence Summaries are contained in F. S. Regs., Part II. and the Staff Manual respectively. Title Pages will be prepared in manuscript.

Place	Date	Hour	Summary of Events and Information	Remarks and references to Appendices
22/12 ES BART	23.12.16		Admitted to 47th Field Amb. Officers Sick Pers. O.R. 15; to D.R.S. 7; to Scabies Station 7; to C.C.S. 1.	
			15th D.R.S. Officers Sick 1; to duty 2; to C.C.S. 1; Remained 6. O.R. 7; to duty 7; to C.C.S. 1; Remained 78. III Corps Scabies. O.R. 9; to duty 2; to C.C.S. 13; Remained 52.	
			Capt. R.S. BLAKER to Company Reinforced Camp 9.71 8th 13th R.F.A. Capt. W.S. WALLACE M.C. to Company Reinforced Camp 8p 6/10 Essex.	PPR
ES BARTS	24.12.16		Admitted to 47th Field Amb. Officers Sick. O.R. 13; to D.R.S. 7; to Scabies 6. 15th D.R.S. Officers Sick; to C.C.S. 3; to Remained. O.R. 11; to duty 5; to C.C.S. 3; to Scabies 1; Remained 78. III Corps Scabies Station. O.R. 9; to duty 3; to D.R.S. 5; to C.C.S. E. Remained 45.	PPR
			Proceeded to WARLOY to Take over HOSPITAL HOSPICE as our Officers Hospital, but are to occupy beds in a few days time.	PPR
ES BART	25.12.16		Admitted to 47th Field Amb. Officers Sick Ads and Jews introduced to A.D.'s M.I. by Divisional Commander. O.R. Officers Sick; 2 to duty; 2 to III Corps Rest Station MILLENCOURT. to 15th D.R.S. O.R. 5; to duty 4; to C.C.S. 26; Remained 57. to III Corps Scabies Station O.R. 4; to C.C.S. 7 Remained 42 Xmas Day. Troops had a Christmas y complete Xmas Scenery.	PPR

Army Form C. 2118

47th Field Ambulance
December 1916

WAR DIARY
or
INTELLIGENCE SUMMARY
(Erase heading not required.)

Instructions regarding War Diaries and Intelligence Summaries are contained in F.S. Regs., Part II. and the Staff Manual respectively. Title Pages will be prepared in manuscript.

Place	Date	Hour	Summary of Events and Information	Remarks and references to Appendices
ESBART	26.12.16		Admitted to 15th D.R.S. Officers nil & kit remain; Officers sick & nil officers. O.R. 3; to duty 2; Sick remain. to III Corps Scabies Sta O.R.S. 1 - D.R.S. 46 remain	J.A.R.
			In 15th D.R.S. and III Corps Scabies Station but to be closed by 12 Both in 9.M. and buildings handed over to III Corps Cavalry Regt. Capt W. H. STEELE having been posted to service at home in Private W.O. Set Ovington.	
ESBART	27.12.16		Admitted to 15th D.R.S. O.R. 16; to 2/2 North. F.A. 1; to duty 3; to C.C.S. 13. 60 remain at III Corps Scabies Station O.R. 7; to duty 4; to C.C.S. 6, 15th D.R.S. 1; 42 remain. Advance party sent to take over buildings and effects of WARLOY. L. HOSPITAL 140 S.P.I.C. is a very suitable modern building and will accommodate about 40 patients (Officers). After fitting up sheer Room and Dry Room.	
ESBART	28.12.16		Admitted to 15th D.R.S. O.R. 1; to duty 20; to C.C.S. 41; sick remain. to III Corps Scabies St. O.R. 4; to 2/2 North. F.A. 15; to duty 2; to C.C.S. 29. sick remain. Today we take over 1st PATRONAGE CONTAY as Medical Officer's Quarters. Cadet A.W.M. MATTHEW in charge. Headquarters today from ESBART to WARLOY. Personnel accommodated in HERES huts in temporary quarters.	J.A.R.

Army Form C. 2118

WAR DIARY
or
INTELLIGENCE SUMMARY
(Erase heading not required.)

47th Field Ambulance
December 1916

Place	Date	Hour	Summary of Events and Information	Remarks and references to Appendices
WARLOY	29.12.16		Admitted to 47th Field Amb. I.R.S; 1t 1/2 S. Irish F.G.3. & 2/2 North. F.G.2. have permission to take over HOSPICE found hot het heating apparatus was badly damaged and heat wouldn't be boiler is cracked & flues & fire tubes broken. The furnace is completely dismantled. Also shaft-turn out in hits and the flange in union does not well. Cast iron feed system also not of upper turn into a long crack in the main pipe. Reported this verbally to D.D.M.S.	P.R.
WARLOY	30.12.16		Some admitted. Remained at work performing WARLOY & CONTAY for reception of sick.	P.R.
WARLOY	31.12.16		Some admitted. Took in sick. Admitted annual report of officer supply heating system & equipment. L.D.M.S. 2 brass extinguisher attached 4 S.ni F.A. 1 Tent Sub-division at CONTAY. Remainder of unit at WARLOY.	P.R.

J.F. Prentice Lt. Colonel
O.C. 47th Field Ambulance

Jan. 1917

Influenza

Vol 18

140/199?

15th Div

Sir

15th Div

of

Lt Colonel T. F. Ritchie RAMC

O.C. 47th Field Ambulance

from 1.1.17 to 31.1.17

Vol. 18

COMMITTEE FOR THE
MEDICAL HISTORY OF THE WA...
Date 4.- APR. 1917

A.A. & Q.M.G.
15th Division

Herewith war diary of this unit
for January 1917.

Please acknowledge receipt

J.F. Patterson Lt Col
O.C. 47th Field Amb

1.2.17

Army Form C. 2118

WAR DIARY
or
INTELLIGENCE SUMMARY
(Erase heading not required.)

47th Bristol Comm Intelligence
January 1917

Instructions regarding War Diaries and Intelligence Summaries are contained in F. S. Regs., Part II. and the Staff Manual respectively. Title Pages will be prepared in manuscript.

Place	Date	Hour	Summary of Events and Information	Remarks and references to Appendices
WARLOY	1.1.17		Lieut Oldfield and Chaplains HOSPITAL HOSPICE WARLOY for the reception of SICK Officers. Seg. Major J. McDOWALL proceeded to England on one months furlough Ely.	PR.
WARLOY	2.1.17		Admitted WARLOY Officers Hospital, Sub. Lieutn. Lionel Bennell of CONTAY (PATRAVA G.E.) Captain MATTHEW his chauffer. Lieut. J. RICKARDS and J.W. CROMBIE reported. Units arrived for duty Ely. Captain VK. WALLACE M.C. returned from N.Z. Stationary Hospital (attachment to study) and proceeded Ely for temporary medical charge of 6/Canadians Infantry on Bde. Brickfield Camp at HENENCOURT WOOD CAMP	PR. PR. PR.
WARLOY	3.1.17		Lt. H.F. BELLAMY proceeded Ely for temporary duty of 72nd Bde R.F.A. Capt. J.V. BROWN returned from leave Ely.	PR. PR.
WARLOY WARLOY WARLOY	4.1.17 5.1.17 6.1.17		D.D.M.S. visited Hospital Ely. 2L RICKARDS proceeded to 45th F.A. for temporary duty Ely. Capt. E. ROBINSON A/45th F.A. arrived for temporary duty Lieut Q/M E. DAVIS returned from leave Ely. Q.Mr. S. WILLS on return from leave forwarded for duty at 9.0.19 Adv. Depot Medical Stores. 75th No. Field Amb. rejoined to transport & in Brigade 9 HOSPITAL HOSPICE from 1/2 South Midland Field Ambulance and 34 Dressings from 15th Fd. Amb. Rest Station WARLOY	PR.
WARLOY	7.1.17		Capt. E. ROBINSON proceeded Ely for temporary duty in 9/Black Watch. Lt Bar Officer Hospital frontmg Qn.d. Lieu will be transferred to us from III Corps Rest Station	PR.
WARLOY	8.1.17		Officer Hospital Bennell Ely.	PR.
WARLOY	9.1.17		Capt F. H.M. VICKERS proceeded Ely for temporary Brickoul church of 8/10 Gordons.	PR.
WARLOY	10.1.17		Lieutn. DEC & W.C.T.G. Gordons on 17 Bde. is Rest Station	PR.

Army Form C. 2118

WAR DIARY
or
INTELLIGENCE SUMMARY
(Erase heading not required.)

47th Field Ambulance
January 1917

Instructions regarding War Diaries and Intelligence Summaries are contained in F.S. Regs., Part II. and the Staff Manual respectively. Title Pages will be prepared in manuscript.

Place	Date	Hour	Summary of Events and Information	Remarks and references to Appendices
H.Q.T. WARLOY	11.1.17		Received 2 A&St T/ 1 N.C.O and Two men without kits	92R.
WARLOY	12.1.17		Captain E. ROBINSON rejoined from 9/Black Watch Btlry	92R.
WARLOY	13.1.17		O.i/c II CONTAY with D.A.D.M.S.	
WARLOY	14.1.17		Started our huts in progress to 3rd Australian Field Ambulance Staff. Seconded product S to C.R.S. accept Urgent cases to VADENCOURT	92R.
WARLOY	15.1.17		Captain E. ROBINSON proceeded to temporary charge of 8/7 Roy. Scots. Brigade.	92R.
WARLOY	16.1.17		2nd CROMBIE proceeded to ENGLAND for interview by Selection Committee War Office.	92R.
WARLOY	17.1.17		Heavy fall of Snow Storm.	92R.
WARLOY	18.1.17		Heavy fall of Snow Storm. Anti-transport to kits.	92R.
WARLOY	19.1.17		Capt P.S. BLAKER rejoined Ambulance from 71st 13th R.F.A. Lt H.F. BELLAMY rejoined Ambulance from 72nd 13th R.F.A.	92R.
WARLOY	20.1.17		Capt Bishop of importance to kits	92R.
WARLOY	21.1.17		1 N.C.O. and 13 Pts sent to 46th F.A. Btry and 1 sent month returned	92R.
WARLOY	22.1.17		Capt. H.M. VICKERS rejoined Ambce from 6/13 Gordons	92R.
WARLOY	23.1.17		3 N.C.O's and 21 Pts to 48th F.A. and an Equal number returned. Snow Hard Storm.	92R.
WARLOY	24.1.17		Lt H.F. BELLAMY proceeds on leave to ENGLAND from Staff Gordons	92R.

Army Form C. 2118

WAR DIARY
or
INTELLIGENCE SUMMARY
(Erase heading not required.)

47th Field Ambulance
January 1917

Place	Date	Hour	Summary of Events and Information	Remarks and references to Appendices
WARLOY	25.1.17		General health continues satisfactory.	9AR
WARLOY	26.1.17		Capt. W.S. WALLACE M.C. returned from temporary duty with C/Cameron Highlanders	SBR
WARLOY	27.1.17		General health. Some few officers in Hospital. D.D.M.S. II Corps on visit inspected today.	SBR
WARLOY	28.1.17		Sanitary & H.E. health still fine serum.	9AR
WARLOY	29.1.17		Lt W.M. CROMBIE having been appointed for one month to the Indian Pension Force in Paris. Off his Regr from 20.1.17. A.D.M.S. inspected Hospital today. 12 O.R. posted to 45th Field Ambulance today. 6th Batallion casualties.	9AR
WARLOY	30.1.17		Capt MATTHEW takes on medical charge of III Corps School today in addition to his other duties.	9AR
WARLOY	31.1.17		49 O.R. returned today from 45th Field Ambulance. Capt H.M. VICKERS and Capt P.S. BLAKER with 20 O.R. attached temporarily to 48th Field Amb.	SBR

J.P. Quinten Lt Colonel
OC 47th Field Ambulance

CONFIDENTIAL. U.1)

Feb 1917

140/1991

15th Div

Vol 19

WAR DIARY.
of
Hq². 'Zeal Ambulance
FEBRUARY. 1917
by
Capt. J V BROWN R A M C
NZ Med Amb. Co.

COMMITTEE FOR THE
MEDICAL HISTORY OF THE WAR
Date 4 APR.1917

Army Form C. 2118

WAR DIARY
or
INTELLIGENCE SUMMARY

(Erase heading not required.)

Instructions regarding War Diaries and Intelligence Summaries are contained in F. S. Regs., Part II. and the Staff Manual respectively. Title Pages will be prepared in manuscript.

Place	Date	Hour	Summary of Events and Information	Remarks and references to Appendices
WARLOY	1.2.17.		Lt RICKARDS returned from 45th F.A. and proceeded to 46th F.A. in relief of Capt P.S. BLAKER sick	PPR.
WARLOY	2.2.17		All sick returns in Brigade transferred. Ambulance 1 in good order. Weather continues very cold. Snow frost all day.	PPR.
WARLOY	3.2.17		Nothing to note. Received new issue winter blankets all transport complete & ready for the road.	PPR.
WARLOY	4.2.17		Dressing Station. Only very small number of sick being admitted. 46th Infantry Brigade now billetted in village.	PPR.
WARLOY	5.2.17		Roll on Sun attended and transferred to C.R.S. or evacuated to C.C.C. Army and A.D. returned.	PPR.
WARLOY	6.2.17		Received a draft of N.6 PWs letter.	PPR.
WARLOY	7.2.17		Capt H.M. VICKERS returned from temporary duty with 46th Field Amb.	PPR.
WARLOY	8.2.17		Lieut Philip McDOWALL returned from leave today.	PPR.
WARLOY	9.2.17		Received warning order of move to new area Capt. VICKERS again attached to 46th Field Ambulance	PPR.
WARLOY	10.2.17		English Group (Hamilton McCabe) sent to new III Corps Area Area. Red Cross stores sent to be returned. At me was attached to 1st ANZAC Corps.	PPR.
WARLOY	11.2.17		Capt. H.M. VICKERS returned from 46th Field Ambulance. Visited new area with A.D.M.S. being near recovered from 46th Bde. Byte as to movement, attachment with 46th Field Amb & afterwards	PPR.
WARLOY	12.2.17		Remainder of III Corps equipment sent in today.	PPR.
WARLOY	13.2.17		About noon Motor Hospital Lorry of Red Cross store handed to A.D.M.S. Red Cross appreciation sent forwarded to C.C.S. CONWAY. Smith TW leave England Thanchet 12th & Capt WALLACE	PPR.

1875 Wt. W593/826 1,000,000 4/15 J.B.C. & A. A.D.S.S./Forms/C. 2118.

Army Form C. 2118

WAR DIARY
or
INTELLIGENCE SUMMARY
(Erase heading not required.)

Instructions regarding War Diaries and Intelligence Summaries are contained in F.S. Regs., Part II. and the Staff Manual respectively. Title Pages will be prepared in manuscript.

Place	Date	Hour	Summary of Events and Information	Remarks and references to Appendices
WARLOY BEAUVAL	14/2/17		Lt. Col. RITCHIE D.S.O. proceeded on leave to England. Went to the 4th L. Infty. Bgd. to BEAUVAL via HÉRISSART, le VAL-de MAISON. Corner in billets at about 2 P.M. S. volunteered to GÉZAINCOURT.	notes
BRETEL	15/2/17		Proceeded from BEAUVAL to BRETEL via GÉZAINCOURT. Evacuated sick to DOULLENS + GÉZAINCOURT reaching billets at noon.	notes
FORTEL	16/2/17		Marched for BRETEL to FORTEL via HEM, Nr Rue AUTHIE, FRÖHEN-le-GRAND & VILLERS-l'HÔPITAL reaching billets at 12.57 P.M. Sick evacuated to DOULLENS + FRÉVENT	notes
HERICOURT	17/2/17		Marched from FORTEL to HÉRICOURT via LIGNY-sur-CANCHE, NUNCQ + ECOIVRES reaching billets at 11.45 A.M. Sick evacuated to Stationary Hospitals at St. POL.	notes
NEUVILLE au CORNET	18/2/17		Marched to this place from HÉRICOURT via PETIT HOUVIN, Station and BILNEVILLE. Billets were reached at 12.15 P.M. Owing to the thaw precautions taken, and all traffic reduced to a minimum. Evacuated to No 12 Stationary Hospital at St. POL. A.D.M.S. at D'WISANS.	notes
"	19/2/17		Still in billets here. Roads very soft. J.B.C. 44th Infy Bgde called to ask if we were comfortable. 32nd Sanitary Section left us to go to D'WISANS	notes
"	20/2/17		Owing to the thaw horse ambulances used to collect sick. DADMS X? Corps visited the unit.	notes
"	21/2/17		Nothing to note. Very few sick being admitted.	notes

Army Form C. 2118

WAR DIARY
or
INTELLIGENCE SUMMARY

(Erase heading not required.)

Instructions regarding War Diaries and Intelligence Summaries are contained in F. S. Regs., Part II. and the Staff Manual respectively. Title Pages will be prepared in manuscript.

Place	Date	Hour	Summary of Events and Information	Remarks and references to Appendices
NEUVILLE AU CORNET	22/2/17		Nothing to note. Received and instructions from A.D.M.S. re Inc. to collect and of the 45th Infy Bgde from + 23/2/17.	notes
"	23/2/17		45th Infy Bgde left this area. Still very frozen.	notes
"	24/2/17		Capt. MATTHEW A.W. granted leave to England from the 25/2/17 until 10/3/17. Capt L. BLAKER. P.S. returned from No. 3 New Zealand Stationary Hospital AMIENS. 45th Infy Bgde left this area.	(not 2a)
"	25/2/17		Nothing to record.	notes
"	26/2/17		Lt. Col. RITCHIE returned from leave resumed command of detourn[?]	notes
NEUVILLE-AU-CORNET	26.2.17		Returned from his H.Qrs. J.S.Ritchie Lt Col	W.J.Wallace Capt. P.A.me. D.A.R.
NEUVILLE-AU-CORNET	27.2.17		2t H.F. BELLAMY proceeded to Infanty Medical Camp O. 10/11 & 2.9 & Div. Lt. BULLOCK A.D.M.S. admitted to R.O.12 Stationary Hosp. his return not to C/Div. Dr Griffins & R 2nd.	D.A.R.
NEUVILLE-AU-CORNET	28.2.17		Capt W.S. WALLACE M.C. proceeded home to Infanty Medical Camp O/command Proceeded to this H.Q. and handed over command of unit to Capt. J.V Barr Ritchie. J.S.Ritchie Lt Col.	D.A.R.

140/0+3 Vol 20

15th Division
B.E.F. France
by
Lt Colonel T F Richie Return.
O.C. 47th Field Ambulance
from 1.3.17 to 31.3.17

COMMITTEE FOR THE
MEDICAL HISTORY OF THE WAR
Date 11 MAY 1917

Vol. 20

Army Form C. 2118

WAR DIARY
INTELLIGENCE SUMMARY
(Erase heading not required.)

47th Field Ambulance
March 1917

Place	Date	Hour	Summary of Events and Information	Remarks and references to Appendices
NEUVILLE au CORNET	3/1/17	9 am	Assumed temporary charge of 47th Field Ambulance, during Lt Col Ritchie's absence as acting A.D.M.S. 1st Division. Officers + 7 O.R.	JM
NEUVILLE au CORNET	3/2/17		No Cases admitted. 2 Officers + 7 O.R. Capt VICKERS from company medical charge of 37th D.I. to School for FELIX RICHMES + 1st Div Company at ABERDOIN St. Box Respirator sent to all ranks.	JM
NEUVILLE au CORNET	3/3/17		No cases admitted to Hospital. Officers Nil - 3 O.R. - 1 case Measles. Practice with Box Respirator + instruction by Capt BLAKER in Gas + Gas attacks.	JM
NEUVILLE au CORNET	3/4/17		No cases admitted to Hospital - Officers Nil - 2 O.R. Conference at 1st Corps H.Q. Officers J.D.D.M.S. No cases admitted - 1 Officer + 8 O.R. - Officer suffering from measles.	JM
NEUVILLE au CORNET	3/5/17		1 Officer Capt BLAKER + 74 N.C.O.s trans. sent to 4th? Field Ambulance ARRAS today. Admitted to Hospital Officers Nil - 7 O.R.	JM
NEUVILLE au CORNET	3/6/17		No cases admitted - Officers Nil - O.R. 5.	JM
NEUVILLE au CORNET	3/7/17		CAPT P.S. BLAKER Returns from Hosp at 46th Field Ambulance. No sick admitted. 1 Officer + 11 O.R. Sgt Major J. MACDOWELL R.A.M.C. mentioned in Sir Douglas HAIG's despatch - London Gazette dated 29-12-16.	JM
NEUVILLE au CORNET	3/8/17		No sick admitted to Hospital. Officers Nil - 14 O.R.	JM
NEUVILLE au CORNET	3/9/17	9 am	Moved from NEUVILLE au CORNET to HABARCQ. To take over Hospital in Chateau from the 37th Field Ambulance. Jos of Patients handed over Officers 6 + 116 O.R. including Lieut. Special Abdominal Hospital. Lt Walter RHINE in charge taken over in Chateau HABARCQ.	JM

1875 Wt. W593/826 1,000,000 1/15 J.B.C. & A. A.D.S.S./Forms/C. 2118.

Army Form C. 2118

WAR DIARY
or
INTELLIGENCE SUMMARY

(Erase heading not required.)

47th Field Ambulance
March 1917

Instructions regarding War Diaries and Intelligence Summaries are contained in F.S. Regs., Part II. and the Staff Manual respectively. Title Pages will be prepared in manuscript.

Place	Date	Hour	Summary of Events and Information	Remarks and references to Appendices
HABARCQ	9/3/17		Visited A.D.M.S. & D.D.M.S. DUISANS.	
HABARCQ	10/3/17		No cases admitted. Officers 1 - O.R. sick 21- wounded 3. CAPT E. Robinson R.A.M.C. reported from 46th D.S. Amb. for duty. Lieut. Bellamy R.A.M.C. returned from Company medical charge of 10/11 H.L.I. 1 N.C.O. & 11 men returned from 6th D.M. Ambulance for duty here. Visit from General commanding VI Corps GENERAL HALDANE & Colonel THOMPSON A.D.M.S. VI Corps. 1 patient died from wounds -	
HABARCQ	11/3/17		No cases admitted. Officers sick 2. wounded Nil. O.R. sick 37- wounded 1.	
HABARCQ	12/3/17		No cases admitted. Officers sick 1. wounded 1. O.R. sick 3 wounded 5. increase receiving Officers 6 sick. 1 wounded. O.R. sick 10 - 5 wounded. 1 Officer - 1 O.R. died from wounds. Visit by D.A.D.S. III Army - D.D.M.S. VI Corps.	
HABARCQ	13/3/17	3 p.m	No cases admitted. Officers wounded Nil sick 1 - O.R. sick 25. wounded Nil. Visit from A.D.M.S. II Div. (Case sepsis found admitted visited Newmaid Pots in ARRAS & 15 ADSN Front line.	
HABARCQ	14/3/17		No cases admitted. Officers sick 1 - wounded Nil - O.R. sick 16. wounded Nil. CAPT MATTHEW. Visiting from here.	
HABARCQ	15/3/17		No cases admitted. 1 Officer & 1 wounded - Officers 3 sick - nil wounded. Conference of A.D.M.S. & O.C. Field Ambulances at office of D.D.M.S. VI Corps.	
HABARCQ	16/3/17		Nothing of importance took place. O.R. 17 sick & 4 wounded - 1 died of wounds. Admitted Officers Nil. 2 cases of measles.	

1875 Wt. W593/826 1,000,000 4/15 J.B.C. & A. A.D.S.S./Forms/C. 2118.

WAR DIARY or INTELLIGENCE SUMMARY

Army Form C. 2118

47th Field Ambulance
March 1917

Place	Date	Hour	Summary of Events and Information	Remarks and references to Appendices
HABARCQ	17/3/17		Capt W.S. WALLACE R.A.M.C. rejoined from 6th Canadians. 2 S.-Reinforcements arrived. Attended Conference at Office of A.D.M.S. 1st Army. Visit by A.D.M.S. & 15th D.H.Q. - Inspection of Hospital - O.R. 18 sick & wounded & cases admitted. Officers sick nil - O.R. wounded 4 - sick nil. 1 case invalid.	RAL
HABARCQ	18/3/17		Capt W.S. WALLACE to the acting Sanitary Officer 1st Div: during the absence of Capt JORY. No cases admitted. Officers wounded 1 - sick nil - 1 Officer airs ground. O.R. sick 31 - wounded 3 - sick ground. 1 case N.Y.D. organic	RAL
HABARCQ	19/3/17		No cases admitted. Officers sick nil - O.R. sick 29 - wounded 5 - 1 case invalid. 1 N.Y.D. case reported fit duty - with Pulmonic Hospital.	RAL
HABARCQ	20/3/17		No case admitted. Officers wounded 1 - O.R.9 - Officers sick nil - O.R. sick 34. Main: CAPT ERROBINSON + CAPT BLAKER with 3 Ord: and men proceed on advance Party to main dressing Station at NOUVEAU QUAI: ARRAS. Opening the heavy shelling at Pont RAUDIMONT - Capt ERROBINSON + SgT ROBINSON E. were killed + Capt BLAKER + Pte WEBBER wounded. - one Officer changed also lost - probably wounded.	RAL
HABARCQ	21/3/17	a.m.	Handed over Rest Station + special Hospital to 4th U.S. Ambulances. 3 Officers + 5 Or proceed to NOUVEAU QUAI: ARRAS, M CALLANAN, MORGAN, M rand now expressively shelled. - Transport Unit + D UISANS, No 3 + 2, 3 & the R.M.T.R. a appointed acting Corporal with Pay.	RAL
ARRAS	2/3/17		Advanced dressing Station at Pet Aud: + meeting Days.	RAL

1875 Wt. W593/826 1,000,000 4/15 J.B.C. & A. A.D.S.S./Forms/C.2118.

WAR DIARY or INTELLIGENCE SUMMARY

Army Form C. 2118

47th Field Ambulance
France 1917

Place	Date	Hour	Summary of Events and Information	Remarks and references to Appendices
NOUVEAU QUAI ARRAS	23.3.17		Construction work – Sandbagging used Contract to Strengthen building. Nothing else of importance took [place]	AM
NOUVEAU QUAI ARRAS	24.3.17		Service this adopted Commences at 11 am. Visited Cellars in Grand Place intended for nearer reserves – Weather turning snowy.	AM
ARRAS	25.3.17		Nothing of importance took [place].	AM
ARRAS	26.3.17		Lt. Col. Ritchie D.S.O. resumed Command of the ambulance on the return of the A.D.M.S. 1st Div. Snow on ground at 4 pm	AM
NOUVEAU QUAI ARRAS	26.3.17		Returned war diary. 98 Return 21st.	AM / 98R
ARRAS	27.3.17		Visited Aid Posts & Relay Posts in area allotted to unit for clearing. Work carried on at NOUVEAU QUAI Sandbagging &c.	98R
ARRAS	28.3.17		Carried work on building &c. Weather very wet.	98R
ARRAS	29.3.17		15 Other ranks Infantry from temporary attachment from Sanitary Section 3rd attached for duty & fatigue	98R
ARRAS	30.3.17 11 a.m. 2.30 pm		D.M.S. and D.D.M.S. inspected NOUVEAU QUAI Relay. Attended conference at D.D.M.S. Quarters.	98R
ARRAS	31.3.17		C.R.E. visited building & inspected progress of work. Windows closed & circulated in ARRAS. Transport at DUISANS	98R

J.A. Ritchie Lt. Col.
OC 47th Field Ambulance

98R

SECRET. 140/21

VOLUME No 22

War Diary for April 1917.
By Lieut: T.F.RITCHIE R.A.M.C.
O.C. 47th Field Ambulance

Vol 21

COMMITTEE FOR THE
MEDICAL HISTORY OF THE WAR
Date   10 JUL. 1917

Army Form C. 2118

47th Field Ambulance

WAR DIARY
or
INTELLIGENCE SUMMARY
(Erase heading not required.)

Instructions regarding War Diaries and Intelligence Summaries are contained in F.S. Regs., Part II. and the Staff Manual respectively. Title Pages will be prepared in manuscript.

Place	Date	Hour	Summary of Events and Information	Remarks and references to Appendices
ARRAS (NOUVEAU QUAI)	1.4.17		Capt. A.W. MATTHEW proceeded to R.O.B Casualty Clearing Station today for temporary duty.	9.B.R.
ARRAS	2.4.17		Attended conference at A.D.M.S. Office today.	9.B.R.
ARRAS	3.4.17		Work was completed on NOUVEAU QUAI. Orders allotted to this unit in GRANDE PLACE have fallen in. Reported this to A.D.M.S. who approves of allotment. Orders of Lordship up there tonight before zero.	9.B.R.
ARRAS	4.4.17		Took over R.A.T. Rating Post at OIL FACTORY from 46th F.C. (8 men + 2 Rated Stretchers). Relieved 45th by 13th at accommodation of total personnel. Arranged number of trains to Rating Post 15-16.	9.B.R.
ARRAS	5.4.17		Too wet, was Posted at 15th under A.D.S. Capt THOMPSON and 1 TN.T Retention of 45th F.C. attached today for temporary duty.	9.B.R.
ARRAS	6.4.17		Capt J.A. SMITH and L.t MacDOUGALL arrived for duty from 45 Bde. D.D.M.S. in field meeting station today. 2 Motor Ambulances of 15th M.A.C. with 1 N.Co. Ranks reported for duty all on Corps Card and was attached to 15th M.A.C for duty. Field Ambulance	9.B.R.
ARRAS	8.4.17		Capt. J.A. SMITH proceeded on duty to 8/10 Borderers Capt. A.S. TAYLOR and Lt Crowell Arnold joined and assumed duties of Cleaning with S.O.C. 44th Inf. Bde.	9.B.R.

WAR DIARY or INTELLIGENCE SUMMARY

Army Form C. 2118

47th Field Ambulance

Place	Date	Hour	Summary of Events and Information	Remarks and references to Appendices
ARRAS	8.4.17	8 p.m.	Capt. W.S. WALLACE L⁺ H.F. BELLAMY and 2 Hours Orderlies (detailed to Relay Post in M. Gutting, 20 Rank & file) attached to 2nd Regt Aid Post all Oth ambulance sent to M.A.C. for duty.	P&R
ARRAS	9.4.17		Troops attacked at 5:30 a.m. Beaux commenced work at once and clearing proceeded satisfactorily. 180 m and 50 U.R. Infantry and Walking wounded fell from Relay Post. Wounded going into A.D.S. in increasing numbers evacuated to M.A.C. proceeding very well. Our trip to Relay Post R.A.P.s as far as O.G.I. system for battle above held. Capt VICKERS proceeded to 7/F K.T. R.B. And Capt PARKER attached. Capt WIGHTMAN 11/2.15 D.A.C. is attached to us for temporary duty. P.D.M.S. VI Apps visited the dressing station. 5 Private killed by shellfire while clearing 2nd objective, 4 3" P.R. in clearing 3rd objective & is at HERMES Trench but his Bearer Subunit arrived & arranged to carried to suffered moving to battles about Feuchin area.	P&R
ARRAS	10.4.17			P&R
ARRAS	11.4.17		D.M.S. 3rd Army, A.D.M.S. Bigade. Dressing Station today. A large No 7/87th Division wounded but being cleared here. Beaus into advanced Reference A.D.M.S. 17th Division came in. Regt Bhy were cleared to Feuchy and established attached to him heads have had back burns + friendly area. Received many men to clear RIVAGE and Baux ECOLE NORMALE. Reinforcing to the large numbers of wounded and various ones. When due to Baux of broken arm. Referred to an things	P&R
ARRAS	11.4.17	9 p.m.	Beaux returned a lamp has been picked at the 57th Field Ambulance.	
	12.4.17		Took he Madlenes and Army to ECOLE to him in compress D.D.M.S. Ovisited dressing station.	P&R
ECOLE NORMALE	do	6 p.m.	Formed up at ECOLE NORMALE.	P&R

Army Form C. 2118

WAR DIARY
or
INTELLIGENCE SUMMARY   47th 2nd N. Ambulance

(Erase heading not required.)

Instructions regarding War Diaries and Intelligence Summaries are contained in F.S. Regs., Part II. and the Staff Manual respectively. Title Pages will be prepared in manuscript.

Place	Date	Hour	Summary of Events and Information	Remarks and references to Appendices
ARRAS ECOLE NORMALE	13.4.17		D.D.M.S. inspected billets today. One half is occupied by 57th 2.G. the other half by this unit. Recommended in billets in upper storeys of building. 6 Tanks attended sick. Officers on alarm days and 515.2.6. Received division 45th F.A. a also relieved in the building and one of the officers and received in stores of 46th F.A.	P.A.R.
ARRAS	14.4.17		All our transport has been moved in from DUISANS. Cleaning up building and moving in. Rather busy day sick and wet.	P.A.R.
ARRAS	15.4.17		Capt. H.M. VICKERS returned from medical charge of 7/8 K.O.S.B. today. Camp transfer to sick list C.R.S.	P.A.R.
ARRAS	16.4.17		D.M.S. inspected building today.	P.A.R.
ARRAS	17.4.17		Small numbers of wounded are being about sick. Self and two sent to WARLUS for attendance	P.A.R.
ARRAS	18.4.17		Surgeon General Sir C. BOWLBY visited the today and approved of arrangements.	P.A.R.
ARRAS	19.4.17		Nothing of importance to state. Usual routine pursued.	P.A.R.
ARRAS	20.4.17		Nothing of importance to state	P.A.R.
ARRAS	21.4.17		Colonel H.W.M. GRAY C.B., Consulting Surgeon from a Section today to all Officers & N.C.O.T in Building of Schedule: A.D.M.S. in General Hospital today.	P.A.R.
ARRAS	22.4.17		Needed witnessing. Quiet but routine used.	P.A.R.

WAR DIARY or INTELLIGENCE SUMMARY

Army Form C. 2118

47th Field Ambulance

Place	Date	Hour	Summary of Events and Information	Remarks and references to Appendices
ARRAS	23.4.17	7.45 a.m.	First 81 wounded cases received from front. 3 Horse Amb. Wagons & 2 Fords sent to 45th Field Amb. at 4.45 a.m.	
		10 a.m.	Sent up Horse Conv. to assist 45th Field Ambulance in clearing.	
		4.0 p.m.	Capts W.S. WALLACE and Capt. H.M. VICKERY with 2 Orderly Pack drivers sent to 45th F.A.	28.R
		11 p.m.	162 lying cases evacuated to C.C.S. from C.A. to Station.	
ARRAS	24.4.17		Horse and Motor Amb. in. From 6 p.m. 23/4/17 to 6 a.m. 24.4.17 116 lying cases. Large quantity of kit to be dealt with. Kit bag sent after being seen to BASTION for evacuation by buses.	28RR
		8	Capt. J.I. LAWSON S.R. reported for duty from BASE	
		6 p.m.	91 lying cases evacuated since 6 a.m.	
ARRAS	25.4.17	6.6 a.m.	87 lying evacuated since 6 p.m. 24.4.17	98RR
ARRAS		6 p.m.	53 lying evacuated since 6 a.m. today	
ARRAS	26.4.17	6 a.m.	53 lying evacuated since 6 p.m. 25.4.17	98RR
		6 p.m.	24 lying evacuated since 6 a.m. today	
ARRAS	27.4.17	6 a.m.	26 lying evacuated since 6 p.m. 26.4.17	79RR
		6 p.m.	28 lying evacuated since 6 a.m. today	
			Enquiry from came in this week showed that an according bout on & C.C.S. was present. Capt. J.I. LAWSON evacuated to C.C.S. suffering from P.U.O.	
ARRAS	28.4.17	6 a.m.	48 lying cases evacuated since 6 p.m. 27.4.17	99R
			24 lying cases evacuated since 6 a.m. today	
ARRAS	29.4.17	6 a.m.	D.O.M.S. II Corps and D.D.M.S. II Corps to special Resting Stat. 21 H.E. BELLAMY evacuated to C.C.S. 21 lying evacuated since 6 p.m. 26.4.17 Capts. WALLACE and VICKERY will return uninjured today.	98R
		6 p.m.	14 lying evacuated since 6 a.m. today. Stretcher Bearer Pte W. BARTIE V.C. with D.M.S. Third Army inspected Resting Stat. Since Admitted on out action. I.O.R. has been treated unasted wise Commenced to Operation on 28.4.17	98R

1875 Wt. W 593/826 1,000,000 4/15 J.B.C. & A. A.D.S.S./Forms/C. 2118.

WAR DIARY or INTELLIGENCE SUMMARY

Army Form C. 2118

47th Field Ambulance

Place	Date	Hour	Summary of Events and Information	Remarks and references to Appendices
ARRAS	29.4.17		Captain J.V. BROWN proceeded to England on Annual Leave (14 days).	O.B.R.
ARRAS	30.4.17		Weather continues fine. Small parties of wounded coming in. In WAR list in bow in ECOLE NORMALE. Act/Major J. McDOWALL proceeded to HAVRE France on leave as in orders to a Garden Party in A.S.C. 14 T. J.P. Robertson Lt Colonel O.C. 47th Field Ambulance.	S.P.R.

B.E.F.

SUMMARY OF MEDICAL WAR DIARIES OF 47th F.A. 15th Div. 6th Corps.

3rd ARMY.

18th Corps from May 6th.

19th Corps from 22nd May.

WESTERN FRONT OPERATIONS - 1917 - April - May.

Officer Commanding - Lt.Col. J.F. Ritchie.

Summarised under the following heading :-

PHASE "B" - Battle of Arras - April - May 1917.

1st Period - Attack on Vimy Ridge - April.
2nd Period - Capture of Siegfried Line - May.

B.E.F.

47th F.A. 15th Div. 6th Corps. 3rd ARMY.   WESTERN FRONT.
Officer Commanding - Lt.Col. J.F. RITCHIE.   April 1917.

Headquarters at ARRAS.

PHASE "B" - Battle of Arras - April - May 1917.
   1st Period - Attack on Vimy Ridge - April.

April 4th. Medical Arrangements. R. Relay P. (Oil Factory) taken over from 46th Field Ambulance.

6th. 15th Div. A.D.S. opened at Rivage Arras.

7th. Transport. All motor ambulances attached to 15th M.A.C.

8th. Medical Arrangements. 20 bearers attached to each R.A.P.

9th. Operations. 15th Division attacked at 5.30 a.m.

Casualties.) Wounded arrived at A.D.S. in large numbers.
Evacuation.)
Evacuation proceeded satisfactorily. 50 Inf. wheeled wounded from Relay Post to A.D.S.

Casualties R.A.M.C. Capt. Parker wounded. O & 5 wounded.

11th. Casualties. Large number of 37th Division wounded arrived.

12th. Medical Arrangements. A.D.S. transferred to Ecole Normale ARRAS worked in conjunction with 51st F.A.

13-22nd. Operations R.A.M.C. Routine.

23rd. Operations. 15th Divisiion attacked.

Moves Transport.   ) 3 Horse Ambulances and 2 Fords
Medical Arrangements.)
sent to 45th Field Ambulance at 4.45 a.m. Larger cars at 10 a.m.

Casualties.) First wounded arrived 7.45 a.m.
Evacuation.)
    162 wounded evacuated to Casualty Clearing Station.

24th. Casualties.) 6 p.m. 23rd - 6 a.m. 24th/116 wounded.
Evacuation.)
    6 a.m. - 6 p.m. 91 wounded.

Large number of sick dealt with. Sent to Bastion for evacuation by buses.

B.E.F.

47th F.A.   15th Div.   6th Corps.   3rd ARMY.   WESTERN FRONT.
Officer Commanding - Lt. Col. J.F. RITCHIE.   April 1917.

Phase "B" contd.

   1st Period contd.

April 25th. Casualties.)   6 p.m. 24th - 6 a.m. 25th 87 wounded (lying) evacuated
          Evacuation.)   6 a.m. - 6 p.m.   53 wounded   "   "

26th.   6 p.m. 25th - 6 a.m. 26th 53 wounded   "   "

                    6 a.m. - 6 p.m.   24   "   "   "

27th.   6 p.m. - 26th - 6 a.m. 27th 26   "   "   "

                    6 a.m. - 6 p.m.   28   "   "   "

                    Majority of cases arrived well dressed and sent
to Casualty Clearing Station as soon as possible.

28th.   6 p.m. 27th 6 a.m. 28th   46 wounded (lying) evacuated

                    6 a.m. - 6 p.m.   34   "   "   "

29th.   6 p.m. 28th - 6 a.m. 29th 26   "   "   "

                    6 a.m. - 6 p.m.   14   "   "   "

Military Situation. 15th Division relieved by 56th Division.

Medical Arrangements. Unit acted as C.M.D.S.

Casualties R.A.M.C. 0 & 11 wounded since 23rd.

30th.   Casualties. Small number of wounded arrived.

B.E.F.

47th F.A. 15th Div. 6th Corps. 3rd ARMY.   WESTERN FRONT.
Officer Commanding - Lt.Col. J.F. RITCHIE.   April 1917.

Headquarters at ARRAS.

PHASE "B" - Battle of Arras - April - May 1917.
   1st Period - Attack on Vimy Ridge - April.

April 4th. Medical Arrangements. R. Relay P. (Oil Factory) taken over from 46th Field Ambulance.

    6th.   15th Div. A.D.S. opened at Rivage Arras.

    7th. Transport. All motor ambulances attached to 15th M.A.C.

    8th. Medical Arrangements. 20 bearers attached to each R.A.P.

    9th. Operations. 15th Division attacked at 5.30 a.m.

        Casualties.) Wounded arrived at A.D.S. in large numbers.
        Evacuation.)
        Evacuation proceeded satisfactorily. 50 Inf. wheeled wounded from Relay Post to A.D.S.

        Casualties R.A.M.C. Capt. Parker wounded. O & 5 wounded.

   11th. Casualties. Large number of 37th Division wounded arrived.

   12th. Medical Arrangements. A.D.S. transferred to Ecole Normale ARRAS worked in conjunction with 51st F.A.

13-22nd. Operations R.A.M.C. Routine.

   23rd. Operations. 15th Divisiion attacked.

        Moves Transport.   ) 3 Horse Ambulances and 2 Fords
        Medical Arrangements.)
        sent to 45th Field Ambulance at 4.45 a.m. Larger cars at 10 a.m.

        Casualties.) First wounded arrived 7.45 a.m.
        Evacuation.)
                 162 wounded evacuated to Casualty Clearing Station.

   24th. Casualties.) 6 p.m. 23rd - 6 a.m. 24th./ 116 wounded.
        Evacuation.)
                  6 a.m. - 6 p.m. 91 wounded.

        Large number of sick dealt with. Sent to Bastion for evacuation by buses.

B.E.F.

47th F.A. 15th Div. 6th Corps. 3rd ARMY.   WESTERN FRONT.
Officer Commanding - Lt. Col. J.F. RITCHIE.   April 1917.

Phase "B" contd.
    1st Period contd.

April 25th. Casualties.) 6 p.m. 24th - 6 a.m. 25th 87 wounded(lying)evacuated
          Evacuation.)
                     6 a.m. - 6 p.m.   53 wounded   "   "
26th.   6 p.m. 25th - 6 a.m. 26th 53 wounded   "   "
                     6 a.m. - 6 p.m.   24   "   "   "
27th.   6 p.m. 26th - 6 a.m. 27th 26   "   "   "
                     6 a.m. - 6 p.m.   28   "   "   "

              Majority of cases arrived well dressed and sent
to Casualty Clearing Station as soon a possible.

28th.   6 p.m. 27th 6 a.m. 28th   46 wounded(lying)evacuated
                     6 a.m. - 6 p.m.   34   "   "   "
29th.   6 p.m. 28th - 6 a.m. 29th 26   "   "   "
                     6 a.m. - 6 p.m.   14   "   "   "

Military Situation. 15th Division relieved by 56th Division.

Medical Arrangements. Unit acted as C.M.D.S.

Casualties R.A.M.C. O & 11 wounded since 23rd.

30th. Casualties. Small number of wounded arrived.

SECRET

Vol 22

23

Diary for May 1917
for the advance of
41st Field Ambulance by
Capt. J.V. Brown, Rank
of a Copy of ...

COMMITTEE FOR THE
MEDICAL HISTORY OF THE W...
Date 10 JUL 1917

WAR DIARY
or
INTELLIGENCE SUMMARY

Army Form C. 2118

(Erase heading not required.)

Place	Date	Hour	Summary of Events and Information	Remarks and references to Appendices
ARRAS (ECOLE NORMALE)	1.5.17		Probably Sickels has been forwarded by Capt. Commander to the following N.C.O.s and men:- Unit unit Sergt. G.H. LONG. Sergt. J. WOODHALL Pro McCREARY J. MARSH A. GREENWOOD L. DOODY	9 B.R.
ARRAS	2.5.17		Made arrangements for treatment of wounded of sections in addition to hostile bombardment did 60 percent with the return to D.D.M.S. wished to select another Field Ambulance in the building.	9 B.R.
ARRAS	3.5.17		51st 2nd Field Ambulance left us this half of Workshop Square to Relief by 89th Field Ambulance 98th Field Ambulance is instructed in part 7/4 On holding and so ordered	9 B.R.
ARRAS	4.5.17		Relief operate has been resumed and instructed are troop in Sinclair. Captain S. BRYSON expected his arrival for duty today, however still arrival in but 2nd in Corps Ambulance.	9 B.R.
ARRAS	5.5.17		Only small routine movement are being dealt with.	9 B.R.
ARRAS	6.5.17		15th division (proceeds to XVIIIth Corps. Its unit dominant however is Ant 9 Corps Area returning Station (R1/M.D.S. VI Corps) working in conjunction with 89th Field Ambulance	9 B.R.
ARRAS	7.5.17	1.30 pm	Small casualties as usual. Only Small Intention of wounded, Captain S. BRYSON and 2nd J.B. McDOUGALL with 50 O.R. proceeded to temporary duty as VII Corps Rect Station (36th Field Ambulance)	9 B.R.
ARRAS	8.5.17		Return of hindrance to R.T.O.	9 B.R.
ARRAS	9.5.17		D.D.M.S. VI Corps visited M.D.S.	9 B.R.

Army Form C. 2118

WAR DIARY
or
INTELLIGENCE SUMMARY
(Erase heading not required.)

Instructions regarding War Diaries and Intelligence Summaries are contained in F.S. Regs., Part II. and the Staff Manual respectively. Title Pages will be prepared in manuscript.

Place	Date	Hour	Summary of Events and Information	Remarks and references to Appendices
ARRAS	10.5.17		On walking took the dressing station at BASTION, but walking wounded will be taken in our half of buildings and kept in 89th field amb^ce. Proceeded to inspect the accessory arrangements.	PWR
ARRAS	11.5.17		Arrangements for "walking" are now practically completed. Ec Open from Sunday 12.4 to 6 p.m. in S. wing D. Bn Staff of BASTION will be attached to us for duty.	PWR
ARRAS	12.5.17	6 p.m.	Walked round collecting Post Bearer & F.A. Hospl. Lying cases to 89th F.A. in S. wing D. ECOLE NORMALE. 6 Officers and 3 tent subdivisions from F.A. of 92nd 29th & 58th shipping attached.	99 R.
ARRAS	13.5.17		Normal inspection to units.	99 R.
ARRAS	14.5.17		Routine inspection to units.	99 R.
ARRAS	15.5.17		Capt. J.V. BROWN returned from short leave. Wrote note from D.D.M.S. that his Capt Aitken in XVIII Corps area on 16th inst.	99 R. 99 R.
ARRAS	16.5.17		Weather continues fine.	99 R.
ARRAS	17.5.17		Arranged for train to convey personnel, bedding etc. 294 F.A. handed on to 88th sitArms.	99 R.
ARRAS	18.5.17	9 a.m.	Handed over ECOLE NORMALE & 28th F.A. 122 & appx. 150 S.R. befors from II Corps Rept Station, their officers to break – the train leaving 10.15am down – to SOMBRIN Stn WARLUS – BARLY.	99 R.
SOMBRIN	18.5.17/ 1 Sept		Arrived at SOMBRIN, hut in theatre (franc). Had accommodation for orderly & small bread fr Bulk. Officers Sub are sent to XVIII Corps Rept Sta in Station in C.C.S.	
SOMBRIN	19.5.17		Capts S WALLACE & A VICKERS Amb'd record returned from 21.5.17	99 R.
SOMBRIN	20.5.17		Capt Bruett Arnov telephoned handed over to Capt J.V. BROWN. J.F. Ritchen Ph.Lt.	

WAR DIARY
or
INTELLIGENCE SUMMARY.
(Erase heading not required.)

Army Form C. 2118.

Place	Date	Hour	Summary of Events and Information	Remarks and references to Appendices
SOMBRIN	20/5/17		Took on temporary charge of 7th Ambulance. Lt Col RITCHIE T.F. on leave. Stafford. Capt S. BRYSON rejoined from VI Corps Rest Station.	AM
	21/5/17	6.45 p.m	Left SOMBRIN at 6 a.m. & marched under 4th Brig. & orders to MAISON LEBLOND on the main DOULLENS - PREVENT Road. No personal casualties en route - Nil. Adv party of Officers, NCO's & men sent to take over CHATEAU HAUTE CLOQUE at WAIL	AM
	22/5/17	6.45 p.m	Left MAISON LE BLOND & proceeded with HQ Brig to WAIL. - My personnel underfoot out on march. Nil. casualties about 20 Nil.	AM
WAIL	23/5/17		Opened as a Rest Station for divisional area. Visit from A.D.M.S. 15th Divn - 2 sick men to Hospital -	AM
WAIL	24/5/17		18 cases in Hospital - Principal disease P.N.O. myalgia + injuries & Enuresis. Lt & Qm F. DAVIS Grants leave to England till June 1/17	AM
WAIL	25/5/17		25 cases in Hospital - 8 Evacuated to 63 C.C.S.	
WAIL	26/5/17		11 Cases Admitted Hospital. Principal diseases P.U.O. Pirie & Tonsillitis. Visit from D.D.M.S. XIX Corps, A.D.M.S. & A.D.D.M.S. 1st Divn. Capt H.H. HEPBURN joined from 2n/10 General Hospital.	AM

Army Form C. 2118.

WAR DIARY
or
INTELLIGENCE SUMMARY.
(Erase heading not required.)

Instructions regarding War Diaries and Intelligence Summaries are contained in F. S. Regs., Part II. and the Staff Manual respectively. Title pages will be prepared in manuscript.

Place	Date	Hour	Summary of Events and Information	Remarks and references to Appendices
WAIL	27/7		12 Cases admitted Hospital - Sprain Ain - 13 Evacuated 14 Remaining.	8M
		7	O.R. reinforcements reported for duty from Base.	
WAIL	28/7		9 admissions - 18 Remaining in hospital	8M
WAIL	29/7		CAPT MATTHEWS & 2 O.R. rejoined from 2 W. 2 C.C.S.	
		11	Admissions. 15 Remaining	
			To Hospital	
WAIL	30/7	13	Admissions. Principally P.U.O. Sct. & myalgia - 14 Remaining	
WAIL	31/7		16 admissions - 5 Evacuations, 25 remaining.	8M
			Nothing of importance to note	

J.M. Brown Capt. R.A.M.C.
O/C. 47th Fld Ambulance

B.E.F.

SUMMARY OF MEDICAL WAR DIARIES OF 47th F.A. 15th Div. 6th Corps.

3rd ARMY.

18th Corps from May 6th.

19th Corps from 22nd May.

WESTERN FRONT OPERATIONS - 1917 - April - May.

Officer Commanding - Lt.Col. J.F. Ritchie.

Summarised under the following heading :-

PHASE "B" - Battle of Arras - April - May 1917.

1st Period - Attack on Vimy Ridge - April.
2nd Period - Capture of Siegfried Line - May.

B.E.F.   1.

<u>47th F.A. 15th Div. 6th Corps. 3rd ARMY. WESTERN FRONT.</u>
                                                                May 1917.
<u>Officer Commanding - Lt.Col. J.F. Ritchie.</u>

18th Corps from May 6th.

<u>Phase "B" - Battle of Arras - April - May 1917.</u>
  <u>2nd Period - Capture of Siegfried Line - May.</u>

May 1st.   <u>D</u>ecorations.

          Sgt.   Long G.H.   )
)
          Sgt.   Woodhall J.   )
)
          Pte.   Mc.Cready.   ) Awarded M.M.
)
          "   Marsh J.   )
)
          "   Greenward A.   )
)
          "   Doody L.   )

3rd.   <u>Medical Arrangements.</u>   51st Field Ambulance relieved
            by 89th Field Ambulance.
            <u>Operations.</u> Operations resumed.
3rd.to   <u>Casualties.</u> Wounded arrived in small
5th.   numbers.
6th.   <u>Transfer.</u> 15th Division transferred to 18th Corps.

47th F.A. 15th Div. 18th Corps. 3rd ARMY.   WESTERN FRONT.
                                                May 1917.
Officer Commanding - Lt.Col. J.F. Ritchie.

19th Corps from May 22nd.

PHASE "B" - Battle of Arras - April - May 1917.
    2nd Period - Capture of Siegfried Line - May.

May 6th.	Transfer. 15th Div. transferred to 18th Corps.
	Medical Arrangements. Unit acted as C.M.D.S. working in conjunction with 89th Field Ambulance.
7th.	Casualties. Small number of wounded dealt with.
	Moves. Detachment. 2 & 50 to 36th Field Ambulance (C.R.S.). Rejoined 18th.
12th.	Medical Arrangements. Walking Wounded Collecting Post transferred to Ecole Normale from Bastion 6 and 3 T.S.Ds. of Field Ambulances of 82nd, 89th, and 56th Division attacked.
18th.	Medical Arrangements. C.M.D.S. handed over to 89th F.A.
	Moves. To Sombrin.
21st-22nd.	Moves.) To Wail.
	Med. Arr.)
	Div. Rest Station opened.
22nd.	Transfer. To 19th Corps.

B.E.F.

47th F.A.   15th Div. 19th Corps.   3rd ARMY.   WESTERN FRONT.
                                                    May 1917.
Officer Commanding - Lt.Col. J.F. Ritchie.

Phase "B" - Battle of Arras - April - May 1917.
   2nd Period - Capture of Siegfried Line - May.

May 22nd. Transfer. To 19th Corps.

Casualties Sick.		Remaining.	Admitted.	Evacuated.
Evacuation.	24th.	18.		
	25th.	25.		8.
	26th.		11.	
	27th.	14.	12.	13.
	28th.	19.	7.	
	29th.	17.	11.	
	30th.	14.	13.	
	31st.	24.	16.	5.

B.E.F.   1.

47th F.A.   15th Div.   6th Corps.   3rd ARMY.   WESTERN FRONT.
                                                  May 1917.
Officer Commanding - Lt.Col. J.F. Ritchie.

18th Corps from May 6th.

Phase "B" - Battle of Arras - April - May 1917.
2nd Period - Capture of Siegfried Line - May.

May 1st.   Decorations.

        Sgt.   Long   G.H.   )
        Sgt.   Woodhall J.   )
        Pte.   Mc.Cready.   ) Awarded M.M.
         "   Marsh J.   )
         "   Greenward A.   )
         "   Doody L.   )

3rd.   Medical Arrangements.   51st Field Ambulance relieved by 89th Field Ambulance.

            Operations.   Operations resumed.

3rd. to   Casualties.   Wounded arrived in small
5th.   numbers.

6th.   Transfer. 15th Division transferred to 18th Corps.

B.E.F.

47th F.A. 15th Div. 18th Corps. 3rd ARMY. WESTERN FRONT.
May 1917.
Officer Commanding - Lt.Col. J.F. Ritchie.

19th Corps from May 22nd.

PHASE "B" - Battle of Arras - April - May 1917.
   2nd Period - Capture of Siegfried Line - May.

May 6th.	Transfer. 15th Div. transferred to 18th Corps.
	Medical Arrangements. Unit acted as C.M.D.S. working in conjunction with 89th Field Ambulance.
7th.	Casualties. Small number of wounded dealt with.
	Moves. Detachment. 2 & 50 to 36th Field Ambulance (C.R.S.) Rejoined 18th.
12th.	Medical Arrangements. Walking Wounded Collecting Post transferred to Ecole Normale from Bastion 6 and 3 T.S.Ds. of Field Ambulances of 82nd, 89th, and 56th Division attacked.
18th.	Medical Arrangements. C.M.D.S. handed over to 89th F.A.
	Moves. To Sombrin.
21st-22nd.	Moves.) To Wail.
	Med. Arr.)
	Div. Rest Station opened.
22nd.	Transfer. To 19th Corps.

B.E.F.

47th F.A.   15th Div.   19th Corps.   3rd ARMY.   WESTERN FRONT.
Officer Commanding - Lt.Col. J.F. Ritchie.   May 1917.

Phase "B" - Battle of Arras - April - May 1917.
  2nd Period - Capture of Siegfried Line - May.

May 22nd.	Transfer. To 19th Corps.			
	Casualties Sick.	Remaining.	Admitted.	Evacuated.
	Evacuation. 24th.	18.		
	25th.	25.		8.
	26th.		11.	
	27th.	14.	12.	13.
	28th.	19.	7.	
	29th.	17.	11.	
	30th.	14.	13.	
	31st.	24.	16.	5.

SECRET 17

War Diary for
June 1917
by
Lt Colonel H.C. Monteith, R.A.M.C
O.C. 147th Field Ambulance

Volume No 24
Vol 23

COMMITTEE FOR THE
MEDICAL HISTORY OF THE WAR
Date —7 AUG. 1917

Army Form C. 2118.

WAR DIARY
or
INTELLIGENCE SUMMARY.
(Erase heading not required.)

Instructions regarding War Diaries and Intelligence Summaries are contained in F. S. Regs., Part II. and the Staff Manual respectively. Title pages will be prepared in manuscript.

Place	Date	Hour	Summary of Events and Information	Remarks and references to Appendices
WAIL	1/6/17		16 O.R. admitted to Hospital, 11 Evacuations including 1 case of measles.	SM
			27 Remaining in Hospital.	SM
			Capt. M.W. MATTHEW granted 3 days leave to PARIS.	SM
			1 R.E. Reinforcement joined.	
WAIL	2/6/17		13 O.R. admitted to Hospital including 1 case measles & 1 case recurrent dysentery.	SM
			17 Evacuations to Remaining.	
			1 O.R. evacuated home to England, 10 duty.	
WAIL	3/6/17		14 O.R. admitted to Hospital including 3 cases of Scarlatina.	SM
			Stores held for units. Very successful.	
			Lt Col Ritchie, Capt Wallace, Capt Norton returned from leave to England.	SM
			Started our visit to St bat. F.F. Ritchie	SM
			J Norton Capt Ritchie	
WAIL	4.6.17		Returned from leave last night having been delayed at ETAPLES.	SAR
			T.R.m. from Captain J.V. BROWN 9th Rifles Lt Col Ritchie	
			Letter sent to Tenth Army stating in letter 1 heavy E.O.R. 1 Heavy E.O.R. in CHATEAU HAUTE CLOQUE WAIL	
			32 Sick Remaining.	SAR

Army Form C. 2118.

WAR DIARY
or
INTELLIGENCE SUMMARY.
(Erase heading not required)

Instructions regarding War Diaries and Intelligence
Summaries are contained in F. S. Regs., Part II.
and the Staff Manual respectively. Title pages
will be prepared in manuscript.

Place	Date	Hour	Summary of Events and Information	Remarks and references to Appendices
WAIL	5.1.17		Weather continues fine. 376th Coy can be seen kitchen is being constructed but materials being supplied really made by XIX Corps R.E.	PRR
WAIL	6.1.17		Weather fine. Route usual. Captain J.V. BROWN awarded Military Cross	PRR
WAIL	7.1.17	3 p.m.	D.D.M.S. inspected Ambulance Park. Gave instructions as to appoint- ments in the certain trip given up. Received instructions to proceed on temporary duty in office of D.D.M.S.	PRR
WAIL	7.7.17	4:30 pm	Assumed charge first ambulance - for Lt Col Ritchie J.F. who is acting D.A.D.M.S. XIX Corps.	PRR
WAIL	8.7.17		24 cases admitted. 7 stopped. 17 evacuations. 3 of returning. 1 OR. granted leave to England for 10 days. Daily training & manoeuvre carried out by units (E.G.) - Stretcher bearing, tent moving, lectures etc.	P.R.

2353 Wt. W2544/4454 700,000 5/15 D. D. & L.   A.D.S.S./Forms/C. 2118.

Army Form C. 2118.

WAR DIARY
or
INTELLIGENCE SUMMARY.
(Erase heading not required.)

Instructions regarding War Diaries and Intelligence Summaries are contained in F. S. Regs., Part II. and the Staff Manual respectively. Title pages will be prepared in manuscript.

Place	Date	Hour	Summary of Events and Information	Remarks and references to Appendices
Wailly	9th		20 Admits 15 Hospital 19 Evacuations stating + 3's remaining - new grounds.	SJB
Wailly	10th		Nothing of importance - Route - Nr Admissions - 14 Evacuations, stating + 28 remaining in hospital.	
Wailly	11th		18 New admits - 3 evacuated totaling 21 Evacuations + 22 remaining. Principal diseases Trench Feet P.U.O. + V.D.T. Lt Col Ritchie returned to unit. Very Stormy rain. J. Brown Capt.	
			Returned to duty from D.D.M.S. Office. Been in orchard from 3rd in Army. Proceeded to 20 & 20 C.C.S. on appointment to command 56th Division and hand over Command Captain J.V. BROWN M.C. assumes temporary command of his Ambulance pending the arrival of any successor. J.J. Ritchie Lt. Col Rhc.	PBR
Wailly	12/7 6pm		Handed over Company Command to Capt N.S. WALLACE 47th RAMC until acting under instructions of A.D.M.S. XV Div. took over temporary command of the unit for Capt J.V. BROWN. J. Brown Capt ADMS. 19 cases admitted to hospital, 15 evacuations, 1 to duty & 26 remaining 1 case of Scabies	

2353 Wt. W2514/1454 700,000 5/15 D.D.&L. ADSS/Foras/C. 2118.

Army Form C. 2118.

WAR DIARY
or
INTELLIGENCE SUMMARY.
(Erase heading not required.)

Place	Date	Hour	Summary of Events and Information	Remarks and references to Appendices
WAIL	13/6/17		Nothing noteworthy has occurred. Day fine also admitted.	who
WAIL	14/6/17		Lt. J.B. McDOUGALL took over temporary charge of the 9th Gordon Highlanders. 1st Lt. J.A.C. COLSTON, M.O.R.C. U.S. Army reported for duty.	who
WAIL	15/6/17		1st Lt. J.A.C. COLSTON, M.O.R.C. U.S. Army detailed for duty with the 46th & 2nd Ind. Unit ordered to move as all cases evacuated (46 2 all) to No 6 Stat. H.S. Move cancelled.	who
WAIL	16/6/17		Capt. H.G.M. ONTEITH D.S.O. R.A.M.C. reported his arrival for duty & took over command of the unit. W.J. Wallace Capt. M.O. R.A.M.C.	who
WAIL	17/6/17		Nothing noteworthy has occurred. 10 cases admitted. 8 evacuated. 2 remaining. Monteith Capt. R.A.M.C.	who
WAIL	18/6/17		Visit from Branch Requisition officer. Third Army command. Examination of leave of Chateau Haute Blogue.	who

Army Form C. 2118.

WAR DIARY
or
INTELLIGENCE SUMMARY.
(Erase heading not required.)

Instructions regarding War Diaries and Intelligence Summaries are contained in F. S. Regs., Part II. and the Staff Manual respectively. Title pages will be prepared in manuscript.

Place	Date	Hour	Summary of Events and Information	Remarks and references to Appendices
WAIL	19/6/17		8 admitted, 10 evacuated, 4 remaining. P.V.O principal dinner Red Cross Stores removed by B.R.C.	MMontiitt
WAIL	20/6/17		Capt. A.W. Matthew RAMC assumed charge of 9th Royal Highlanders. Capt H.H. Hepburn & Capt S. Bryson RAMC and 2 NCO's proceeded on to H.Q. 15th Div. Visit from Branch Registration Officer, Third Army, who terminated leave of Chateau Haute Bergue from 21.6.17. 22 admitted, 25 evacuated, 1 remaining.	MMontiitt
GAUCHIN	21/6/17		March from WAIL to GAUCHIN, under orders of 44th Bde. Reached billets about 9 AM. 32 admitted, 4 remaining.	MMontiitt
MAREST	22/6/17		March from GAUCHIN to MAREST at 4 AM, reaching billets at 8.30 AM. 13 admitted, 13 evacuated, 1 remaining.	MMontiitt
NOEUX FONTES	23/6/17			

Army Form C. 2118.

WAR DIARY
or
INTELLIGENCE SUMMARY.
(Erase heading not required.)

Instructions regarding War Diaries and Intelligence Summaries are contained in F.S. Regs., Part II. and the Staff Manual respectively. Title pages will be prepared in manuscript.

Place	Date	Hour	Summary of Events and Information	Remarks and references to Appendices
NORRENT-FONTES	23/6/17		March from MAREST at 8.30 A.M. to NORRENT FONTES, reaching billets 12.15 P.M. Weather cool. Cases sent to 58 C.C.S. LILLERS. 10 admitted. 10 evacuated, 1 remaining.	
NORRENT-FONTES	24/6/17		Inspection of smoke helmets, box respirators, urine respirators, at 58 C.C.S. LILLERS. Admitted 11, evacuated 11, remaining 1.	
THIENNES	25/6/17		March from NORRENT FONTES at 9 A.M. Arrived THIENNES 11.40 A.M. Weather cool. Admitted 24. Evacuated 24 to 39 Station Hosp at AIRE. Remaining 1.	
CAESTRE	26/6/17		March from THIENNES at 4.20 A.M. Arrived CAESTRE 9.30 A.M. Weather cool. Admitted 15. Evacuated 15 to 15 C.C.S. HAZEBROUCK.	
VLAMERTINGHE MILL	27/6/17		March from CAESTRE at 5.45 A.M. Arrived at VLAMERTINGHE MILL at 10.45 A.M. Took over Mill from holding party of 46 F.A. Weather cool. Admitted 11 sick, 12 wounded. Evacuated 11 sick and 12 wounded, 1 sick remaining.	
VLAMERTINGHE MILL	28/6/17		Admitted 24 sick, 3 wounded O.R. 05 jnis wounded 1. All evacuated. Weather warm. Lt. J.B. McDougall RAMC rejoined unit from temporary	

Army Form C. 2118.

WAR DIARY
or
INTELLIGENCE SUMMARY.
(Erase heading not required.)

Place	Date	Hour	Summary of Events and Information	Remarks and references to Appendices
VLAMERTINGHE MILL	29/6/17.		Temporary medical charge of 9th Gordon Hghrs. At 2.45 AM H.V. still burst in horse-lines, killing 7 H.D. & 3 mules, & wounding 1 D.M. & 3 mules. Four other mules received very slight injuries. Admitted 22 sick & 2 wounded. Evacuated 24. 1 remaining. Transport moved to H.7.d. 2.8. Sheet 28. 1/40,000.	
Do.	30/6/17.		Visited Right & Left Bn R.A.P.s, R.A.P., & 46th F.A. A.D.S. & Collecting Post. Capt. H.H. Hepburn R.A.M.C. sent to 72nd Brig. R.F.A. for duty. Capt. A.W. MATTHEN R.A.M.C. sent to 8th Seaforth H.I. for temporary duty. Admitted & evacuated. 1 remaining. 19 sick & 5 wounded	

W.V. Renwith
Lt. Col. R.A.M.B
O.C. 47th Field Ambulance

B.E.F.

SUMMARY OF MEDICAL WAR DIARIES OF

47th FIELD AMBULANCE,

15th Div., 19th Corps, 5th Army.

(from 18/6/17.)

WESTERN FRONT, JUNE 1917.

Officer Commanding: Lieutenant-Colonel H. G. Monteith.

Summarised under the following heading:

PHASE "D": BATTLE OF MESSINES, JUNE 1917.

B.E.F.

47th FIELD AMBULANCE, WESTERN FRONT, JUNE 1917.

15th Div., 19th Corps, 5th Army.

O.C. Lieutenant-Colonel H. G. Monteith.

PHASE "D": BATTLE OF MESSINES, JUNE 1917.

1917. H.Q. at VLAMERTINGHE MILL.

June 18th <u>Transfer, Moves</u> Unit transferred with 15th Div. from 3rd Army to 19th Corps, 5th Army, and commenced march to new area.

19th/27th <u>Moves</u> To VLAMERTINGHE MILL and took over from holding party of 46th F.A. <u>Medical Arrangements</u> Unit opened for local sick and wounded.

29th <u>Operations</u> Enemy H.V. shell burst in horse lines - number of animals killed and wounded.

B.E.F.

SUMMARY OF MEDICAL WAR DIARIES OF

47th FIELD AMBULANCE,

15th Div., 19th Corps, 5th Army.

(from 18/6/17.)

WESTERN FRONT, JUNE 1917.

Officer Commanding: Lieutenant-Colonel H. G. Monteith.

Summarised under the following heading:

PHASE "D": BATTLE OF MESSINES, JUNE 1917.

B.E.F.

47th FIELD AMBULANCE,   WESTERN FRONT, JUNE 1917.

15th Div., 19th Corps, 5th Army.

O.C. Lieutenant-Colonel H. G. Monteith.

PHASE "D": BATTLE OF MESSINES, JUNE 1917.

1917.	H.Q. at VLAMERTINGHE MILL.
June 18th	Transfer. Moves Unit transferred with 15th Div. from 3rd Army to 19th Corps, 5th Army, and commenced march to new area.
19th/27th	Moves To VLAMERTINGHE MILL and took over holding party of from 46th F.A. Medical Arrangements Unit opened for local sick and wounded.
29th	Operations Enemy H.V. shell burst in horse lines - number of animals killed and wounded.

SECRET

VOLUME 25
Vol. 24

47th Field Ambulance

War Diary for June 1917
by Lt Colonel H.C. MONTEITH R.A.M.C
O/C 47th Field Ambulance

COMMITTEE FOR THE
MEDICAL HISTORY OF THE WAR
Date 10 SEP.1917

Army Form C. 2118.

WAR DIARY
or
INTELLIGENCE SUMMARY.
(Erase heading not required.)

Place	Date	Hour	Summary of Events and Information	Remarks and references to Appendices
VLAMERTINGHE MILL	1/7/17		15 sick, 10 wounded admitted & <s>directed</s> evacuated. 1 remaining. 1 officer died of wounds in F.A.	MSmowtoth
Do.	2.7.17		1 officer 13 O.R. sick admitted & evacuated <s>admitted</s>. 13 O.R. wounded admitted & evacuated. Weather warm.	MSM
Do.	3.7.17		Visited adv. dressing station & reg. aid posts. O.R. 13 sick, 1 officer & 18 O.R. wounded admitted & evacuated.	MSM
Do.	4.7.17.		O.R. 24, Officer 1 admitted & evacuated sick. Wounded O.R. 1. 1 O.R. sick remaining. During the night some shelling abt. of neighbouring area. 1 shell landed in camp, causing no damage.	MSM
Do.	5.7.17		Officer 1, O.R. 12 sick, 2 officers 1, O.R. 12 wounded admitted & evacuated neighbouring area during the evening. Weather cool. H.V. gun shelled	MSM
Do.	6.7.17.		O.R. 7 sick & 10 wounded admitted & evacuated. Weather warm.	MSM

WAR DIARY
or
INTELLIGENCE SUMMARY.
(Erase heading not required.)

Army Form C. 2118.

Place	Date	Hour	Summary of Events and Information	Remarks and references to Appendices
VLAMERTINGHE MILL	7/7/17		Visited A.D.S's & aid-posts. Lt. L.E. DOUGALL R.A.M.C. evacuated sick to No. 10 C.C.S. 5 sick admitted & evacuated. 21 wounded admitted, 20 evacuated, 1 returned to duty. ADSS	
Do.	8/7/17		Officers 2, O.R. 8 sick & O.R. 4 wounded, admitted & evacuated. Heavy rain. ADSS	
Do.	9/7/17		Reconnoitred ground in front area for evacuation of walking wounded. Capt. R. Arthur R.A.M.C. rejoined unit from temporary medical charge of 8th Seaforth Hldrs. 10 wounded & 19 sick admitted & evacuated. DDMS	
Do	10/7/17		Sgt. BROWN R.A.M.C. proceeded to 61 C.C.S. for duty & struck off the strength of the unit. 17 wounded admitted, 16 evacuated, 1 died. 17 sick admitted & evacuated. ADSS	
Do.	11/7/17		15 sick & 18 wounded admitted, including 1 officer wounded. Two wounded returned to duty. Remainder evacuated. ADSS	

Army Form C. 2118.

WAR DIARY
or
INTELLIGENCE SUMMARY.
(Erase heading not required.)

Instructions regarding War Diaries and Intelligence Summaries are contained in F.S. Regs. Part II. and the Staff Manual respectively. Title pages will be prepared in manuscript.

Place	Date	Hour	Summary of Events and Information	Remarks and references to Appendices
VLAMERTINGHE MILL	12/7/17		Reconnoitred sites for Govn N.W. Dressing Station in the neighbourhood of Ypres, in the event of an advance. All available officers attended lecture by Consulting Surgeon, 5th Army. Area considerably shelled during the night. Two H.V. shells landed in this camp, causing no damage. 27 sick & 41 wounded, including 2 officers sick & 2 wounded, admitted. Two O.R. died. Remainder evacuated. Two officers & 3 O.R. N.Y.D ? gas amongst the sick.	ASM
Do.	13/7/17		Lt BRAYAC M.O.R.C. U.S. Army reported arrival for duty. Heavy shelling of area during the night. Sick, officers 5, O.R. 122 admitted & evacuated. Of these, 4 officers & 116 O.R. were N.Y.D ? gas. Wounded, officers 1, O.R. 25 admitted & evacuated. Of Two O.R.s died.	23 7 ASM
Do.	14.7.17		Sick admitted & evacuated. officers 3, O.R. 63, including 36 N.Y.D ? gas. Wounded O.R. 35. Returned to duty. Remainder evacuated. Heavy rain at night.	ASM

2353 Wt. W3514/1454 700,000 5/15 D.D.&L. A.D.S.S./Form/C. 2118.

WAR DIARY
or
INTELLIGENCE SUMMARY.
(Erase heading not required.)

Army Form C. 2118.

Place	Date	Hour	Summary of Events and Information	Remarks and references to Appendices
VLAMERTINGHE MILL	15/7/17		Sick, admitted MTM 8 O.R. & evacuated 8 O.R. Wounded admitted 11 O.R. / child. remainder evacuated. Weather warm. H&TP.	
Do.	16/7/17		Off sick, officers 1, O.R. 1, admitted & evacuated. Wounded officers 2, O.R. 34 admitted & evacuated. Weather warm. MTM	
Do.	17/7/17		Inspected Asylum, YPRES, with a view to something use of it as a Corps H.W.D.S. in the future. Capt. S. BRYSON rejoined unit from temporary duty c 8/10 Scottish. Two officers & 3 O.R. admitted & evacuated sick. MTM 8 O.R. admitted & evacuated wounded.	
Do.	18/7/17		8 O.R. sick and 1 officer & 26 O.R. wounded admitted & evacuated, including 1 officer & 9 O.R. "W" gas lack Shell. Weather showery. MTM	
Do.	19/7/17		Took over evacuation of wounded from R. outlets of Dunnival front. 2 N.E.O's & 7 men sent to Zunin Rd Collecting Post.	

Army Form C. 2118.

WAR DIARY
or
INTELLIGENCE SUMMARY.
(Erase heading not required.)

Place	Date	Hour	Summary of Events and Information	Remarks and references to Appendices
VLAMERTINGHE MILL	20/7/17		Sick admitted & evacuated, 19 O.R. including 5 NYDN cases. Wounded, 20 O.R. admitted. 1 returned to duty, remainder evacuated. ADMS.	
	21/7/17		Inspected Bearer Post on Brown Road, & roads for evacuation of wounded. Sick admitted & evacuated, 1 Officer, 5 O.R. including 1 NYD General. Wounded, 1 Officer returned to duty, & 3 O.R evacuated & 1 died. ADMS.	
Do.	21/7/17		Sick admitted & evacuated 2 O.R. Wounded - admitted 62. Two died of wounds, Two discharged to duty, remainder evacuated. ADMS	
Do.	22/7/17		Visited Bearer Post, Brown R⁴, & advanced collecting post on railway embankment. Sick admitted & evacuated Officers 1, O.R. 3. Wounded admitted Officers 5. O.R. 26. All evacuated except 3 O.R. discharged to duty. ADMS	
Do.	23/7/17		Sick admitted & evacuated O.R. 3. Wounded 1 Officer & 18 O.R. ADMS	
Do.	24/7/17		Sick admitted & evacuated 2 Officers & 3 O.R. Wounded 25 O.R. one of whom returned to duty. ADMS	

WAR DIARY
or
INTELLIGENCE SUMMARY.
(Erase heading not required.)

Army Form C. 2118.

Place	Date	Hour	Summary of Events and Information	Remarks and references to Appendices
			To duty.	
			1st Lt. GATLIN J.S. M.O.R.C. U.S.A. & 1st Lt. WALL J.P. M.O.R.C. U.S.A. reported arrival for duty.	AJS
VLAMERTINGHE	25.7.17		Inspected MENIN Rd. bearing Post. Sick admitted & evacuated Officers 1, O.R. 13, including 8 NYD Gassed. Wounded admitted & evacuated Officers 1, O.R. 28, civilian 10, 1 W. Gas Lachrymal.	AJS
Do.	26.7.17		Sick - Officers 2, O.R.; Wounded - Officers 1, O.R. 14, (1 W. Gas Lethal). Inspected route for evacuation of walking wounded by light Railway.	AJS
Do.	27.7.17		Visited bearing Post at MENIN Rd.; relay post on railway embankment, & advanced bearer post. Sick, Officers 1, O.R. 6 admitted & evacuated. Wounded, Officers 3, O.R. 18 admitted. 108 & 30.R. died of wounds; remainder evacuated.	AJS

WAR DIARY or INTELLIGENCE SUMMARY

Army Form C. 2118.

Place	Date	Hour	Summary of Events and Information	Remarks and references to Appendices
VLAMERTINGHE MILL	28/7/17		Showed O.C. 113 F.A. & representative 112 F.A. 18th Div'l front over. Visit from ADMS XIII Corps. Sick Officer 1, O.R. 2 admitted & evacuated. Wounded Off'r 1, O.R. 13 admitted. Two of these died & 4 returned to duty.
Do.	29/7/17		Attended conference at ADMS' office. Weather wet. Lt. LOGAN ASC reported for temporary duty. Sick O.R. 1, wounded Off'r 1, O.R. 13, 3 of these died of wounds. Remainder evacuated.	
Do.	30/7/17		4 Officers (composed of 1 tent division of 110th F.A. reported for temporary duty. 1 sick & 12 wounded admitted & evacuated, & 1 wounded officer. Sgt. MATTHEW & Lt. GRAY proceeded to MENIN Rd collecting post.	
Do.	31/7/17		Active operations commenced 3.50 A.M.. The first casualties up arrived here at 6.40 A.M. Fifteen bearers & two lorries had been placed at my disposal for evacuating cases from the front	

WAR DIARY
or
INTELLIGENCE SUMMARY.
(Erase heading not required.)

Army Form C. 2118.

to C.C.S. Cars were also brought here from Belgian Batt. corner CH 24 a 3.8) by light railway, & the main course of evacuation from here to C.C.S. REMY siding was by broad gauge railway.

Casualties at till 12 midnight were:-

	Officers	O.R.
15th Div.	17	972
16th Div	2	63
	-	37
31		
55	26	959
Corps troops } Collins groups }	19	1256
4 comands	-	218
Total	58	3,505

Of these, roughly 3,700 were evacuated by train.

At 1 A.M. CAPT. WALLACE & CAPT BRYSON proceeded with bearers to the trenches.

Weather fine till 7 P.M. Steady rain all night.

H. G Monteith
Lt Col.
O.C. 47 F. AMBULANCE.

Secret
August '17
Vol 25

Aug 1917

140/236+

War Diary for August 1917
of 47th Field Ambulance
Lt Colonel H C MONTEITH. R.A.M.C.
O.C. 47th Field Ambulance

COMMITTEE FOR THE
MEDICAL HISTORY OF THE WAR
Date −1 OCT.1917

WAR DIARY
or
INTELLIGENCE SUMMARY.
(Erase heading not required.)

Army Form C. 2118.

Place	Date	Hour	Summary of Events and Information	Remarks and references to Appendices
VLAMERTINGHE MILL	1/8/17		Admissions & evacuations = Officers 17, O.R. 874, including 12 Germans. The greater part of the casualties arrived during the night, — the result of a German counter-attack in the afternoon. Constant rain during the whole 24 hours. Visit from DDMS II Corps & ADMS 15th Div. Visited scouting post at MENIN Rd. Work there proceeding satisfactorily. Evacuations from here now being carried out entirely by bus & lorry, the train service having been discontinued by order of DMS Fifth Army.	
Do.	2/8/17		Admissions & evacuation .. { Wounded, officers 10. O.R. 580 { Sick officers 1 O.R. 178 Germans wounded 2 Capt. W.S. WALLACE RAMC and 8 O.R. of this ambulance wounded & evacuated. Visit from DDMS XIV Corps. Heavy rain all day & night.	

Army Form C. 2118.

WAR DIARY
or
INTELLIGENCE SUMMARY.
(Erase heading not required.)

Instructions regarding War Diaries and Intelligence Summaries are contained in F.S. Regs., Part II. and the Staff Manual respectively. Title pages will be prepared in manuscript.

Place	Date	Hour	Summary of Events and Information	Remarks and references to Appendices
VLAMERTINGHE MILL	3/8/17		Relieved by 112th F.A. 16th Division. Relief completed at 7 P.M. March to LUNA PARK (at L9 G 2.3. Sheet 27.). The personnel at MENIN Rd COLLECTING Post relieved by 113 F.A. 16th Div at 12.30 P.M. Admissions & evacuations up till 7 P.M. { Wounded officers 2, O.R. 121 Sick officers 1, O.R. 87. } & arranged relief. HSM	
LUNA PARK (L 9 G 2.3. Sheet 27)	4/8/17		Heavy rain all day. Visited Menin Rd. C. Post, & arranged 399 patients taken over at Luna Park. Bearer sections arrived at LUNA PARK at 7 AM. 176 sick & 185 wounded remaining. Heavy rain all day. Visited ADMS 15th Div., & made arrangements with O.C. Delancey St. for attaching Aid of patients & Stements. Also arranged with Area Commandants for bathing personnel.	
Do.	5.8.17.		Admitted, sick 1, wounded 1. Discharged sick 51, wounded 57. Evacuated sick 5, wounded 8. Remaining sick 121, wounded 121. Shrine admitted & wounded 3.	

Army Form C. 2118.

WAR DIARY
or
INTELLIGENCE SUMMARY.
(Erase heading not required.)

Instructions regarding War Diaries and Intelligence Summaries are contained in F. S. Regs., Part II. and the Staff Manual respectively. Title pages will be prepared in manuscript.

Place	Date	Hour	Summary of Events and Information	Remarks and references to Appendices
LUNA PARK	6.8.17		Visit from DDMS XIX Corps. Weather fine.	
			Sick admitted 7, evacuated 9, To duty 11, remaining 108. Eliminate 4 [admin & evac]	
			Wounded " 1, " 1, " 11, " 110	
Do.	7.8.17.		CAPT. H.P. HERBERT M.D.R.C. & LT. BAUGHMAN M.O.R.C. U.S.A	DGMS
			reported arrived for duty.	
			Capt. BRYSON R.A.M.C proceeded on 10 days leave to England.	
			Visit from ADMS 15th Divn. All available men in unit sent to baths.	
			Weather hot.	
			Sick, To duty 13, evacuated 5, Remaining 90.	
			Wounded " 27, " 2, " 81	DGMS.
Do.	8.8.17		Sick. To duty 9, evacuated 4, Remaining 97	
			Wounded " 6, " 0, " 75.	
			Weather hot. Heavy thunderstorm at night	DGMS
Do.	9.8.17		DDMS XIX Corps inspected the camp.	
			Sick. To duty 13, evacuated 2, remaining 60.	
			Wounded " " 35, " 0, " 40.	MDY.

Army Form C. 2118.

WAR DIARY
or
INTELLIGENCE SUMMARY.
(Erase heading not required.)

Instructions regarding War Diaries and Intelligence Summaries are contained in F. S. Regs. Part II. and the Staff Manual respectively. Title pages will be prepared in manuscript.

Place	Date	Hour	Summary of Events and Information	Remarks and references to Appendices
LUNA PARK	10/8/17		Sick, To duty 12, evacuated 5, Remaining 43.	
			Wounded, " " 3, " 0, " 37.	
			Weather fine.	
Do.	11/8/17.		Sick, To duty 7, evacuated 3, Remaining 33	
			Wounded, " 1, " 1, " 34	MO.
			Weather wet.	
Do.	12.8.17.		Sick, To duty 2, evacuated 1, Remaining 31	
			Wounded, " 3, " 3, " 28	MO.
			Weather fine.	
Do.	13.8.17.		Sick, To duty 8, evacuated 2, Remaining 22	
			Wounded, " 4, " 1, " 23	
			1 Officer sick admitted & evacuated.	
			Visit from DDMS XII Corps. Weather fine	
			Inspection & address by S.O.C. 15th Div⁻.	
Do.	14.8.17.		Sick, To duty 2, evacuated 2, Remaining 18	MO.
			Wounded, " 3, " 1, " 20	

Army Form C. 2118.

WAR DIARY
or
INTELLIGENCE SUMMARY.
(Erase heading not required.)

Place	Date	Hour	Summary of Events and Information	Remarks and references to Appendices
LUNA PARK	15.8.17		Sick, To duty, 3. Evacuated 1. Remaining 14. Wounded " 4 " 0 " 16	MSM.
Do.	16.8.17		Sick Admitted 23. Evacuated 0. To duty 1. Remaining 46. Wounded " 4 " 31 " 4 " 32 Weather fine.	MSM.
Do.	17.8/17		DADMS XIX Corps inspected the camp. Sick Admitted 11, Evacuated 2, To duty 1. Remaining 54. Wounded " 0 " 2 " 1 " 29. Weather fine.	MSM.
Do.	18.8.17		Capt. WALL M.O.R.C. & Lt. BAUGHMAN M.O.R.C. with 3 brown sub-divisions temporarily attached to 45 F.A. for duty in the forward area. Lt. GRAY M.O.R.C. attached for temporary duty to 8th Surgeon the High ??. Sick. Admitted 39. Evacuated 7. To duty 2. Remaining 84. Wounded " 6 " 2 " 2 " 31.	MSM.
Do.	19.8.17		Sick Admitted 42. Evacuated 109. To duty 17. Remaining 0. Wounded " 0 " 28 " 3 " 0 CAPT. BRYSON RAMC returned from leave to England.	MSM.

Army Form C. 2118.

WAR DIARY
or
INTELLIGENCE SUMMARY.
(Erase heading not required.)

Place	Date	Hour	Summary of Events and Information	Remarks and references to Appendices
LUNA PARK	20.8.17		Left LUNA PARK 9A.M. & took over RED FARM C.M.D.R. at 65 d 25 sheet 28. from 108 F.A. 31st Divn. LUNA PARK closed, & a guard left over stores.	
			CAPT. BRYSON RAMC with 15 O.R. proceeded to the HOSPICE at WATOU (E 28 d. sheet 27) for care of local sick, taking over from 113 F.A. 16th Divn.	
			CAPT. HERBERT MORC & 8 O.R. proceeded to XIV Corps Reinforcement camp for duty. RED FARM closed.	
RED FARM 21.8.17. G.S.d.25(sheet 28)			CAPT. WALL MORC returned to duty from 45 F.A.	
			CAPT. VICKERS RAMC proceeded to A.D.S. POTIJZE for temporary duty vice	M.O.
DO.	22.8.17.		Lt. GRAY MORC. returned from temporary duty with 8th Seaforth High.d	
			Capt. MATTHEW RMDS proceeded to front area for brevet duty.	M.O.
DO.	23.8.17.		CAPT WALL MORC & Lt. GRAY MORC. proceeded to 45 F.A. for temporary duty	M.O.
DO.	24.8.17		CAPT. BRYSON after returned to HdQr. having been relieved at WATOU by 11 East Lancs F.A. 42nd Divn.	MOT.
			Lt. GRAY M.B. Re took over temporary charge of 13th Royal Scots	

WAR DIARY
or
INTELLIGENCE SUMMARY.

(Erase heading not required.)

Army Form C. 2118.

Place	Date	Hour	Summary of Events and Information	Remarks and references to Appendices
RED FARM 6.5.d.2.5 (Sheet 28)	25/8/17		Relieved at RED FARM by 1/2 East Lancs. F.A. 42nd Div'n, & proceeded to BRANDHOEK. G.12.b.7.8. (Sheet 28.) Holding party at LUNA PARK rejoined unit, having handed over to 1/3 E. Lancs. 42nd Div". CAPT WALL M.O.R.C. recalled from 45 F.A. & proceeded for temporary duty to 70 Bde R.F.A. CAPT BRYSON R.A.M.C. recalled from 45 F.A. & proceeded for temporary duty to 10/11 H.L.I.	H.H.M. H.H.M.
Do.	26/8/17		Nothing noteworthy occurred. Heavy rain all night.	H.H.M.
Do.	27/8/17		Visited ADS at Prisons YPRES, & POTIJZE. Heavy rain all day.	H.H.M.
Do	28/8/17		CAPT G. BUCHANAN R.A.M.C & LT W.L. STUART R.A.M.C reported for duty with this unit. LT. GRAY M.O.R.C. attached for permanent duty to 13th Royal Scots. & struck off the strength of this unit accordingly.	H.H.M. H.H.M.

WAR DIARY
or
INTELLIGENCE SUMMARY
(Erase heading not required.)

Army Form C. 2118

Place	Date	Hour	Summary of Events and Information	Remarks and references to Appendices
BRANDHOEK	29/8/17.		CAPT. A.W. MATTHEW R.A.M.C. evacuated & evacuated to C.C.S. Scattered party returned from front. Casualties sustained since being committed into front area from 18.8.17 amount to :- Officers wounded 1. O.R. Killed 1 O.R. wounded 5. 17577 L.19 & L.3 sheet 27. 4m)	
BRANDHOEK	30/8/17.		Left BRANDHOEK & marched to WATOU, No.2 Area.	
L.19 B/3	31/8/17.		Marched to CAESTRE & entrained to ARRAS.	

17th......
Lt. Col.
O.C. 43 F.A.

SECRET. N° 29

25

Oct 1917   140/2438

VOLUME 1

Id 26

War Diary for September 1917 of
1st Field Ambulance, by
Lt Colonel H.C. MONTEITH, R.A.M.C.

COMMITTEE FOR THE
MEDICAL HISTORY OF THE WAR
Date — 5 NOV. 1917

1-10-17

WAR DIARY
or
INTELLIGENCE SUMMARY

(Erase heading not required.)

Army Form C. 2118

Place	Date	Hour	Summary of Events and Information	Remarks and references to Appendices
WATOU AREA L9B63 Sheet 27.	1/9/17		Moved to CAESTRE & return to ARRAS. Arriv at ARRAS at midnight. Weather showery. Lt. BAUGHMAN M.O.R.C. left at CAESTRE with a car, to remain at station until entrainment of Brig. completed. BTM motor lorry at 8 P.M.	
AGNEZ R17A (Sheet 5/c.)	2/9/17		March from Arras, on completion of detrainment, & proceed to camp East of AGNEZ, arriving 5 A.M. Lt. BAUGHMAN rejoined unit 10 P.M.	mtry
Do.	3/9/17		Capt. NALL M.D.A.C. rejoined from temporary duty with 70 Bde. R.F.A. Sick admitted 12, transferred 11, evacuated 1.	mtry
Do.	4/9/17		Visited dressing station at BLANGY, & A.D.S's at FAMPOUX & FEUCHY. Sick admitted 14, transferred 9, evacuated 3, remained 2.	mtry
Do.	5/9/17		Capt. BUCHANAN R.A.M.C. & Capt. NALL M.O.R.C. & 20 O.R. proceeded to A.D.S. at FAMPOUX & FEUCHY, as advance parties. Sick admitted 16, transferred 11, evacuated 7.	mtry

Army Form C. 2118

WAR DIARY
or
INTELLIGENCE SUMMARY
(Erase heading not required.)

Instructions regarding War Diaries and Intelligence Summaries are contained in F.S. Regs., Part II. and the Staff Manual respectively. Title Pages will be prepared in manuscript.

Place	Date	Hour	Summary of Events and Information	Remarks and references to Appendices
AGNEZ	6.9.17.		March to Oil Factory, BLANGY (G23.d.0.5 Sheet 51B) & take over evacuation of Division at short notice from 10th F.A. 4th Div". 2 officers & 43 O.R's take over A.D.S. FANPOUX A.23.a.8.5 & Lt. BAUGHMAN in charge. Capt. VICKERS & Capt. HALL with 4 O.R's take over A.D.S. FEUCHY H21.c.2.9 & advanced posts.	
BLANGY G.23.d.0.5 Sheet 51B.	7.9.17.		Inspected Advance Dressings Stations, Carrier relay posts & Reg. Aid. Posts. Weather warm. Work proceeding smoothly. Things quiet.	
do.	8.9.17		Visited A.D.S. FEUCHY & leading point for patients evacuated by train. Inspected Second. ARRAS with a view to its suitability	
do	9.9.17		Accompanied A.D.M.S. to A.D.S. & R.A.P. on CRUMP Lane. Visited B" H.Q. at WILDERNESS Camp. H.18.a.1.2.	
do	10.9.17		Visited A.D.S. FEUCHY, posts on Orange Hill & gunpits & R.A.P. R. Sector. Much artillery. Line quiet.	

Army Form C. 2118

WAR DIARY
or
INTELLIGENCE SUMMARY
(Erase heading not required.)

Instructions regarding War Diaries and Intelligence Summaries are contained in F. S. Regs., Part II. and the Staff Manual respectively. Title Pages will be prepared in manuscript.

Place	Date	Hour	Summary of Events and Information	Remarks and references to Appendices
BLANGY G.23.d.2.5 Sheet 51.b.	11/9/17.		Lieut Col. A.G. MONTEITH. proceeded on leave to the united Kingdom. Capt H. VICKERS assumed temporary command of unit during his absence; D.A.D.V.S. visited and inspected the horses & mules. Visit from D.D.V.S. Third Army. — A.M.K.B. Capt.	
do.	12/9/17.		Reconnoitred ground in vicinity of Decauville Railway, from H.21.c.2. as far as H.34.d.6.5. and thence over to Orange Hill and "Lone Pile" with a view of utilizing track in conjunction with our evacuation of wounded; forward posts at SAMPOUX & FEUCHY crates. HMK	
do.	13/9/17.		Visited Posts at SAMPOUX & FEUCHY. HMK	
do.	14/9/17.		O.R. O.R. slightly wounded. HMK	
do.	15/9/17.		Visited A.D.S. at FEUCHY & explored route with S.A.D.M.S. Kerr running from H.29.c.4.4. to H.35.a.6.2. (approximately) with a view to reclaiming same for transport of wounded. HMK	
do.	16/9/17.		Fine day. HMK	

Army Form C. 2118

WAR DIARY
or
INTELLIGENCE SUMMARY
(Erase heading not required.)

Instructions regarding War Diaries and Intelligence Summaries are contained in F.S. Regs., Part II. and the Staff Manual respectively. Title Pages will be prepared in manuscript.

Place	Date	Hour	Summary of Events and Information	Remarks and references to Appendices
BLANGY. G.23.a.9.5. sht 51.b	17/9/17		Visited A.D.S. Feuchy. JMW	
do.	18/9/17		Lieut W.L. STUART R.A.M.C. proceeded to No. 6 Stationary Hospital, FREVENT, for duty. JMW	
do.	19/9/17		Visited A.D.S. FEUCHY. Capt. DALE, R.A.M.C., R.M.O. to A.D.S. Feuchy, reports that 31 shells fell in the village between 6.30 p.m. - 6.45 p.m. JMW	
do.	20/9/17		Visited A.D.O. Zampoux, foun O.R. returned from XIV Corps Reinforcement Camp. JMW	
do.	21/9/17		Ten O.R. men joined for duty as stretcher bearers. Visited A.D.S. Feuchy. JMW	
do	22/9/17		Visited A.D.S. Fampoux, Lieut Col. H.G. MONTEITH returns from leave to U.K. & resumes command. JMW	
do.	23/9/17		Visited A.D.S FEUCHY. Capt VICKERS R.A.M.C. departed on 10 days leave to U.K.	

Army Form C. 2118.

WAR DIARY
or
INTELLIGENCE SUMMARY.
(Erase heading not required.)

Instructions regarding War Diaries and Intelligence Summaries are contained in F.S. Regs., Part II. and the Staff Manual respectively. Title pages will be prepared in manuscript.

Place	Date	Hour	Summary of Events and Information	Remarks and references to Appendices
BLANGY	24.9.17		Visited R.A.P. Right sector, & R.A.P. posts in Infant Trench & gun-pits. Visited the M.O.s of the 2 battalions on the R. sector.	
do.	25.9.17		Visited A.D.S. FAMPOUX & R.A.P. in Crump Trench. Work on new R.A.P.) under course of construction, is proceeding satisfactorily.	
do.	26.9.17		Reconnoitred light Railway system on R. sector with a view to evacuation of casualties by tram from R.A.P. Attended lecture on "Gas" by Capt. Douglas A.S.M.C. of Mond. St Gen.	
do.	27.9.17		Visited R.A.P. now being work on new R.A.P. proceeding satisfactorily. Visited BHQ & M.O. (Capt Inman) of 8th Seaforth Highlanders. Inspected A.D.S. FAMPOUX. Capt. WALL M.O.R.C. departed for duty with 38 D.D.S., & is struck off strength of this unit. Lt. SMITH F.C. M.O.R.C. temporarily attached to this unit from 46 F.A.	

Army Form C. 2118.

WAR DIARY
or
INTELLIGENCE SUMMARY.
(Erase heading not required.)

Place	Date	Hour	Summary of Events and Information	Remarks and references to Appendices
BLANGY	28.9.17.		Lt Keyes M.O.R.C. attached for temporary duty from 46 F.A. with M.O. ½ 6/7 R.S.F., made a tour of front line of R. Batt. front of R. sector. Visited H.Q. of this battalion (6/7 R.S.F.) & discussed with O.C. the advisability of forming an R.A.P. nearer to the front line than the present R.A.P.	
do	29.9.17		Visited R.A.P. R. sector, & with M.O. ½ 6 & 7 another High ᵗ. went round the trenches of L. Batt. R. sector, visiting the 2 Coy. H.Q. of companies in front line.	
do.	30.9.17.		Visited A.D.M.S. & discussed advisability of constructing a new R.A.P. for the R. Bn. of R. sector, & also a dug-out, near the present combined R.A.P. for the 2 Batt⁽ˢ⁾ R. sector, to accommodate 12-15 lying cases. (Sheet 51B, H.36 c.1.9.) Capt J B RAE M.O.R.C. & Lt. E.D. LOUGHMAN M.O.R.C. Temporarily attached to this unit for instruction. Lt. KEYES B.L. M.O.R.C. attached for permanent duty with this unit from 29.9.17.	

W S Monteith
Lt. Col.
O.C. 47 F.A.

SECRET 24

Oct. 1917

Volume N°28

Vol 27

14/2499

War Diary of 47th & 2nd Ambulances
for October 1917 by
Lt Colonel H.G.MONTEITH late
Comm'dg 47=th Field Ambulance

COMMITTEE FOR THE
MEDICAL HISTORY OF THE WAR
Date -8 DEC. 1917

Army Form C. 2118.

WAR DIARY
or
INTELLIGENCE SUMMARY.
(Erase heading not required.)

Instructions regarding War Diaries and Intelligence Summaries are contained in F. S. Regs., Part II. and the Staff Manual respectively. Title pages will be prepared in manuscript.

Place	Date	Hour	Summary of Events and Information	Remarks and references to Appendices
BLANGY G.23.d.2.5/Sht 57.B)	1/10/17		Visited R.A.P. R. outer & gun-pits (H.36.c.1.9), & consulted also G.O.C. 45th Bgd. re building a new advanced R.A.P. for R. Batt. R. outer. Consulted O.C. 73 R.E. Coy., & saw Area Commandant about billeting men R.A.M.C. personnel in Happy Valley (H.36.c.5) for working party. Lt BAUGHMAN M.O.R.C. attached to 12th H.L.I. for temporary duty.	MSM
do	2/10/17		Visit from D.A.D.M.S. (Sam) Third Army, accompanied by a Russian Red Cross officer, a French officer & O.C. No.2 Stationary Hospital. Showed them round A.D.S? & explained methods of evacuation of wounded. Lt. Smith M.O.R.C. temp. attached to this unit, was transferred for temp. duty to 1/1 R.S.F.	MSM
do	3/10/17		Visited R.A.P. Lone Copse. Work on new dug-outs proceeding satisfactorily; also visited R.A.P. & Right outer and ADS FAMPOUX.	MSM

Army Form C. 2118.

WAR DIARY
or
INTELLIGENCE SUMMARY.
(Erase heading not required.)

Place	Date	Hour	Summary of Events and Information	Remarks and references to Appendices
BLANGY	4.10.17		Visited R.A.P. R. Scots & H.Q 45th Bde Brig. to obtain information about a forthcoming raid; Capt. Walker R.A.M.C. accompanied me, & gave advice to M.O. on the question of "shock". Visited A.D.M.S. & construction of new R.A.P. for R. Bn. R. Scots. DDMS XVII Corps convened H.Q. at BLANGY & A.D.S?	
do	5.10.17		Weather cold & unsettled.	
do	6.10.17		Visited H.Q. 45th Brig., H.Q. Argyl & Suth. Highrs & R.A.P. A. & S. Highrs. Weather cold & wet. Lt F.C. Smith M.O.R.C. has this day been put on the strength of this unit. Lt. & Qr.M. Davis returned from leave to U.K.	
do	7.10.17		Lt KEYES M.O.R.C. proceeded to 11th A.C.S. Hosp. for temporary duty. Spent the night at R.A.P. L.Bn. R. Scots, A. & S. Highrs. A raiding party of 47 went over at 9.15 P.M. Casualties slight, but a certain number of the party failed to return.	
do	8.10.17		Visited R.A.P. R. Scots, Bn. H.Q. of L. Bn. R. Scots & H.Q 45th Bgde. Weather wet.	

WAR DIARY
or
INTELLIGENCE SUMMARY.
(Erase heading not required.)

Army Form C. 2118.

Place	Date	Hour	Summary of Events and Information	Remarks and references to Appendices
	9.10.17.		Weather wet. Nothing noteworthy occurred. HJH.	
	10.10.17.		Visited O.C. I.W.T. Coy. re. heating of barges for conveying casualties up the SCARPE from FAMPOUX. Visited R.E. officer i/c of workmen party on the new R.A.P. for R. Batt. R. sector. Capt. W.H. HERBERT M.O.R.C. proceeded to take over medical charge of 8/10 Gordon His. vice Capt. J.A. Smith R.A.M.C. Capt. H.M. VICKERS R.A.M.C. returned from leave to U.K. Was shewn and toured A.D.S. & R.A.P. of Division on our right by O.C. 36 F.A. Capt. HERBERT M.O.R.C. struck off the strength of this unit. HJH.	
	12.10.17.		Visited R.A.P. CRUMP Trench in R Bn. of R. sector. new R.A.P. is however acting extent. Visited ADS FAMPOUX. Work is being done, strengthening the roof of dressing station & cook house. Weather wet. HJH.	

Army Form C. 2118.

WAR DIARY
or
INTELLIGENCE SUMMARY.
(Erase heading not required.)

Place	Date	Hour	Summary of Events and Information	Remarks and references to Appendices
BLANGY 13.10.17	13.10.17.		Inspected work being done on new R.A.P for R Bn. R. section.	
Do.	14.10.17.		Visited Relay posts & ADS FEUVRY. Transport inspected by O.C. No. 4 Coy. 18th Div. Train. Lt. Col. GRAY C.B. Consulting Surgeon Third Army with a Danish Doctor visited the ambulance, & were shown A.D.S.'s & method of evacuation. Heavy shelling during the afternoon by our artillery owing to raid by 12th Div on our Right. Guns again active at 9.30 P.M. in consequence of a small raid by 61st Div: on our left.	ADMS ADMS
Do.	15.10.17.		Visited R.A.P., & R batt, L section, & ADS FAMPOUX.	ADMS
Do.	16.10.17.		Nothing noteworthy occurred	
Do.	17.10.17.		Inspected ADS's. Work being done at FAMPOUX, strengthening roof of dressing station & erecting shelter for attention stand.	ADMS
Do.	18.10.17.		Visited ADS FEUVRY. Nothing noteworthy occurred on Div? front.	ADMS
Do.	19.10.17.		Attended Third Army conference on "Surgical Shock".	m
Do.	20.10.17.		Inspected new R.A.P. in process of construction at in Right section. Visited R.A.P. R. section & bearer relay post. D.D.M.S. XVII Corps & ADMS 18th Div? inspected F.A. Headquarters at BLANGY.	ADMS

Army Form C. 2118.

WAR DIARY
or
INTELLIGENCE SUMMARY.
(Erase heading not required.)

Instructions regarding War Diaries and Intelligence Summaries are contained in F.S. Regs., Part II. and the Staff Manual respectively. Title pages will be prepared in manuscript.

Place	Date	Hour	Summary of Events and Information	Remarks and references to Appendices
BLANGY	21/10/17		Inspected new R.A.P. now in use, in L Sector; Left B⁴⁵ Visited ADS FAMPOUX & R.A.P. at TRIPLE ARCH.	MM.
Do.	22.10.17.		Maj. S. Lloyd & Capt. J.F. McKERNAN M.O.R.C. reported for instruction in work in the front area. Capt. Lt. F.C. SMITH M.O.R.C. attached off the strength of this unit from 21.10.17 for permanent medical charge of 6/7 R.S.F.	MM
Do.	23.10.17.		Attended conference on surgical shock at GRÉVILLERS	MM
Do.	24.10.17.		Visited A.D.S FEUCHY & R.A.P. R.Suton. Very heavy firing on the 51st Div. front on our left. Quiet on our front.	MM
Do.	25.10.17.		Visited R.A.P. L.B⁴⁵ Left SUTON & A.D.S FAMPOUX. Weather fine. Front quiet.	MM.
Do.	26.10.17		Visited by DADM.S (Bar) Third Army & 2 American Officers. Showed them round ADS⁵ & R.A.P. L suton. Weather wet.	MM HATS
Do.	27.10.17.		Inspected R.A.P. R.B⁴⁵ L suton & ADS FEUCHY. Road between FEUCHY & FAMPOUX slightly shelled.	

Army Form C. 2118

WAR DIARY
or
INTELLIGENCE SUMMARY
(Erase heading not required.)

Instructions regarding War Diaries and Intelligence Summaries are contained in F.S. Regs., Part II. and the Staff Manual respectively. Title Pages will be prepared in manuscript.

Place	Date	Hour	Summary of Events and Information	Remarks and references to Appendices
BLANGY	28/10/17		Major S. LLOYD & Capt. J.F. MCKIERNAN M.O. R.A.M.C. returned to their unit. Weather fine. HSM.	
DO.	29/10/17		Lt. B.L. KEYES M.O. R.A.M.C. rejoined unit from temporary medical charge of 11th A. & S.H. 71. Inspected A.D.S. FEUCHY, Relay Posts at Orange Hill & Grenadier, & R.A.P., which is in process of construction in CURLS SWITCH SOUTH Trench, for Right Bn, Bn, R. Iniskn. HSM.	
DO	30.10.17		Visited A.D.S. FEUCHY. Nothing noteworthy occurred. HSM	
DO.	31.10.17		Major G.W. PINKSTON U.S.M.C. & Major C.C. DEMMER U.S.M.C. reported for a week's temporary duty with this unit.	

H. Wentworth
Lt. Col.
O.C. 47 Field Ambulance.

SECRET 15

VOLUME N° 29

War Diary of 47th Field Ambulance
for November 1917
by
Lieut Col AG Monteith RAMC
Lt ½ 7th R.M.C.

COMMITTEE FOR THE
MEDICAL HISTORY OF THE WAR
Date 17 JAN. 1918

Army Form C. 2118

WAR DIARY
or
INTELLIGENCE SUMMARY
(Erase heading not required.)

Place	Date	Hour	Summary of Events and Information	Remarks and references to Appendices
BLANGY	1/11/17		Lt. R. L. D LUKENS M.O.R.C. ⎫ Leave this day from Estrum on the Lt. B. W. DAY " ⎬ Transfer of the Field Amb. B.B. Mc.BLUER " ⎭	
Do.	2/11/17		Capt. N.C. GRAHAM R.A.M.C. arrived for temporary duty for the purpose of selecting tents & lines. Lt. BAUGHMAN M.O.R.C. rejoined the unit from temporary medical charge of 69th 14.C.I. Visited R.A.P. L.B² L.Brig²ᵈ & A.D.S. FAMPOUX.	
Do.	3/11/17		Visited R.A.P. R.Sector & A.D.S. FEUCHY.	
Do.	4/11/17		DADMS 3rd Third Army & an American Officer I visited here, & were shewn round A.D.S³ & R.A.P.	
Do.	5/11/17		CAPT. N.C. GRAHAM R.A.M.C. returned to his unit. Inspected R.A.P. R.Sector, which is in process of construction. Visited A.D.S³ & current R.A.P. R.Sector. Lt. KEYES M.O.R.C. proceeded on leave to PARIS.	

Army Form C. 2118

WAR DIARY
or
INTELLIGENCE SUMMARY
(Erase heading not required.)

Instructions regarding War Diaries and Intelligence Summaries are contained in F. S. Regs., Part II. and the Staff Manual respectively. Title Pages will be prepared in manuscript.

Place	Date	Hour	Summary of Events and Information	Remarks and references to Appendices
BLANGY	6/11/17		Paid out company. Showed the 2 American officers our Coys lowatin, Disp. Bath etc. Nothing of importance occurred in front area.	MSY
BLANGY	7/11/17		Visited R.A.P. L.B⁶ L. Bgd. & ROEUX Caves. Attended meeting at A.D.M.S. office.	MSY
do.	8/11/17		Maj. Pinkston & Maj. DENNER U.S.M.C. observed for duty attd. to 43 C.C.S. Visited A.D.S⁶ & R.A.P. R. scutto & made arrangements for raid by 7/8 KOSB which took place during the night 8/9ᵗʰ.	MSY
do.	9/11/17		Lᵗ BAUGHMAN M.O.R.C. Attached to 8/10 Gordon Hrs. for temporary duty. Lᵗ KEYES M.O.R.C. returned from leave to Paris. A.D.S. FAMPOUX, & relay posts han'd. stretcher handed over to 4 & 6 F⁴ Amb⁶. 8 casualties occurred amongst the raiding party of KOSB last night	MSY
do.	10/11/17		Nothing noteworthy occurred.	MSY
do.	11/11/17		Lᵗ KEYES M.O.R.C Attached to 8/10 Gordons for permanent duty Lᵗ BAUGHMAN M.O.R.C. Attached to 6 Cameron Hrs. for temporary duty	MSY
do.	12/11/17		Visited R.A.P.⁶ & relay posts. During last night, the enemy bombarded FEUCHY & FAMPOUX with gas shells, making use apparently of both Phosgene & Lachrymatory shells	MSY

WAR DIARY
or
INTELLIGENCE SUMMARY

Army Form C. 2118

(Erase heading not required.)

Instructions regarding War Diaries and Intelligence Summaries are contained in F. S. Regs., Part II. and the Staff Manual respectively. Title Pages will be prepared in manuscript.

Place	Date	Hour	Summary of Events and Information	Remarks and references to Appendices
BLANGY	13/11/17		Gas shells again fell in the neig'bourhood of Feuchy & road between FEUCHY & FAMPOUX.	HWM
do.	14/11/17.		9 gassed cases passed through A.D.S. FEUCHY. Visited R.A.P. R. Scots. Capt E. BUCHANAN R.A.M.C. proceeded to 10th Scottish A/Amb for temporary duty. Nothing noteworthy occurred.	HWM
do.	15.11.17			HWM
do.	16.11.17.		Enemy 'planes generally quiet. Raid by 3/12 Seaforth H.H. lukewarm & lightly retaliated.	HWM
do.	17.11.17.		Capt. L. BUCHANAN R.A.M.C. rejoined unit. Visited R.A.P. R. Scots & Seafor.	HWM
do.	18.11.17.		All available officers attended classes meeting at S.E.C.S. Road firing covering by 10th A/g'ls. 2 casualties. Sent to S.B. E.S. Day M.O.R.C., Lt. LORENS M.O.R.C., 2 M.O.'s & 12 privates were visited R.A.P. Johnston Lane & inspected CHINSTRAP LANE.	HWM
do	19.11.17		Road by 2nd R.Scots. 1 o.r. wounded. Visited R.A.P. R. Scots. 10 gassed casualties received.	HWM
do.	20.11.17		Sent a supply of Gas to R.A.P. Johnston Lane with a view to using it as an A.D.S. in the event of an advance. Visited No. Bn. H.Q. Road artillery urgent 19/20 by 9th Fusiliers. 10 casualties evacy to heavy force wounded.	HWM

Army Form C. 2118

WAR DIARY
or
INTELLIGENCE SUMMARY
(Erase heading not required.)

Instructions regarding War Diaries and Intelligence Summaries are contained in F.S. Regs., Part II. and the Staff Manual respectively. Title Pages will be prepared in manuscript.

Place	Date	Hour	Summary of Events and Information	Remarks and references to Appendices
BLANGY	21/11/17		Two raids took place this morning in R. sector by 19/11 H.L.I. & 8th Gamerons. 4 casualties resulted. Weather wet.	
do.	22/11/17		Capt. N.P. HERBERT M.O.R.C., on return from leave to U.K., has been taken on the strength of this unit.	
do.	23/11/17		Inspected new R.A.P. in Trenches of contraction in R. sector, view railroad of light railway N.of MONCHY, with a view to connecting walking wounded by it in the event of an advance.	
do.	24.11.17		Visited A.D.S. Feuchy. No casualties during the 24 hours.	
do.	25.11.17		Visited R.A.P. Lyt. R's R. sector. A supply of surgical materials etc. is near & truck there to serve an A.D.S. in the event of an advance on this front.	
do.	26.11.17		Nothing noteworthy occurred.	
do.	27.11.17		Visited A.D.S. FEUCHY.	
do.	28.11.17		4th Div. took over the R. sector from 15th Div. Pos B in burst & visited.	
do.	29.11.17		15th Div. relieve 61st Div in the line. FAMPOUX A.D.S. taken over by me from 48th F.A., & general posts from 61st Div. During the afternoon FAMPOUX A.D.S. shelled, causing 15 casualties. One O.R. of this unit died of wounds.	
do.	30.11.17		Visited R.A.P. & relays per R. Enemy artillery very active.	Lt. Bd. O.C. 47 F.A.

Dec 17

Dec 1917

Hostilities up to 4th Dec 1917 Relieved
December 1917
by 4th HM Vickers R.A.O
OC Lt Fd Ambulance

28 Novr 30
14/2018
VA 29

47th Field Ambulance

COMMITTEE FOR THE
MEDICAL HISTORY OF THE WAR
Date — 1 FEB. 1918

Army Form C. 2118

WAR DIARY
or
INTELLIGENCE SUMMARY
(Erase heading not required.)

Instructions regarding War Diaries and Intelligence Summaries are contained in F.S. Regs., Part II. and the Staff Manual respectively. Title Pages will be prepared in manuscript.

Place	Date	Hour	Summary of Events and Information	Remarks and references to Appendices
BLANGY	1.12.17		Visited ADS FAMPOUX & RAP Johnson Lane H 30 & 8.0. (Sheet 51.R.) Front quiet	Map reference Sheet 51/B
do.	2.12.17		Inspected ROEUX farm, a visited RAP GROUP Trench H24.f.7.2, & Beaver/Post. Hostile artillery active on FEUCHY - FAMPOUX road near lumen lane. Capt. HERBERT & Sergeant proceeded on gas-course for 5 days. ITD'Y.	
do.	3.12.17		Nothing noteworthy occurred. ITD	
do.	4.12.17		Visited RAP & B'n H'qrs of centre R'y R. Brig. & discussed the new positions for AAP. Inspected Posts at Triple & Drijle [illegible] ITD'Y	
do.	5.12.17		Attended meeting at A.D.M.S. office. Visited ADS FEUCHY. Front quiet.	
do.	6.12.17		Inspected all Advanced Posts. Front quiet. In the evening the enemy attempted a raid on R.B'n of R. Brig. Three casualties resulted. ITD'Y	
do.	7.12.17		With DADMS 15"Div" visited R.A.P. & relay posts. Front quiet. ITD'Y	
do.	8.12.17		Three shell-gas cases passed through ADS FAMPOUX. ITD'Y	
do.	9.12.17		Nothing noteworthy occurred.	
do.	10.12.17		FAMPOUX heavily shelled during the afternoon, 5 shells falling within ADS compound. Attempted hostile raid on B'n. 8. of the third S.Royle repulsed. 11 casualties occurred. ITD'Y	
do.	11.12.17		Visited ADS FAMPOUX. Front quiet	
do.	12.12.17		Visited ADS Fampoux & consulted with an R.E Officer about strengthening ITD'Y 1st F.B. A.ELLWER MORT 90th our Company during absence of station	
do.	13.12.17		Visited ADS FAMPOUX. FAMPOUX - FEUCHY Road shelled intermittently all day. ITD'Y Discussed with CRE 15th Div'n advisability of making an ADS at Triple Arch	
do.	14.12.17		Visited ADS FEUCHY & FAMPOUX & Ruby Post Triple Arch. Inspected the latter place with a view to building a new ADS. ITD'Y	

Army Form C. 2118

WAR DIARY
or
INTELLIGENCE SUMMARY
(Erase heading not required.)

Instructions regarding War Diaries and Intelligence Summaries are contained in F. S. Regs., Part II. and the Staff Manual respectively. Title Pages will be prepared in manuscript.

Place	Date	Hour	Summary of Events and Information	Remarks and references to Appendices
BLANGY	15.12.17		Visited O.C. Light Railway Co. On completion of line up to TRIPLES ARCH, the trolley will be allowed at my disposal for carrying evacuations to FAMPOUX.	
do.	16.12.17		Inspected work being done on A.D.S. FAMPOUX. The front side of the building being reinforced with concrete.	
do.	17.12.17		Party of 30 m.n. detailed for work with 9th Gordon Highrs to construct new A.D.S. at Taylor's Arch. Attended meeting at 192 B.S.	
do.	18.12.17.		Nothing noteworth to report.	
do.	19.12.17		Inspected work being done on new A.D.S. Triple Arch. Present A.D.S. at FAMPOUX being reinforced with concrete. Showed A.D.Ms French Div3 round A.D.S.? R.A.P.s etc.	
do.	20.12.17.			
do.	21.12.17.		Nothing worthy of report. H.M.Vickers took over.	
do.	22.12.17.		Lieut. Col. H.S.MONTEITH, D.S.O. proceeded on leave to U.K. and Capt. H.M.VICKERS, R.A.M.C. took over command of the ambulance.	
do.	23.12.17.		Nothing to report.	
do.	24.12.17.		Funeral party at Fampoux. Funday was kept.	
do.	25.12.17.		Xmas day, men collected in billets, the men had a dinner and a concert. Men amongst themselves jollily carried on in the evening. Snow fell during the day.	

WAR DIARY
or
INTELLIGENCE SUMMARY

Army Form C. 2118

Place	Date	Hour	Summary of Events and Information	Remarks and references to Appendices
BLANGY.	26.XII.17.		Lieut. LEUKENS, R.O.R.C. took over T.M.C. of 7/8 R.C.F.B. H.N.VICAR Capt.	
do	27.XII.17		Lieut. McCLUER, B.B. R.O.R.C. took over T.M.C. of 12th H.L.I. H.N.VICAR Capt.	
do	28.XII.17		Visited aid posts at Fervez & Pampoux. H.N.VICAR Capt.	
do	29.XII.17		Nothing of note. H.N.VICAR Capt.	
do	30.XII.17		Arrangements were made with O.C. No.9 J.A. to taking over the line encountered. Lieut LEUKENS R.O.R.C. D.O.R.C. will attend them over (permanent residue only) of 7/8 R.O.R.B. the Ming to from 25th eight both Batty. H.N.VICAR Capt.	
do	31.XII.17.		Nothing of note. H.N.VICAR Capt.	

H.N.VICAR
Capt.
O/C 4? R.F.A. Amb

PACKET 24

War Diary of
1/1 Highland
Field Ambulance

H.C. Monteith
& 1/2 Highland
Field Ambulance

Packet 31

VIII 30
1918 15

COMMITTEE FOR THE
MEDICAL HISTORY OF THE WAR
Date -4 MAR 1918

47th FIELD AMBULANCE
No.
Date 1/2/19

WAR DIARY
or
INTELLIGENCE SUMMARY

(Erase heading not required.)

Army Form C. 2118

Instructions regarding War Diaries and Intelligence Summaries are contained in F.S. Regs., Part II. and the Staff Manual respectively. Title Pages will be prepared in manuscript.

Place	Date	Hour	Summary of Events and Information	Remarks and references to Appendices
BLANGY	1.1.18		The A.D.S. at Fampoux & Feuchy and the advanced posts were relieved by the advance party of No. 9. F.A., and hostling points of This Ambulance arrived at H.Q., a hosting party was sent to ALLONVY-LE-COMTE.	WON/V/18 Capt. James
BLANGY to AVESNES-LE-COMTE at J.26.d.3.4. Sheet 51/	2.1.18.		The Ambulance was relieved by No. 9 F.A. of the Guards Division, & no left, marched from Blangy at 9 a.m. and arrived at AVESNES-LE-COMTE (J.26.d.3.4) at 1 p.m., and took over from 1st H.F.A. of the Guards Division. Four patients belonging to the 2me Divisions were taken over. Ambulances cars were sent out on the Glorieux 45th & 46th C.C.S.s. Took over motor ambulance cars from the 45th & 46th C.C.S.s. Took in making arrangements for the evacuation. The Lieut Medical Charge of Ambulance of 45th & 46th Brit Hospls	
AVESNES-3.1.18. LE-COMTE	3.1.18.		The War was on 15 other horse (officer & squad) with back for 15 patients. The above were proceeding over patch arranged for Mongre & Shoe-smiths enlisted. 3 Jnr Privates (1st & Communic. 2nd & R.C.D. and 2nd Rows) Rata missions to be trained in the use of the Lewis gun (Pattern admitted 15 – 10 discharged to duty – nil) Deaths 2 Remaining on strength 20.	A.A. Potter Lt. Col. H.M. Arlington R.A.M.C.

WAR DIARY
or
INTELLIGENCE SUMMARY

(Erase heading not required.)

Army Form C. 2118

Place	Date	Hour	Summary of Events and Information	Remarks and references to Appendices
AKENNSTEAD COMTE	4.1.18		General work on Camp continued — in building just erected new dressings and Camp Zone for Patients admitted ...... 8 Other Ranks ...... 6 Average holding — nil Admissions — nil Evacuations — 22	
do.	5.1.18		Capt. F. Best Lunn RAMC. posted on Base ? U.K. Patients kept in most cases pended till Gentlemen? T? minutes being inclemently cold. Patients: to: admitted — 90 to: Dismissed — 7 " Transferred — nil " remains in hosp. — 35.	G.R.O. ? ? ? ?
do.	6.1.18		Bath Ph.? 50 other Patients were completed today and opened for the reception of patients. to: admitted — 18 to: Dismissed — 4 " Evacuated " in enemy — 49. H.O. Vickers Capt. RAMC	Lt. A. Pitter? RAMC also crew arr. & second time.
do.	7.1.18		Patients To: admitted — 28 To: Discharged — 7 " Discharged 2 " remaining — 65	

H.A. Vickers

Army Form C. 2118

WAR DIARY
or
INTELLIGENCE SUMMARY
(Erase heading not required.)

Instructions regarding War Diaries and Intelligence Summaries are contained in F.S. Regs., Part II. and the Staff Manual respectively. Title Pages will be prepared in manuscript.

Place	Date	Hour	Summary of Events and Information	Remarks and references to Appendices
AVESNES-LE-COMTE	8.1.17.		Lieut Col. H.C. MONTEITH D.S.O. returned from leave to U.K. & took over command of the Ambulance vice Capt:- No. admitted 10. No. Davidson -1 discharged -1 remaining -55 "To C.C.R.S & 1	
do.	9.1.17.		Capt. H.M. VICKERS proceeded on leave G.O.K. Patients. No. admitted 29 No. evacuated 14 " discharged 0 " remaining 78 " To C.C.R.S. 9	HCM Lt Col
do.	10.1.17.		Patients No. admitted 10. No. evacuated 8 " discharged 3 " remaining 75 " B.R.S. 2	HCM
do.	11.1.17		Patients No. admitted 35 No. evacuated 5 " discharged 10 " remaining 91 HCM " S.R.C. 4	
do.	12.1.17		Lt. D. HOLROYDE A.M.C. reported for duty, & taken on the strength accordingly Patients No. admitted 13 " discharged 1 " C.A.S. 3 " evacuated 20 " remaining 80 ADMS XVIII Corps inspected the camp. HCM	

Army Form C. 2118

WAR DIARY
or
INTELLIGENCE SUMMARY
(Erase heading not required.)

Place	Date	Hour	Summary of Events and Information	Remarks and references to Appendices
AVESNES LE COMTE	13.1.18		Patients. No. admitted 11. No. discharged 3. " To C.R.S. 3 Remaining 75 " Evacuated 10	
do.	14.1.18		Patients " Admitted 19 No. discharged 4 " C.R.S. 1 Remaining 83 " Evacuated 6	
do.	15.1.18		Patients No. admitted 18 No. discharged 7 " C.R.S. — Remaining 85 " Evacuated 9 V. heavy rain all day.	
do.	16.1.18		Patients No. admitted 22 No. discharged 1 " C.R.S. 1 Remaining 92 " Evacuated # 13	
do	17.1.18		Lt. B.B. McGuire M.O.R.C. rejoined from temporary duty Lt. & Q.M. Davis R.A.M.C. proceeded on leave to U.K. Patients No. admitted 15 No. discharged 5 " C.R.S. 5 Remaining 79 " Evacuated 18	
do.	18.1.18		Patients No. admitted 20 No. discharged 7 " C.R.S. 9 Remaining 80 " Evacuated 3	

Army Form C. 2118

WAR DIARY
or
INTELLIGENCE SUMMARY
(Erase heading not required.)

Instructions regarding War Diaries and Intelligence Summaries are contained in F.S. Regs., Part II. and the Staff Manual respectively. Title Pages will be prepared in manuscript.

Place	Date	Hour	Summary of Events and Information	Remarks and references to Appendices
AVESNES LE COMTE	19.1.18		Patients No. admitted 22 " wounded 3 " C.R.S. 6 No. discharged 1. Remaining 92	M2
do.	20.1.18		Patients No. admitted 11 " wounded 6 " C.R.S. 6 No. discharged 4 Remaining 87	M2
do.	21.1.18		Patients No. admitted 19 " wounded 5 " C.R.S. 6 - G.12.S.H. 1 diphtheria No. discharged 7 Remaining 847	M2
do.	22.1.18		Capt HERBERT M.O.R.C. wounded to 19 B.G.S. No. admitted 10ff 160.R. " wounded 1 " 9 " " C.R.S. - 3 Discharged 4 Remaining 87	M2
do.	23.1.18		Capt BUCHANAN RAMC returned from leave to U.K. No. admitted 25 " wounded 9 " C.R.S. 10 Duty 3 Remaining 90	M2
do.	24.1.18		Hospital & camp inspected by A.D.M.S. 15th Div. Consent given to patients No. admitted 22 Discharged 3 " wounded 9 Remaining 95 " C.R.S. 5 Transport inspected by O.C. No. 4 Bry. Div. Train	V.Montgomery

Army Form C. 2118

WAR DIARY
or
INTELLIGENCE SUMMARY
(Erase heading not required.)

Place	Date	Hour	Summary of Events and Information	Remarks and references to Appendices
AVESNES LE COMTE	25/1/18		Patients. No. admitted 14 " evacuated 2 " to 8 RS 6 No. discharged 5 " Remaining 96	
do.	26/1/18		No. admitted again 1 / O.R. 14 " wounded " / O.P. 2 CRS — 5 Discharged 3. Remaining 100	
do	27/1/18		No. admitted 18 " wounded 3 " CRS 7 Discharged 5 Remaining 103	
do.	28/1/18		No. admitted 22 " evacuated 8 " C.R.S. 5 " to 12 Stat. Hosp. 1. NYD diphtheria 1. Capt. H.F.N. SCOTT R.A.M.B is this day taken on the strength of their unit. Discharged 6 Remaining 107	
do.	29/1/18.		Patients No. admitted 22 " wounded 11 " 6 RS 4 Lt. B.B. 2: Blица MODL reported for temporary duty to 8 Garrison Hosp. Discharged 9 Remaining 105	
do	30/1/18		Patients admitted off: 1 O.R. 22 evacuated " 1 O.R. 18 CRS " 11 To 12 Stat. Hosp. " 1 (? Diphtheria) Discharged 8 Remaining 91	
do	31/1/18		Patients admitted 27 " evacuated 14 " CRS 3 Discharged 10 Remaining 91	

H.W.Montifford O.C. 42 F.A.

Secret 14
28/10/18

Volume 32

WA31

140/784

War Diary of 47th Field Ambulance
for the month of 1918
by
LC.OE.G. MONTEITH D.S.O. Rank C
Commdg. 47th Fd Amb. eg

Army Form C. 2118.

WAR DIARY
or
INTELLIGENCE SUMMARY.
(Erase heading not required.)

Instructions regarding War Diaries and Intelligence Summaries are contained in F. S. Regs., Part II. and the Staff Manual respectively. Title pages will be prepared in manuscript.

Place	Date	Hour	Summary of Events and Information	Remarks and references to Appendices
AVESNES	1/2/18		Patients. No. admitted 26 To duty 7	
			" wounded 22 Remaining 81	
LE CONTE			" CRS 7	
J. Col. 3. G. (about 5 G.)			Capt M.W. Littlewood RAMC reported for duty & taken on the strength	
				March 3/18
do	2/2/18		No. admitted 14 To duty 4	
			" wounded 19 Remaining 50 MOC	
			" CRS 22	
do	3/2/18		Patients. No. admitted 28. 1 O.R.18 To duty 6	
			No. wounded 18 Remaining 33 MOC	
			" CRS 1 - 13	
do	4/2/18		Patients. Admitted 30 Duty 5	
			Evacuated 21 Remaining 17 MOC	
			CRS 20	
do	5/2/18		Patients Admitted 21 Duty 2	
			Evacuated 19 Remaining Nil MOC	
			CRS 21	
Hospital St Jean	6/2/18		Handed over ambulance site at AVESNES to W.R.F.A. 4th Div.	
ARRAS			Marched to ARRAS at 9 AM arriving at 1 PM & took over Hosp. St Jean	
			from 45th F.A.	
			Patients. No. transferred from 45th F.A. 38 No. to CRS 19 7 NYD Div. O.R. SC Myal.	
			" admitted 62 " wounded 24 Remaining 57 MOC	

WAR DIARY
or
INTELLIGENCE SUMMARY.
(Erase heading not required.)

Army Form C. 2118.

Place	Date	Hour	Summary of Events and Information	Remarks and references to Appendices
Hop N°Jean ARRAS	7/2/18		Patients Admitted Off 1 OR 33 To R SET P 1 wounded — 1 — 13 CRS — — 6 Remaining 19 NYD	
do	8/2/18		Lecture by ADMS 15th Div: to MO's XVIII Corps on Trench Feet. Patients Admitted 66 Remaining 98 NYD wounded 23 CRS 13	
do	9/2/18		Patients admitted Off 1 OR 38 Duty 5 1 NYD Diphtheria to 12CCS/B54 wounded — 1 — 11 — 6 CRS Remaining 112 NYD	
do	10/2/18		Patients admitted SO Duty 1 wounded 18 CRS 24 Remaining 128 NYD	
do	11/2/18		Patients admitted Off 2 OR 48 Duty 4 wounded — 1 — 23 CRS — 1 — 23 Remaining 114 NYD	
do	12/2/18		Patients admitted Off 1 OR 37 Duty 7 wounded — — 19 CRS — 1 — 12 Remaining Off 1 OR 112 NYD	
do	13/2/18		Patients admitted Off 1 OR 45 Duty Off 1 OR 6 1 Scarlet to NYD wounded — — 21 To ILSt Hoch OR 3 1 NYD Diphtheria CRS — 1 — 19 Remaining 108	

Army Form C. 2118.

WAR DIARY
or
INTELLIGENCE SUMMARY.
(Erase heading not required.)

Instructions regarding War Diaries and Intelligence Summaries are contained in F. S. Regs., Part II. and the Staff Manual respectively. Title pages will be prepared in manuscript.

Place	Date	Hour	Summary of Events and Information	Remarks and references to Appendices
Nok St Jean ARRAS	14/2/18		Patients Admitted Off 1 OR 49 To Duty 4 evacuated — 1 — 19 Remaining 113 CRS	MO
do.	15/2/18		Capt. H.M. VICKERS returned from leave to U.K. CAPT. M.M. LITTLEWOOD RAMC proceed on Exchange dug to 9th R.H. Patients Admitted Off 1. OR 26 To duty 4 evacuated — — 11 Remaining Off 1. OR. 13 CRS	MO
do	16/2/18		Patients Admitted OR 58 To duty 6 evacuated OR 12 To R.R.H.Met 1 NYD & others Remaining Off 1 OR 129 CRS	MO
do.	17/2/18		Patients Admitted 33 To duty 11 To 12 SCR 1 NYD & others evacuated 13 Remaining 124 Off 1. OR 13 CRS	MO
do	18/4/18		Patients Admitted off 1 OR 43 (including 2 N.G. wound) Duty 7 evacuated — 18 CRS — 22 Remaining 120 MO	MO
do	19/2/18		Patients Admitted Off/NO OR 48 2 Duty OR. 2 evacuated Off 1 OR 13 Remaining sick 124. wounded 2. MO — 27	
do	20/2/18		Patients Admitted Off 1 OR 32 Duty OR 2 evacuated — 7 Remaining OR 136 CRS — 13	MO

Army Form C. 2118.

WAR DIARY
or
INTELLIGENCE SUMMARY.
(Erase heading not required.)

Instructions regarding War Diaries and Intelligence Summaries are contained in F. S. Regs., Part II. and the Staff Manual respectively. Title pages will be prepared in manuscript.

Place	Date	Hour	Summary of Events and Information	Remarks and references to Appendices
Hot. Styran ARMY	21/2/18		1st DAY MOBL Proceeded en route to the south of France	
			Patients admitted Off 1. O.R. 38 To duty O.R. 4	
			wounded — 10 Remaining O.R. 128	
			C.R.S. — 22	MOY
do.	22/2/18		Patients admitted Off 1. O.R. 57 To duty O.R. 11	
			wounded — 24 Remaining — 131	
			C.R.S. — 19	MOY?
do.	23/2/18		Patients admitted O.R. 43 To duty 4	
			wounded — 26 Remaining 120	
			C.R.S. — 16	MOY
do.	24/2/18		Patients admitted 59 To duty 7	
			wounded 28 Remaining 127	MOY
			C.R.S.	
do.	25/2/18		Patients admitted Off 4 O.R. 41 To duty 1	
			wounded — 4 — 10 Remaining 132	
			C.R.S. — 24 1(Death)	10 MOY
			To 12 Stat.Hosp.	
do.	26/2/18		Patients admitted Off 1. O.R. 34 Duty 5	
			evacuated — 1 — 19 Remaining 128	MOY
			C.R.S. — 14	

WAR DIARY
or
INTELLIGENCE SUMMARY.

Army Form C. 2118.

Place	Date	Hour	Summary of Events and Information	Remarks and references to Appendices
Hosp. 8°Jeu ARRAS	27/2/18		Patients Admitted 60 evacuated 17 CAS 34 To duty 4 Remain 133	
do	28/2/18		Patients Admitted 52 evacuated 29 CAS 36 To duty Remain 129	O.O. Monteith Lt Col. O.C. 47 F.A.

SECRET.

Volume 33

29

140/249

War Diary of 47th Field Ambulance
for March 1918
by Lieut. Col. H.C. Monteith DSO RAMC
Commdg. 47th F Amb.

YB 32

COMMITTEE FOR THE
MEDICAL HISTORY OF THE WAR
Date 12 MAY 1918

WAR DIARY
or
INTELLIGENCE SUMMARY.
(Erase heading not required.)

Army Form C. 2118.

Place	Date	Hour	Summary of Events and Information	Remarks and references to Appendices
Hosp. ARRAS	1/3/18		Inspection by Col. E.B. KNOX A.D.M.S. 15th Div. Capt. W.P HERBERT M.O.R.C. U.S.A. rejoined from hospital, & is taken on the strength on rejoining. Patients Admitted 98 / O.R 36 Duty 5 wounded 20 Remain 127 C.R.S 23	
do	2/3/18		Patients Admitted O.R 53 Duty 7 wounded 27 To 15.Cast. H. 10 R. Measles. C.R.S 14 Remain 131	
do	3/3/18		Patients Admitted of 2 O.R. 41 Duty 5 wounded — 17 — 13 Remain 125 C.R.S 63 Capt. R Buchanan R.A.M.C. proceed to 6 Somerset L.I. for temporary duty Capt. Littlewood R.A.M.C. rejoined from temporary duty with 9 R.H. Arty.	
do	4/3/18		Patients Admitted of 3 O.R 55 Duty 4 wounded — 21 Remain 130 C.R.S — 26	
do	5/3/18		Patients Admitted of 1 O.R 56 Duty 10 wounded " 20 To 15 Cast. H. 1 munises C.R.S " 28 Remain 127	

WAR DIARY
or
INTELLIGENCE SUMMARY.
(Erase heading not required.)

Army Form C. 2118.

Instructions regarding War Diaries and Intelligence Summaries are contained in F. S. Regs., Part II. and the Staff Manual respectively. Title pages will be prepared in manuscript.

Place	Date	Hour	Summary of Events and Information	Remarks and references to Appendices
Hosp. St Jean	6/3/18		Capt F.H.N. SCOTT RAMC transferred to 15th Machine Gun Bn, & attached to 15th Army HQ for duty.	
ARRAS			Patients admitted CCS 41 OR 55 — 105 / CRS — 1 — 32 / Duty 18 / Remaining 26	MTM
ECOLE NORMAL ARRAS	7/3/18		Moved from Hosp. St Jean to ECOLE NORMAL. Move complete by 10.40 A.M.	
			Patients admitted Off 1 OR 42 / evacuated — 23 / CRS — 1 — 11 / Duty 2 / Remaining 31	
			Visit from DDMS XVII Corps.	
			Arrangements made to function as Corps Main Dressing Station.	MTM
do.	8/3/18		Patients admitted 31 / evacuated 27 / CRS 4 / Duty 2 / 12 STRA 28 / Remaining 38	MTM
do.	9/3/18		Patients admitted 45 / evacuated 35 / CRS 12 / Duty 2 / Remaining 24	MTM
do.	10/3/18		Patients admitted 36 / evacuated 26 / CRS 10 / Duty 5 / Remaining 19	MTM
			U. Day. M.O.R.C. returned from leave to U.S. Forces.	MTM

WAR DIARY
or
INTELLIGENCE SUMMARY.
(Erase heading not required.)

Army Form C. 2118.

Place	Date	Hour	Summary of Events and Information	Remarks and references to Appendices
ECOLE NORMAL	10/3/18		Pte E. Unger MM Lt. Boy RAMC returned from leave to G.S. Front. Opened as Corps Main Dressing Station, XVIII Corps.	
ARRAS			Inspected by DDMS XVIII Corps.	
			Patients: Admitted sick – Offrs 2 O.R. 62 XVIII Corps wounded – 4 – 35 O.R. 8 1st Div – 1 – 3 1 Corps Troops C.R.S. O.R. 3 (wounded) Died Duty Remaining Wounded O.R. 19 Div: O.R. 19 Offrs. 4 & 120.O.R. wounded gas W. MM	
do	12/3/18		Inspected by DA&QMG & DDMS XVII Corps Patients: Admitted sick 19. O.R. 50 wounded O.R. 5 15th Div – 48 – 5 Corps Troops C.R.S. 1 – 5 2 Div & E.Hosp. 1 2 "Guards Div" Wounded 2 offs & 18 O.R. including 130 R gassed. MM	
do			Left Capt. E. Bitchener RAMC reported from leave 6th Division train. MM	
do	13/3/18		Patients: Admitted sick O.R. 38 wounded O.R. 6 1st Div forming 28 – 5 C.R.S. 1 (wounded) L.O.T. 12 R.A.M. 11 "Guards" received Div" wounded 16 gassed 8 sick, 3 mustard MM	

Army Form C. 2118.

WAR DIARY
or
INTELLIGENCE SUMMARY.
(Erase heading not required.)

Instructions regarding War Diaries and Intelligence Summaries are contained in F. S. Regs., Part II. and the Staff Manual respectively. Title pages will be prepared in manuscript.

Place	Date	Hour	Summary of Events and Information	Remarks and references to Appendices
ECOLE NORMAL ARRAS	14/3/18		Patients 15th Div. A.C.T. { Admitted evacuated C.R.S. No 12. Stat H. 9 Guards Div. General } sick. Off 1 O.R. 29 Wounded O.R. 2 — 13 — 1 — 2 (MVD Dysent.) (8 Bill. 1 mustard)	MM
do	15/3/18		Patients 15th Div. { Admitted evacuated C.R.S. Guards } sick Off 1 O.R. 29 wounded O.R. 2 — 15 — 1 — 14 — 1 wounded O.R. 2 gassed 4 (1 mustard) 1	MM
do	16/3/18		Patients 15th Div. A.E.T. { Admitted evacuated C.R.S. 12 Stat H. } sick O.R. 82 Wounded O.R. 3 — 21 — 3 — 10 (masks) — 1 Guards Div. Wounded 4 gassed 10. 1 mustard .. 9 Blue cross. S.I. 2	MM
do	17/3/18		Patients 15th { Admitted sick off. OR 26 wounded O.R. 11 C.R.S. — 13 — 7 — 14 — 4 ut gas. Guards O.R. wounded 5 gassed 8 (7 mustard)	MM

2353 Wt. W3544/7454 700,000 5/15 D. D. & L. A.D.S.S./Forms/C. 2118.

WAR DIARY or INTELLIGENCE SUMMARY

Army Form C. 2118.

Place	Date	Hour	Summary of Events and Information	Remarks and references to Appendices
ECOLE NORMAL ARRAS	18/3/18		Capt. LITTLEWOOD RAMC proceeded on leave to U.K. Instructions received to again admit patients here for retention for 7 days. Patients { Admitted sick O.R. 33, wounded O.R. 5 evacuated " 18, " 5 C.R.S. " 8 R. Stat. H " 2 (NYD dysentery & German measles) Remaining " 7 "Genes" Div. Wounded 5. Gassed 5 (evacuated)	
do.	19/3/18		Patients { Admitted sick O.R. 1, O.R. 22, wounded O.R. 2 evacuated " 1, " 13, " 2 C.R.S. " 8 Remaining " 11 "Genes" Div. 1 wounded, 1 gas (evacuated)	
do.	10/3/18		Patients { Admitted sick 26, W. 12 evacuated " 12, " 12 to C.R.S. 8 Remaining 17 "Genes" Div: gassed 4 (evacuated)	

Army Form C. 2118.

WAR DIARY
or
INTELLIGENCE SUMMARY.
(Erase heading not required.)

Place	Date	Hour	Summary of Events and Information	Remarks and references to Appendices
ECOLE NORMAL ARRAS.	21/3/18.		ARRAS intermittently shelled, numerous casualties resulting. XVIII Corps Divisional Defence Scheme put into operation. Capt. Pascall RAMC & 22 O.R. from 4th F.A. 4th Div. attached for temporary duty. Adv. Hdqrs. 15th Div. & Captures { admitted wounded 4. O.R. 131. sick offi 1. O.R. 32 C.R.S — 3 — 9 — 87 Duty — 1 — — — 10 Died of wounds — — — 3 — — — 12 Gas Cases (included in above) 1 — 12 (9 mustard. 4 Phosgene.) Guards Div. { wounded 28 O.R. 22 to C.C.S. 3 died. 16 duty Gassed — 3 (1 phosgene. 2 mustard.) 4th Div. { wounded 16 O.R. wounded 16 Total wounded 7 offrs. 173 O.R. (S.W.Y.D Bn.) (15th Div. Sgt. 730 O.R.) 1137 22/3/18. Advn Hdqrs 15th Div. & Bat. Jocks { admitted evacuated offi 1. O.R. 8 sick offi 1. O.R. 44 C.R.S — 1 — 4 — 2 — 28 Died — — — 4 — — — 18 — — — — — — — 2 13 W. Gas mustard amongst wounded admitted. Guards Div. wounded 3. gassed & mustard 4th Div. — 5 — Total wounded offi 2. O.R. 58 (included 17 gassed) 1112	

2353 Wt. W2544/1154 700,000 5/15 D.D. & L.   A.D.S.S./Forms/C. 2118.

WAR DIARY
or
INTELLIGENCE SUMMARY.

Army Form C. 2118.

Place	Date	Hour	Summary of Events and Information	Remarks and references to Appendices
ECOLE MILITAIRE ARRAS	23/8/18		Patients Admitted sick. Off 1 O.R. 17 wounded Off 2 O.R. 106 (includes 3 mustard gas) 14 2 102 evacuated 3 4 CCS 1	
do	24/8/18		Patients Admitted sick O.R. 44 wounded Off 2 3 4 4 Transf. to 46 F.A. 4 2 4th Div. wounded Off 1 O.R. 13 Cases hitherto being sent to 5 C.C.S. Warlus now being sent to 46 F.A. at HAUTAVESNES	MM77
do	25/8/18		Patients Admitted sick Off 1 O.R. 17 Wounded Off 3 O.R. 29 15 2 26 To 46 F.A. evacuated 1 2 Died 1 To 46 F.A. 4th Div. wounded 1 Off. 70 O.R.	MM77
do	26/8/18		Admitted sick O.R. 13 wounded O.R. 51 48 evacuated 2 Died 1 To 46 F.A. 13	MM77
do	27/8/18		Ceased to function as a South M.D.S. & are now as 2nd Div. M.D.A. Detachment from 11 from F.A. returned to their unit. Patients Admitted sick Off 1 O.R. 14 wounded O.R. 18 1 13 17 evacuated CRS 1 Died	MM77

Army Form C. 2118.

WAR DIARY
or
INTELLIGENCE SUMMARY.
(Erase heading not required.)

Place	Date	Hour	Summary of Events and Information	Remarks and references to Appendices
ECOLE NORMAL ARRAS	28/3/18		After a very heavy bombardment for several hours, the enemy attacked this morning. Wounded commenced arriving here about 8 A.M.. Shortly before this, a shell struck the operating room, & arrangements made to nurse the wounded in the basement. From 8 A.M. to 1.30 P.M. cars came in in very large numbers, but after 1.30 P.M. relatively few arrived. In addition to cases who passed through our A.D.S., about 170 others passed through this ambulance, whose particulars had been taken in other F.A's, i.e. of 45th F.A. & Ambulances of 4th Div? Cases admitted & passed through my A.D. both:- Admitted . wounded Off. 21. O.R. 894 sick O.R. 33. evacuated 19 873 19 33 To 46 F.A. 1 - - 1 To duty 1 19 - - Died - 2 - - sick include 26 N.Y.D. gas. Figures of cases evacuated up till 12 midnight:- To C.C.S. 541 A party of 1 N.C.O & 4 men proceeded to WARLUS to 46 F.A 34 open a post there for local casualties. Total 575	

Army Form C. 2118.

WAR DIARY
or
INTELLIGENCE SUMMARY.
(Erase heading not required.)

Place	Date	Hour	Summary of Events and Information	Remarks and references to Appendices
ECOLE NORMAL	29/3/18		Considerable shelling in this area in the early hours of the morning. One shell struck the stables, all mules being wounded, & several other shells fell in the yard, causing several M.T.C. cars & lorries damage. During the remainder of the day, little shelling occurred. The Bearer party which had been attached to 95 F.A. are returned, no casualties having been inflicted on them. 1 NCO & 2 men were sent to WARLOS to reinforce party sent yesterday. Lt. B.B. McBRIDE M.O.R.C. proceeded to 9th R.H. for temporary duty. Patients. Admitted. Wounded. Off. 4. O.R. 62. sick O.R. 9. evacuated 4 57 9 to 46 F.A. 3 to Duty 2 MOY	
do.	30/3/18.		Shelling was considerable at intervals during the day in this neighbourhood. One Ford car damaged. Casualties wounded O.R. 38 sick Off. 1, O.R. 34 Admitted 36 8 evacuated 26 to 46 F.A. to Duty 2. Lt. HOLROYD R.M.C. proceeded to take charge of post at WARLUS. MOY	

2353 Wt. W3114/1454 700,000 5/15 D.D.&L. A.D.S.S/Forms/C.2118.

Army Form C. 2118.

WAR DIARY
or
INTELLIGENCE SUMMARY.
(Erase heading not required.)

Instructions regarding War Diaries and Intelligence Summaries are contained in F. S. Regs., Part II. and the Staff Manual respectively. Title pages will be prepared in manuscript.

Place	Date	Hour	Summary of Events and Information	Remarks and references to Appendices
ECOLE NORMAL ARRAS	3/3/18		Intermittent shelling of surrounding area all day. One shell bursting just outside the reception room killed 2 men belonging to this ambulance. Casualties Admitted Off 2 O.R. 23. 7th O.R. 3 4/2 Wounded 2 19 Evacuated 1 3 2 Died	Wentworth Lt. Col. O.C. 47 F.A.

2353 Wt. W2514/1454 700,000 5/15 D. D. & L. A.D.S.S./Forms/C. 2118.

SECRET 27

Volume N° 34

Vol 33

War Diary of 47th Field Ambulance
for April 1918 by
Lieut Col HC MONTEITH DSO RAMC
Commdg 47th Field Ambulance

140/9908

47TH
FIELD AMBULANCE,
R.A.M.C.
No. ....
Date ....

COMMITTEE FOR THE
MEDICAL HISTORY OF THE WAR
Date — 6 JUN. 1918

WAR DIARY
or
INTELLIGENCE SUMMARY.
(Erase heading not required.)

Army Form C. 2118.

Place	Date	Hour	Summary of Events and Information	Remarks and references to Appendices

WARLUS 51c K36d	1/4/18.		Headquarters & 73 O.R. moved from ECOLE NORMAL to WARLUS, being relieved at the ECOLE by O.C. 45th F.A. Three Officers, 1 warrant officer and 90 O.R. remain at ECOLE, attached to O.C. 45 F.A. Casualties :- Admitted wounded Off 3. O.R. 11. sick Off 2. O.R. 29
			                                         3 8 2 3
			                                 To Duty 3 2 28
				MMcN Tuttt Lt. Col.

do.	2/4/18.		Returns Admitted wounded O.R. 1 sick O.R. 10.
			       To 46 F.A. 1 9
			       3 Can F.A. 1
				MMcN

do.	3/4/18.		Admitted sick O.R. 11. To 46 F.A. " 11.	MMcN
do.	4/4/18.		Admitted sick Off 1 O.R. 9 To 46 F.A. 1 8 To 3 Can F.A. - 1 Rain in afternoon & night	MMcN
do.	5/4/18		Admitted sick O.R. 6 wounded O.R. 4 To 8 CCS 2 To 46 F.A. 4 To 3 Can CCS 1 To Duty 1 Remain 1	MMcN

Capt. J. S. GILCHRIST RAMC to & from on the strength of this unit. MMcN

Army Form C. 2118.

WAR DIARY
or
INTELLIGENCE SUMMARY.
(Erase heading not required.)

Place	Date	Hour	Summary of Events and Information	Remarks and references to Appendices
WARLUS.	6/4/18		Admitted sick O.R. 3. Evacuated to 46 F.A. MTZ	
AGNEZ LES DUISANS	7/4/18		Moved from WARLUS to old site of 19 C.C.S. near AGNEZ les DUISANS. Heavy rain in pm. Capt M.H. LITTLEWOOD RAMC returned from leave to U.K. Admitted sick Off 1 O.R. 5. evacuated to 46 F.A. Off 1. O.R. 4. To duty 1. MTZ	
S/c LICSS				
do.	8/4/18		Admitted sick O.R. 2. evacuated to 46 F.A. 1. Remaining 1. MTZ	
			Accommodation ready for 50 slightly sick cases	
do.	9/4/18		Admitted 150.R. To 46 9 O.R. To CCS 1 Remaining 6 MTZ	
do.	10/4/18		Admitted sick Off 5 O.R. 55 To 46 F.A. Off 5 O.R. 39 Remaining O.R. 22 MTZ	
			Admissions include 15 NYD Gas	
do.	11/4/18		Admitted wounded Off 2 O.R. 1 sick Off 1 O.R. 52	
			evacuated CCS 2 9	
			To 46 F.A. 1 27	
			Remaining 1 38 MTZ	
do.	12/4/18		1st Day MORE & MOR9 seconded to take charge of adv. site at Fosseux le complete	
			Admitted sick O.R. 39 wounded O.R. 1	
			To 46 FA 27	
			To CCS 4	
			To duty 2	
			Remaining 44 1 MTZ	

Army Form C. 2118.

WAR DIARY
or
INTELLIGENCE SUMMARY.
(Erase heading not required.)

Instructions regarding War Diaries and Intelligence Summaries are contained in F. S. Regs., Part II. and the Staff Manual respectively. Title pages will be prepared in manuscript.

Place	Date	Hour	Summary of Events and Information	Remarks and references to Appendices
Agnes in Division	13/4/18		Visit from DDMS XVII Corps	
do.	14/4/18		Admitted sick Off. 2 O.R. 48 wounded O.R. 1	
			Evacuated 2 2	
			To 46 FA 46	
			Remain 44	
do.	15/4/18		Admitted sick Off 2 O.R. 43 wounded O.R. 2	
			To 46 FA 35	
			To CCS 2 7	
			Duty 1	
			Remain 44 2	
do.	15/4/18.		Admitted sick Off 5 O.R. 52 wounded Off. 1 O.R. 3	
			To 46FA 4 29 1	
			CCS 1 22 2	
			Remain 39 1	
do.	16/4/18.		Admitted sick Off 5 OR 41 wounded O.R. 6	
			To 46FA 1 28	
			Evacuated 2 7	
			To Duty 6	
			Remain 39 1	

WAR DIARY
or
INTELLIGENCE SUMMARY

Army Form C. 2118.

Place	Date	Hour	Summary of Events and Information	Remarks and references to Appendices
Agny-les-Duisans	17/4/18		Lt. D. HOLROYDE RAMC proceeded for duty to 11 A. & S. H.Ls.	
			Admitted sick Offs. 1 O.R. 70. Wounded O.R. 2	
			To 46 F.A. 47	
			CCS 13	
			To Duty 1	
			Remaining 48	
do.	18/4/18		Admitted sick O.R. 39 W. O.R. 9	
			To 46 F.A. 17	
			CCS 18	
			To Duty 1	
			Remaining 46	1 MT72
do.	19/4/18		Admitted sick Offs 4 O.R. 57 W. 3 O.R. 3	
			To 46 F.A. 2 29	
			To CCS 2 16	
			To Duty 3	
			Remaining 49	1 OT2 ATO
do.	20/4/18		Opened Divl Main Dressing Station, via M.D.S. at ECOLE NORMAL ARRAS.	
			Party at ECOLE NORMAL rejoin unit.	
			Capt. "SEL CHRIST RAMC proceeded to 9 G.R.H. for duty.	

WAR DIARY
or
INTELLIGENCE SUMMARY.
(Erase heading not required.)

Army Form C. 2118.

Place	Date	Hour	Summary of Events and Information	Remarks and references to Appendices
L. of C. S.S. Boat 57.C	20/4/18		Instructions received to increase accommodation for slightly sick cases from 50 to 100 beds.	
			Admitted sick Offr 2, O.R. 42 W. Offr 1, O.R. 18	
			To 42 CCS 20	
			46 F.A. 1 23 14	
			To Duty 4 3	
			Remaining 44	
do	21/4/18		Admitted sick offr 3, O.R. 88 W. Offr 1, O.R. 42	
			To 7 CCS 1 24 27	
			To 46 F.A. 2 26 15	
			To duty 6	
			Remain 76	
			Wounded include 15 gas, mustard	
do	22/4/18		Admitted sick Offr. Nil O.R. 44 W. Offr 3 O.R. 31	
			To CCS 8 3 27	
			To 46 F A 9 4	
			To duty 4	
			Remain 99	

Army Form C. 2118.

WAR DIARY
or
INTELLIGENCE SUMMARY.
(Erase heading not required.)

Instructions regarding War Diaries and Intelligence Summaries are contained in F.S. Regs., Part II. and the Staff Manual respectively. Title pages will be prepared in manuscript.

Place	Date	Hour	Summary of Events and Information	Remarks and references to Appendices
AUCHEL	23/4/18.		Entrained from AGNEZ LES DUISANS to AUCHEL, arriving AUCHEL 5.30 P.M.	
	24/4/18.		Relieved at Agnes by 2/2 London F.A. 56 Div'n, 2 patients remaining in Hosp. handed over to them.	
			Patients admitted Sick Off 1. O.R. 17 wounded O.R. 3.	
			To 46 F.A. 9	
			To C.C.S. 26 1 3	
			To duty 7	
			Transferred to 2/2 London 75	MO
AUCHEL	25/4/18.		Admitted & evacuated to CCS 10 O.R.	MO
do.	25/4/18.		" " " " 1 Off. & 60 O.R.	MO
do.	26/4/18.		" " " 1 " & 16 O.R.	MO
do.	27/4/18.		Admitted O.R. 18. Evacuated to C.C.S 4. To 60th R.S. 4. To 60th Queries R.A.	MO
			To 12 SECT R. 1. Memph	MO
do.	28/4/18.		Admitted O.R. 10. To CCS. 1. To 60th received A.I.	MO
do.	29/4/18.		Order cancelling an order to Proceed to XVII Corps was received at 11.30 A.M. The Horse Transport, which had already started - washed.	
			Patients Admitted & evacuated to CCS. O.R. 10. nil.	MO
do.	30/4/18.		Inspected by Inj. Gen. Reed vc. G.O.C. 1st Div'n ?	
			Admitted O.R. evacuated 8 Remarks by J Moffatt	MO

Lt.Col. O.C. 47. F.A.

SECRET. No 35
140/2983 Volume
WO 34

War Diary for May 1918 of
47 Field Ambulance
by
Lt Colonel H.C. MONTEITH D.S.O. R.A.M.C.
Commdg. 47 Fd Amb

COMMITTEE FOR THE
MEDICAL HISTORY OF THE WA[R]
Date 9 JUL 1918

47TH
FIELD AMBULANCE,
R.A.M.C.

WAR DIARY
or
INTELLIGENCE SUMMARY.

Army Form C. 2118.

Place	Date	Hour	Summary of Events and Information	Remarks and references to Appendices
AUCHEL	1/5/18		Route march and company training	
			Patients admitted O.R. 12 evacuated 9. To/ both sections P.2. Remaining 5	M.9.7/18
do.	2/5/18		Route march & company training	
			Patients Remitted 12, 21 eyto O.C.S. 1 ST & ISOA. TO S.A.S. 4 O.A.	M.9.7
Hosp. at From	3/5/18		Moved from AUCHEL to CALONNE-RICOUART, & entrained from there 6 ACR to ARRAS arriving there 7 P.M. Transport	M.9.7
ARRAS			proceeded by road to BOUVES.	
			Patients admitted sick 17, wounded 1 O.R. evacuated to C.C.S.	M.9.7
do	4/5/18		All R.M.O. posts of R. Brigade, South of the Scarp, taken over from 2nd Canadian F.A. Arranged with O.C. No 3 Canadian F.A. for relief of all posts N. of Scarpe from tomorrow.	
			Patients admitted & evacuated 6 O.R.s. 19 O.R.	M.9.7
do.	5/5/18		Relief of all posts N. of Scarpe completed. Maj. Buchanan & 15 O.Rs with M.O.R. 57/18	
			22 O.R. proceed to A.D.S. L'ABEYETTE, H/14 b.7.1.	
			Capt. Herbert M.O.N.G. & 11 O.R. proceed to A.D.S. Point du Jour. H.9 b.0.9.	
			Patients admitted & evacuated to C.C.S. S.O.R.	M.9.7

WAR DIARY
or
INTELLIGENCE SUMMARY.
(Erase heading not required.)

Army Form C. 2118.

Instructions regarding War Diaries and Intelligence Summaries are contained in F. S. Regs., Part II. and the Staff Manual respectively. Title pages will be prepared in manuscript.

Place	Date	Hour	Summary of Events and Information	Remarks and references to Appendices
Hay St Jean	6/5/18		Visited all posts S. of Scarpe, & A.D.S. L'ABEYETTE. Mt 14/c 52.	51 B
ARRAS			Transport lines moved from GODVES to Agny in Divisional	N.W.
do.	7/5/18		CAPT. W. McCONNELL M.C. R.A.M.C. Td. is taken on the strength of this unit. Inspected RAP L. Bnig H4c unfuel, ADS Point du Jour H3C 8.2, 3 relay post at Lamont at H13a O 3. Visited H6 & 13th R. Scots & 9th R.H.	MTT
			Inspected transport lines & O.M. Stores at Agny in Divisional reserve. Casualties Amoval through A.D.S. 10 wounded.	1055
do	8/5/18		Inspected RAP L.Bn. L. Bing, & ADS Point du Jours & new RAP at Railway Bridge. H19 b S.6. Front quiet.	MT
			2nd A.M. VICKERS MMG Aprovered to AMS office for temporary duty. BT1.	MT
			Casualties 9 O.R. wounded.	
do	9/5/18		Reastin Post at CHANTECLER G6d.0.2. Taken over by 57th Div.	
			Inspected all posts N. of Scarpe, & consulted with R.E. on building a new RAP at Railway Bridge H.19 b S.6.	
			Casualties 7 O.R. wounded.	MT
do.	10/5/18		Casualties 3 O.R.	
			Visited ADS & inspected Hore Lines. Situation in line reversed.	MT

WAR DIARY
or
INTELLIGENCE SUMMARY.

Army Form C. 2118.

(Erase heading not required.)

Instructions regarding War Diaries and Intelligence Summaries are contained in F. S. Regs., Part II. and the Staff Manual respectively. Title pages will be prepared in manuscript.

Place	Date	Hour	Summary of Events and Information	Remarks and references to Appendices
Hd. Qrs. ARRAS	11/5/18		Visited ADS L'ABBEYETTE & portion of Lines to Front. Quiet. Weather fine. 8.	HTT
do	12/5/18		Visited both ADS? RAP, L B?, L Bn. & RAP, R B? R Bn. Weather rainy & no little artillery activity. Casualties 16. Inspected Horse-lines. Areas consistently shelled between 7.30 P.M. & 10 P.M.	HTT
do	13/5/18.		Casualties 10. Quiet day.	HTT
do	14/5/18.		Inspection by Brig. Gen. H.N. THOMPSON CB. CMG DSO. DDS 1st Army. Casualties 2. O.R.	HTT
do	15/5/18		Inspected both ADS? & all RAP? N. of Scarpe. Consulted with O.C. R. Bn. L.Bn. as to best situation for a new R.A.P. Back arrangements with MO % & for L.Bn. for evacuation of any wounded in raid. Fixed for 3.45 to-morrow morning. Blangy heavily shelled. Casualties Off. 2. O.R. 24. Maj. VICKERS RAMC returned from temporary duty at ADMS Office.	HTT

WAR DIARY
or
INTELLIGENCE SUMMARY.

Army Form C. 2118.

Place	Date	Hour	Summary of Events and Information	Remarks and references to Appendices
Hosp. St Jean	16/5/18		A raid was carried out by about 70 men of R. Scots this morning at 3.45 A.M. in L. Sector L. Brigade. Casualties which occurred during the raid :- 1 officer missing 3 men killed 6 wounded. In retaliation 6 O.R. killed & 8 wounded in retaliation. The raid was considered successful, a number of the enemy being killed, i.e. 3 being taken prisoner. The railway A at M.19.b was bombarded with gas shells for about an hour. Casualties from through A.D.S. 34 O.R. including 2 mustard gas cases & 3 N.Y.D gas.	
do.	17.5.18.		Nothing of importance occurred. Casualties 13 O.R. wounded.	
do.	18.5.18.		Visited all posts N. of Yperlee with A/ADMS.	
			Arranged with CRE to commence working on new R.A.P. in Farm Vache. Casualties 18.	
do.	19.5.18.		Quiet day. Hosp. St Jean twice hit by shells. Weatherspoon. Casualties 8.	
do.	20.5.18		Visited RAP R.Bn R.Brig. & Albatros in RAPs proceeded to top Tank. Casualties 5. Weather hot.	

Army Form C. 2118.

WAR DIARY
or
INTELLIGENCE SUMMARY.
(Erase heading not required.)

Instructions regarding War Diaries and Intelligence Summaries are contained in F. S. Regs., Part II. and the Staff Manual respectively. Title pages will be prepared in manuscript.

Place	Date	Hour	Summary of Events and Information	Remarks and references to Appendices
Foot of gun	21/5/18		Quiet day. Casualties 6. Weather hot.	
ARRAS	do.	22.5.18	Enemy R.A.P. in Gun Valley H.15.b.3.6. is now under construction. Visited all posts & R.A.P.'s N. of Scarpe. Weather hot. Inspection of 2 O.R.Ks.	W.D.
do.	23.5.18		With A/ADMS visited M.O. 44th & 46th Bns. Inspected R.A.P. S. of Scarpe & ARRAS & BLANGY. Quarters hot. Weather cool.	W.D.
do.	24.5.18		Inspected work being done on R.A.P. Gun Valley. Very wet morning. Casualties 8.	W.D.
do.	25.5.18		Casualties 5. Nothing of importance occurred. Weather fine	W.D.
do.	26.5.18		Front area heavily shelled during the day, especially PUDDING Trench, H.15.b. After dark the FAUBOURG - S? LAURENT Road, & BLANGY area also heavily shelled. Bombardment with gas at E. end of L'ABBEYETTE. Casualties 22.	W.D.
do.	27.5.18.		Front area heavily shelled with yellow cross gas about 1 A.M. Area chiefly affected was that of left Br⁹, left Brig?, the road E. of S? Laurent. H.13.b was also heavily shelled & area E. of L'Abbeyette. Total casualties = 2 officers & 25 O.R. gassed. 1 off. & 59 O.R. non gas casualties.	W.D.

Army Form C. 2118.

WAR DIARY
or
INTELLIGENCE SUMMARY.
(Erase heading not required.)

Place	Date	Hour	Summary of Events and Information	Remarks and references to Appendices
Hop. à Jean	28/3/18		Uneventful. Artillery activity general. Casualties passing through control of 1 Officer & 17 O.R. Of these 1 Off. & 14 O.R. were gassed - yellow gas. The latter are all gunners. Most casualties seen thickened though sitting on ground which had been gassed the night before.	
ARRAS				
do.	29/3/18.		Visited both A.D.S?. Day quiet. Casualties 14 OR's	
do.	30/3/18.		Casualties 12. Situation normal. Enemy artillery active in front of our area. Area shelled intermittently with HV gun. Visited R.A.P. R.lm. L.Brig. & all along fronts.	
do.	31/3/18.		During the night 31/1ᵃᵐ - 1³⁰, a raid was attempted on R. subsection, L.Brig. in H.H.B.L.d. by 2 Off. & 30 O.R. of 4/5 R.H. Casualties - Evacuated - 1 Off. & 10 O.R. all slight. 1 Off. & 2 O.R. returned to duty. The raid appears to have been a failure, the enemy's trenches not having been reached.	

W.M. Smith
Lt. R.A.C.
O.C. 47 F.A.

SECRET
June 1918

Volume 36
J/1 35

War Diary of 4th Field Ambulance for
June 1918. to June — Chief
Monteith DSO RAMC
Lt Col.

COMMITTEE FOR
MEDICAL HISTORY
Date

16/2/31

Army Form C. 2118.

WAR DIARY
or
INTELLIGENCE SUMMARY.

(Erase heading not required.)

Instructions regarding War Diaries and Intelligence Summaries are contained in F.S. Regs., Part II. and the Staff Manual respectively. Title pages will be prepared in manuscript.

Place	Date	Hour	Summary of Events and Information	Remarks and references to Appendices
Map Sheet 51B Arras	1/6/18		Arras shelled with gas during the night of 1st-2nd. The day has been quiet.	Map sheet 51B
			Casualties 1 Off. & 19 O.R.	MMY
do.	2/6/18		Inspected work done on new R.A.P. 63 in valley H15 C 4.9, a partial ceiling observed. Little artillery activity. Casualties 13, including 2 officers X gas MMY	
do.	3/6/18		Day quiet. Casualties 8, of which 3 yellow cross cases. MMY	
do.	4/6/18		Blaney heavily shelled in the evening. Inspected work on R.A.P. Gown Valley. Owing to a heavy fall, the work has to much interfered with. So casualties 10, including 1 yellow cross MMY	
do.	5/6/18		50 O.R. from 45 & 41 FA reported for temporary duty for the purpose of constructing a new R.A.P. at H13 b 45.6. Casualties 6. Day quiet. MMY	
do.	6/6/18		St Laurent, Blangy heavily shelled during the morning. Visited all posts. No casualties. Casualties Nil. MMY	
			Lt R.L. Leighton M.O.R.C. proceeded for temporary duty to 6 10th Suppl ETO depot MMY	
do.	7/6/18		Blangy heavily shelled in the morning. Inspected work on new R.A.P. Casualties 2 MMY	

WAR DIARY or INTELLIGENCE SUMMARY

Army Form C. 2118.

Place	Date	Hour	Summary of Events and Information	Remarks and references to Appendices
Hospital Farm Huts	8/6/18		Day quiet. Casualties 5.	Sheet 5/3
do	9/6/18	at 2 AM	Arrival wire carried out by 6th Camerons this in R. relies. R. Brig.n on enemy lines at 4.22 a.m. C.T.I. Party consisted of 2 officers & 20 O.R. Casualties 1 killed & 6 wounded all the result of shell fire. At 2.30 A.M. the enemy attempted a raid on 8th Seaforth H.rs in Right Sector of Left Brig.n 26 O.R. Seaforth H.rs wounded. 2 O.R. 47th F.A. killed & 2 R.A.M.C. wounded. Total casualties 43 M.S.M.	M.S.M.
do	10/6/18		Day quiet. Hospital work on over R.A.P.s Casualties 5 including 1 yellow cross.	M.S.M.
do	11/6/18		Visited 63 A.D.M.S 15th Div.n. The day has been quiet. Casualties 6. Capt. Walker R.A.M.C. reported for duty. Visited A.D.S. Situation normal. Casualties 10.	M.S.M. M.S.M.
do	12/6/18		Casualties 4. Nothing of importance occurred.	M.S.M.
do	13/6/18		D.D.M.S. XVII Corps & A.D.M.S 15th Div.n inspected A.D.S. & the R.A.P.s which are in process of construction. Casualties 3.	M.S.M.

Army Form C. 2118.

WAR DIARY
or
INTELLIGENCE SUMMARY.
(Erase heading not required.)

Instructions regarding War Diaries and Intelligence Summaries are contained in F. S. Regs., Part II. and the Staff Manual respectively. Title pages will be prepared in manuscript.

Place	Date	Hour	Summary of Events and Information	Remarks and references to Appendices
Pozt. St Jean APRES	15/6/18		Visited RAP R.B.G R.brig.s & support Bn R. Brig.s Day quiet. During the night ST LAURENT was heavily shelled. My Relay Post was twice struck & a Sunbeam car damaged. 4 gunners casualties resulted from this shelling. Total wounded 7. M17	
Hosp. Styre	16/6/18.		Two raids were carried out simultaneously during the night. Raid 'A' by 1 off. & 36 O.R. of 9/16 Royal Scots operated on enemy's line in H.5.d. 1 & slight casualty was sustained. Three prisoners taken. Raid 'B' by 1 off. & 30 O.R. Seaforth Mn. attacked at H.11.d & H.17.b. 5 men slightly wounded. No prisoners taken. Early in the morning 9/16 Rl St Laurent Relay Post H.13.a.O.2. heavily shelled. Building hit twice & car injured. M13 1 E Day M.O.R.C. evacuated sick. P.U.O.	
do.	17/6/18.		Visited ADS L'Abbeyette & Support Bn. Nothing of importance to record. Casualties 1/2. 7 A.M.T.B evacuated sick with P.U.O. from Sam Valley rents. M17	
do.	18/6/18.		Inspected work on new R.A.P. Day uneventful. M17	

WAR DIARY
or
INTELLIGENCE SUMMARY.

(Erase heading not required.)

Army Form C. 2118.

Instructions regarding War Diaries and Intelligence Summaries are contained in F. S. Regs., Part II. and the Staff Manual respectively. Title pages will be prepared in manuscript.

Place	Date	Hour	Summary of Events and Information	Remarks and references to Appendices
Hesp. Eajea	19/6/18		Visited A.D.S. Pont du Jour & HQ 13th A Regt. Heavy rain in morning. Casualties 2	
do.	19/6/18		Visited A.D.S. P du Jour & made arrangements as said. Casualties to Scots raw RTD	
do.	21/6/18		Trial run carried out by 1st R. Scots in left sector at Hill 8, Hill 2 & H.60 at 3. A.M. Two officers & 22 O.R. were wounded through A.D.S. P. du Jour. The raid was very successful, many of the enemy being killed, & 10 prisoners	
			taken. Our wounded were evacuated through A.D.S. Capt. WALKER RAMC is attached to the 23rd of having proceeded to 39 Div.	
do.	22/6/18		The new RAP in tram volley at Hill of 31 is now in operation.	
			Lt LEIGHTON M.O.R.C. returned from temp. duty with C. Rifles. Evacuation 3 NYD	
do	23/6/18		1 Or R.A.m.C wounded in a telling fire. Total Casualties = 11 Evacuation —	
	24/6/18		Visits to dt. L'ABROUYETTE and dressing posts arranged by 10 H. F. R.W.F with M.O. accompanied by autograph fire. Total nr. D. Casualties — 1.	
"	"		Major Williams M.O.R.C. U.S.A. on a temp. peirschester	BI
"	"		Special arrangements made for new trip Ptes W.K. & T.R. at ad 28 a 55 dram H 28 a 55 50	Bri
"	"		Reconnaissance dressed 6 pm new trip the Pte R. Camilla raid now many R. F. wounded.	
"	"		Capt. Bull FRWC proceed from U.S. F.M. for 4 years duty.	BI
	25/6/18		Nothing to report. Casualties 9	BI

WAR DIARY
or
INTELLIGENCE SUMMARY.

Army Form C. 2118.

Place	Date	Hour	Summary of Events and Information	Remarks and references to Appendices
Wancourt Jenc.	26/6/18		Evacuated Jeancourt through ADS's 29.O.A., including 26 yellow cross gas	
Boiry			Most of P.M. the VICTORY Camp. 6.30.9.3. which was occupied by 71 & 50 SB in Bty'n Reserve were heavily shelled. About 30 men were concussed several killed. MW	
do	27.6.18.		Casualties 12, including 10 minor yellow cross gas. MW	
do	28.6.18		Work on dug-out in 6.18 central canned today. This is being prepared for an ADS in the event of a withdrawal to the TILLOY system. Casualties 10, all yellow cross gas.	
do	29.6.18.		Attended meet g of O.C. F.A. at ADMS's Office. Casualties 5, including 1 mustard gas. MW	
do	30.6.18.		Casualties 6, including 4 yellow cross gas. MW	
			Capt M.W. LITLEWOOD RAMC proceeded to 2/20th "Bn" genty.	

J.J. Mortimer
Lt. Col.
O.C. 47 F.A.

POCKET 6

July 1918.

War Diary of 47 Field Ambulance
for July 1918 by Lieut Colonel
H.G. MONTEITH DSO RAMC
Comm.dg 47 F.Ambce

Major
J. M. Mackenzie

Volume 39.
Vol 36
140/3200.

COMMITTEE FOR THE
MEDICAL HISTORY OF THE WAR
Date 5 OCT. 1918

WAR DIARY
or
INTELLIGENCE SUMMARY.
(Erase heading not required.)

Army Form C. 2118.

Place	Date	Hour	Summary of Events and Information	Remarks and references to Appendices
Hop. S. Jean	1/7/18		Visited O.C. 46 F.A. round ADS: & posts N. of Scarpe. MM3	
ARRAS	2/7/18		Casualties 2. The day been quiet. MM3	
do.	3/7/18		With O.C. 46.F.A. visited R.A.P. R.Bn. R. Brig & support battalions. MM3	
do.	3/7/18		Casualties 3, including 1 gassed (self.) MM3	
do.	4/7/18		Casualties 5, including 2 gassed yellow cross. MM3	
S. CATHERINE	5/7/18		Casualties 3. Visited ADS: Day enemy shld. Moved to S. CATHERINE & took over M.D.S. from O.C. 46"F.A. ADS: & all forward posts relieved by O.C. 46 F.A. Casualties passing through M.D.S.{wounded 187. 12 O.R.	
			admitted sick 39	
			evacuated to 45.F.A. 29 sick & 3 wounded	
			" " C.C.S. 10 " 9 "	
			To details " " 1 officer. MM3	
do.	6/7/18		Adm. H.B. wounded 48.2 O.R. 4. sick O.R. 81	
			evac to C.C.S. 2 57	
			45. F.B. 3)	
			died of wounds 1	
			66 P.D.O. (1 officer) included in the sick. MM3	

WAR DIARY or INTELLIGENCE SUMMARY

(Erase heading not required.)

Army Form C. 2118.

Place	Date	Hour	Summary of Events and Information	Remarks and references to Appendices
ST.CATHERINE G.15.A.2.3.	7/8		Casualties – 2 Off. & 7 OR. evac. & 4 OR.s wounded passed through the M.D.S., 2 neck officers 41 cuts OR.s + 2 wounded OR.s were evacuated to CCS.; 13 cuts & 1 w. OR. were transferred to 45-F.A. 1 W. OR. died & was buried.	A.R.Vickery
do	8/8		Admitted Wounded OR. 9 Sick. 3 76	SR. 46. W. ? 45FA.S.f. 30 W. 8 H.P.Vickery
			Capt. W.P.HERBERT. R.O.R.C. M.f.a. rejoined A.E.F. & took 1/c of the duty the poor to keep rota Lieut. I.G.SHIRREY R.O.R.C. M.f.a. reported of duty & to take on the duty to.	H.P.Vickery
do	9th		Admitted Off. OR. Evacuated: (a) to CCS. Off. 2 OR. 3 Remainder duty W. - 2 W. - 1 1 OR. S. 2 53. (b) to 45FA.S. - 49. Bar. 15/7 of y. W. 1 OR.	A.P.Vickery

Army Form C. 2118.

WAR DIARY
or
INTELLIGENCE SUMMARY.
(Erase heading not required.)

Instructions regarding War Diaries and Intelligence Summaries are contained in F. S. Regs., Part II, and the Staff Manual respectively. Title pages will be prepared in manuscript.

Place	Date	Hour	Summary of Events and Information	Remarks and references to Appendices
S. Ecurie	10/7/18		Patients admitted O.R. 7 sick O.R. 33.	
			evacuated WB. 4 6 4	
			G 45 F.A. 1 29	M.M. Smith
	11.73		Patients admitted. H. O.R. Remainder H. R.	
			S. 1 30. (5) 45 R.A.S.I. S.q.	
			W. - - W. - -	
			(B) C.C.P. S. - 1	
O.C. Reno			The Ambulance was relieved by the first Canadian Field Amb., the	
Agnez			motor lorry does at midnight 11/7/18 - on relief the Amb. moved to Haut	
L.I.C.55			Avesnes at old Cel. and Agnez (L.I.C.6.6.). H.Q. Victor mgr	
GOUY-SERVINS 2ᵀᴴ			Field Amb. marched from site at Agnez at under orders of 4ᵀᴴ Div.	
			Bgte. at 9.25 p.m. and arrived at GOUY-SERVINS @ 35 2/7ᵀᴴ Bn Reg at 1 am 13ᵀᴴ	
do	13ᵀᴴ		Lieut Col. H.R. Portatch D.S.O. proceeded on leave to U.K. a.m. Major	
			H.P. Victor Pearce assumed Command of the Ambulance	
			All units on the Bgte. (45ᵀᴴ) visited. M.O.'s got in touch with	
			A.D.M.S. visited & inspected new site.	

WAR DIARY
or
INTELLIGENCE SUMMARY.
(Erase heading not required.)

Army Form C. 2118.

Place	Date	Hour	Summary of Events and Information	Remarks and references to Appendices
GOUY-SERVINS	14/7/18		Heavy rain.	
do	15/7/18		Lieut N. DAY & Lieut R.L. LEIGHTON, A.R.C. M.A. returned to the unit — Lieut C. BUCHANAN & 2 O.R. went forward with the 43rd Inf. Brigade as Billeting party to a new area. Heavy rain & thunderstorm.	A.R. McR[?]
Gouy-Servins	16/7/18		Full Amb. with transport marched from Gouy-Servins at 7.30 p.m. to Bivouac for the noon. Packed for night & road 2 miles outside AUBIGNY. (E.7.A.06 & 51°)	A.R. McR[?]
AUBIGNY	17/7/18		Bull. Amb. with M.T. transport bivouaced at AUBIGNY Station until 45th Inf. Bgde. at 11.30 a.m. & arrived at LIANCOURT (BEAUVAIS district) at 6.20 a.m. on 18th. M.T. transport arrived at BRYAS. Very heavy thunderstorm to rain at 7.30 p.m.	A.R. McR[?]
LIANCOURT	18/7/18		Billets in Petit Chateau Liancourt — M.T. transport & ground cars at Sant B. Omis. Rained at about 11.30 a.m. to 12 in noon.	
BRYAS (MT Lives)				

Army Form C. 2118.

WAR DIARY
or
INTELLIGENCE SUMMARY.

(Erase heading not required.)

Instructions regarding War Diaries and Intelligence Summaries are contained in F.S. Regs. Part II. and the Staff Manual respectively. Title pages will be prepared in manuscript.

Place	Date	Hour	Summary of Events and Information	Remarks and references to Appendices
LIANCOURT.	19/7/18		2.O. transferred to 46th Inf. Bgde. – Reveille at 3.45 a.m.	
			Started at 5.30 a.m. for TOURTREUCOURT – Re-embussing point of the Brigade. Entrained on French lorries and arrived HAUTE-FONTAINE (SOISSONS 140 S/E) at 6.45 p.m.	
			M.T. transport unable to get up until 10 a.m.	
		6.30 pm	Horse transport under Lieut. Lo Fey & 2/C Ulla moved to MORU (BEAUVAIS Nature).	H.O. Munayey
HAUTE-FONTAINE.	20/7/18		Field Ambs. on bivouacs in Haute-fontaine wood. Run as usual.	
(by cart) (Bivouacs Nature)				HNU
do	21/7		Marched at 11.40 p.m. with 46th Bde. Blown up an hour & a kilometer from "Z" in MONTGOBERT. Point.	
			Bivouaced in wood arriving at 4.30. a.m. 22/7/18 (Poisant map)	HNU
BIVOUACS	22/7/18		Lines were tree – rests most of day – with a view of being called to move at any time – Lieut. King & R.C. Ulla &	
to the town of Ponte.			one Motor Cyclist attached to 46th R.A.Q Temporary duty.	HNU
MONTGOBERT. (Poisant map)				

WAR DIARY or INTELLIGENCE SUMMARY

Army Form C. 2118

Place	Date	Hour	Summary of Events and Information	Remarks and references to Appendices
BIVOUAC, ½ a Kilo. from Route of "L" in MONTGOBERT	23/8		Lieut G.W. DAY, R.A.M.C. U.F.A. 9 20 OR's proceeded to No. 12 Field Hospital. American D.S. for temporary duty. Lieut I.G. SHIRKEY, R.A.M.C. U.F.A. 9 20 OR's proceeded to No. 3 Field Hospital American D.S. for temporary duty. Eighty four horses now attached for temp. duty to 46th F.A. F.A. motor cars & drivers 7 orderlies attached for temp. duty to 46 F.A. Two clerks attached for temp. duty to 46 F.A. Lieut R.L. LEIGHTON, R.A.M.C. U.S.A. proceed for temp. duty to 6th Cavalry HD on A.O.1/C.	JMcL
do	24/8		Lieut I.G. SHIRKEY, R.A.M.C. U.S.A. 9 20 OR's attached for duty to No. 3 American Field Hosp. returned reported their return.	JMcL
do	25/8		Lieut G.W. DAY, R.A.M.C. U.S.A. 9 10 OR's returned from temp. duty at No. 12 American Field Hosp. Lieut R.L. Leighton reported for permanent med. chg. of 6 Cannon Sqn. 9 is chrck of the duty it. Lieut G.C. BOY, R.R.C. permanent med. charge of 10th Cavalry Rifles & is chrck of the duty it.	JMcL

1875 Wt. W593/826 1,000,000 4/15 J.B.C. & A. A.D.S.S./Forms/C.2118.

WAR DIARY or INTELLIGENCE SUMMARY

Army Form C. 2118

Place	Date	Hour	Summary of Events and Information	Remarks and references to Appendices
BIVOUAC ½ a kilo South of the "S" of MONTGOBERT. (Forest of Retz)	26/7/18		25 BPs proceeded for temporary duty to No 63 C.C.S.; 10 BPs returned for temporary duty at No. 1A American Field Hospital. Lieut S. M. KING, A.R.C. M.F.A. having been posted to permanent medical charge of 6th Cameron (who is struck off strength). Heavy rain in afternoon & evening. JMW	
do.	27/7/18		Heavy rain. JMW	
do.	28/7/18		Capt & Qr. Master Rhind returned from leave to O.K. JMW	
do.	29/7/18		Major Buchanan & 23 BPs with medical equipment proceeded to walking wounded retaining post of FA duty under 33 Division to HAUTE ST REMY near VILLERS-COTTERETS. (Command Area). Fine day. JMW	
do.	30/7/18		Lt. D.A.D.M.S. Lieut Colonel C.A. Burichall, visited & inspected the Ambulance. Fine day. JMW	
do.	31/7/18		Lieut J.B. BALDWIN, A.O.R.C. M.F.A. & Lieut B.F. WRAY, A.D.C. M.F.A. reported their arrival (in evening of 30th) for duty & are taken on the strength. JMW J.A. McKee, Lt Col, O.C. 1st F. Amb C.E.F.

7
Aug. 1918.

CONFIDENTIAL.

War Diary

of

Lt Colonel A.G. Monteith DSO. RAMC.

O.C. 47th Field Ambulance

August 1st to 31st 1918.

98 37
14/39-9

Volume 38.

Army Form C. 2118

WAR DIARY
or
INTELLIGENCE SUMMARY
(Erase heading not required.)

Instructions regarding War Diaries and Intelligence Summaries are contained in F. S. Regs., Part II. and the Staff Manual respectively. Title Pages will be prepared in manuscript.

Place	Date	Hour	Summary of Events and Information	Remarks and references to Appendices
BIVOUAC between 1 kilometer East of MONTGOBERT. (Brasseur aus)	1/8/18		Fine day. No thing of note. AMY	
do	2/8/18		Heavy rain. AMY	
do	3/8/18		Major Buchanan & 23 O.R.'s returned from the berry wounded returning Part at Remy. AMY	
do	4/8/18		Fine. Aux. personnel marched from Bivouac in road to Embussing Point at Paris Part of Oncy on the Oncy Cuvres road. 46th M.J. Regt. Arms started Point 12 mid- day – Leave started at 3.15 P.m. – and SACY-LE-GRAND at 8.15 P.m. Major Buchanan with D.A.G. transport moved under B.T.O. H.O. Peterson Major	
SACY-LE-GRAND (Beauvais aus)	5/8/18		Lt Col. Hewlett returned from leave from U.K. AMY	
do	6/8/18		Nothing noteworthy happened. AMY	
do	7/8/18		Landed from Sacy at 2 AM to entrain at PONT St. MAXENCE detrained at 11 PM at PETIT HOUVIN travelled to HOUVIN. Lt. EALY D.B. MORI. & Lt. BECKNER E.J. 2.0.R.G. U.S.A. are this day taken on the strength of this unit. MY	

Army Form C. 2118

WAR DIARY
or
INTELLIGENCE SUMMARY
(Erase heading not required.)

Instructions regarding War Diaries and Intelligence Summaries are contained in F.S. Regs., Part II. and the Staff Manual respectively. Title Pages will be prepared in manuscript.

Place	Date	Hour	Summary of Events and Information	Remarks and references to Appendices
HOUVIN	8.8.18		Admitted & evacuated sick 12 O.R. Wounded (gas) 2 O.R.	MO
do.	9.8.18		do " " 8 O.R. " 1 "	MO
do.	10.8.18		" " 80 A " Nil.	MO
do.	11.8.18		" 12 O.R. & 3 Offrs	
			Lt. BALDWIN J.B. M.O.R.C. & 1 O.R. proceeded to 1st Army School of Instruction	
			Lt. EALY A.B. & Lt. BECKNER J.B. M.O.R.C. & 20 O.R. proceeded to 15 C.C.S. for temporary duty & instruction	
do.	12.8.18.		Admitted & evacuated sick O.R. 5.	MO
do.	13.8.18		" " " 8	
			Four cars sent to E.a. specialist en reconnaissance.	MO
do.	14.8.18.		Admitted 9, wounded sick O.R. 2. Running 7. officers/evacuated	MO
do.	15.8.18		" Off 1, O.R. 7 " Off 1, O.R. 7 " 7	
			Lt. EALY & Lt. BECKNER M.O.R.C. & 20 O.R. rejoined from 15 C.C.S	MO
do.	16.8.18.		Admitted 6 7 wounded. 7 O.R.	
			In accordance parity warning of Army Nether & 9 O.R. proceeded to K28 d.5.3. Mob. S.Tc. to take over Main Dressing Station from 4/1 London F.A. 51st Div?	MO
BRIQUETERIE WANQUETIN	17.8.18.		Marched at 6 AM to WANQUETIN. Took over M.D.S from 4/1 London F.A.	
			Admitted Off. 1 sick, 1 wounded. O.R. 25 sick 2 wounded. 18	
K28 d.53 57 C Imp.			From 6th. Rs. To Div Rest St. 6 O.R.	MO

Army Form C. 2118

WAR DIARY
or
INTELLIGENCE SUMMARY
(Erase heading not required.)

Instructions regarding War Diaries and Intelligence Summaries are contained in F. S. Regs., Part II. and the Staff Manual respectively. Title Pages will be prepared in manuscript.

Place	Date	Hour	Summary of Events and Information	Remarks and references to Appendices
WANQUETIN	18/8/18		Admitted sick off: 3 O.R. 24 wounded O.R. 11 (includes 3 2nd Lord gas)	
			To CCS " 2 " 13 " 9	
			To 46 F.A. " 1 " 9 " 2	
			To 12 Stat: A. - " 1 " -	
do.	19/8/18		Admitted sick off 2 O.R. 34 wounded O.R. 30 2 (S.I.W.)	
			To CCS " - " 2 " 16	
			To 46 F.A. " - " - " 18 " 30	
				MM
do.	20 8/18		Admitted sick O.R. 93 wounded 32 " -	
			To C.C.S. " 17 " 32	
			To 46 F.A. " 76 " -	
			Lt. WRAY MORL rejoined from hosp. medical charge 1/7th Royal Scots N.O.R	
do	21 8/18		Admitted sick off 1. O.R. 76. wounded O.R. 27	
			To CCS " - " 1 " 19 " 24	
			To 46 F.A. " - " 57 " 3	
			Lt. EALY, BECKNER & WRAY MORL proceeded to XVIII Corps Zone	
			drawing 35' with 2 tent sub- divisions	
ST. SAVEUR ARRAS	22/8/18		Took over A.D.S & Med. stores in Left Brig. area from 457 F.A. Marshall at 7 AM	
G-29.c.88			arriving at Sauveur 10 30 A.M.	MM

WAR DIARY
or
INTELLIGENCE SUMMARY.

(Erase heading not required.)

Army Form C. 2118.

Place	Date	Hour	Summary of Events and Information	Remarks and references to Appendices
Hop. St Jean ARRAS	23/8/18		Handed over ADS at ST SAUVEUR & personal kits to O.C. No. 9 San. F.A. Relief complete 5 P.M. Marched to H.Q. St Jean ARRAS. Sick & 2 wounded admitted & evacuated.	MOZ
GOUY-SERVINS	24/8/18		Marched with 41 I.B. to ANZIN at 5.30 AM. Entrained at ANZIN & detrained at CHATEAU de la HAYE. Marched to GOUY SERVINS. Billet from 46 F.A. 6 sick admitted & evacuated.	MOZ
K10 a. 58. 44 B	25/8/18		Marched at 7 AM arriving K10 a. 10 AM. Took over Div. M.D.S. from 46 F.A. Admission on transfer — sick 40 w. I.O.R. Direct admissions 35 To C.C.S. 25 To C.R.S. 6 To 12 S.F.A. 2 Remaining 42 Visit from Lot. Army Consulting physician 1st Army	K10 a. 58. 2nd 44 B MOZ
do.	26/8/18		Admitted sick O.R. 40 wounded O.R. 25 To C.C.S. 16 22 Died — 3 12 S.F.A. 8 Rem. 58 1	MOZ

2353 Wt. W2544/1454 700,000 5/15 D.D.&L. A.D.S.S./Forms/C. 2118.

WAR DIARY
or
INTELLIGENCE SUMMARY.
(Erase heading not required.)

Army Form C. 2118.

Place	Date	Hour	Summary of Events and Information	Remarks and references to Appendices
RUITZ KROQ 58	27/8/18		Admitted sick 36 wounded 10. Died wounded O.R. 1. To CRS (2/4th Lond) 14 — — Officers sick 1. to CCS. — CCS 23 — 9 Remainder sick 52. wounded 1. R Stat H 5 (5 hostages)	maps 44 B.
do	28/8/18		Admitted sick 50 " 12 Died wounded 1 To CRS — 15 — 11 to duty sick 8 CCS 28 Remainder — 42 To 12 SC H 11 (casualties) Officers sick 3. wounded 1. To 1/2 NH FA	
do	29/8/18		Visit from DDMS 1st Corps & trans team. 1st S.Army. Admitted sick 32. wounded 29. To CCS 12 29 To CRS 3 Remainder sick 50, To 12 SF H 8 Remainder include 15" and Tank gas cases MTD	
do	30/8/18		Admitted sick 42 wounded 7. Evac: 6.12 St.A.R. 5 deserters ?. To CCS 26 7 Remainder sick 52. CRS 2 (casualties) Officers adm. & evac. 2 sick To 1/2 NH FA 5 (casualties) wounded include 2 "gas inhaled.	
do	31/8/18		Admitted sick 36 wounded 8 To CCS 24 2 To 12 SCH 9 (inclu 8 dy inhaled) To CRS 9 1 Remainder 4.8. —	

H J Merritt
Lt Col. F.A.
O.C. 47 F.A.

SECRET 29
Vol 38
1.11.18
14/3259
War Diary of 47th Field Ambulance for
September 1918 by Lieut Colonel
A. G. MONTEITH D.S.O. Royal Canadian
47th Field Ambulance

COMMITTEE FOR THE
MEDICAL HISTORY OF THE WAR
Date 9 NOV 1918

WAR DIARY
or
INTELLIGENCE SUMMARY.
(Erase heading not required.)

Army Form C. 2118.

Place	Date	Hour	Summary of Events and Information	Remarks and references to Appendices
K.17.2. K20 a.5.3.	1/9/18.		Patients admitted sick 39 wounded 5 (includes 3 mustard gas.) " wounded 16888 " 16 - 5 " 7 (includes 5 ? dysentery.) Discharged to duty " 125E.A 8 Remaining 60	Maps 44 B.
do.	2/9/18.		Admitted sick 29 wounded 12 (1 gas) To CCS 19 7 To CRS 7 - To duty 3 (6 clinical dysentery) To 12 S.E.A.	W577-W188 LT.88E. Died 1 accidental Remaining 55
do.	3/9/18		Admitted sick 34 wounded 65 To CCS 24 65 To CRS 8 - To duty 9 To 12 S.E.A. 3 To station cutter 36 Remaining	Wounded include 57 gas (yellow cross) gas 45, 6 flammen, 10 M.G. Coy.
do.	4/9/18.		Admitted sick 23 wounded 19 (3 gas mustard) To CCS 14 19 To CRS 11 - To duty 5 To 12 S.E.A. 4 (3 dysentery)	Remained sick 35 Officers wounded 5 exam. & evacuated, includes 2 gas mustard
do.	5/9/18.		Admitted sick 36 wounded 11 To CCS 26 8 To 12 S.E.A. 5 (4 dysentery, 1 T.S.) To duty 1 Remaining 39 wounded 3.	

Army Form C. 2118.

WAR DIARY
or
INTELLIGENCE SUMMARY.
(Erase heading not required.)

Instructions regarding War Diaries and Intelligence Summaries are contained in F. S. Regs., Part II. and the Staff Manual respectively. Title pages will be prepared in manuscript.

Place	Date	Hour	Summary of Events and Information	Remarks and references to Appendices
From S.E.	5/9/18		Admitted sick 40 wounded 63 → 2 {yellow X gas officers 4 O.R. 55	
			To CCS 25 80 - 1 {phosgen. - 3	
			" 12 St. B 3 (casualty) - 1	
			, CRS 2 - - 1st (phosgen gas)	
			To duty 1 - 1	
			Died of wounds - 3 Officers adm. & evac. 4 sick/. 1 wounded 4 OR.	
			Remaining 48	
do.	7.9.18		Admitted sick 43 wounded 55 (includes 52 gas. mustard.)	RDA
			To CCS 21 55	
			To 12 St. B 8 (casualty) - 2	
			To CRS 1 - 1 Officers sick/. adm & evac?	
			To duty 8 -	
			Remaining 47	
do.	8.9.18		Admitted sick 57 wounded 25 includes 22 gas mustard).	HJFry
			To CCS 27 25	
			To 12 St. B 10 -	
			To stain unit 2 - 1 Officers sick 2 wounded/. adm. & evac?	
			To duty 9 - 1	
			Remaining 59	
do.	9.9.18		Admitted sick 62 wounded 18 (all gassed, mustard.)	HJFry
			To CCS 26 17	
			To 12 St. B 8 - (5 urgent cty)	
			To CRS 10 1	
			To duty 4	
			Remaining 55 1	

Army Form C. 2118.

WAR DIARY
or
INTELLIGENCE SUMMARY.
(Erase heading not required.)

Instructions regarding War Diaries and Intelligence Summaries are contained in F. S. Regs., Part II. and the Staff Manual respectively. Title pages will be prepared in manuscript.

Place	Date	Hour	Summary of Events and Information	Remarks and references to Appendices
K20 a 5.8	10/9/18		Admitted sick 43 wounded 4 (1 gas mustard)	
			To CCS 33	
			To 12 SD.R 2 (acquits)	
			To CRS 9	
			Remaining 54	
				1877
do	11/9/18		Admitted sick 40 wounded 3	
			To CCS 23 3	
			CRS 9	
			– sailing order 2	Officers sick 3 men & WAAC
			To 12 SD.R 5 (acquits)	
			To Duty 3	
			Died 1	
			Remaining 51.	1877
do	12/9/18		Admitted sick 26 wounded 39 (5 gas mustard)	
			To CCS 22 39	
			To CRS 2 (acquits)	Officers sick 2 men & WAAC
			To 12 SD.R 8	
			To Duty 2	
			Died 1	
			Remained 44	1817
do	13/9/18		Admitted sick 48 wounded 36 (13 gas mustard)	
			To CCS 17 34	
			To CRS 14	
			To administration 1	
			To 12 SD.R 9 (acquits)	
			To Duty 1	
			Died 2	1877

WAR DIARY
or
INTELLIGENCE SUMMARY.
(Erase heading not required.)

Army Form C. 2118.

Place	Date	Hour	Summary of Events and Information	Remarks and references to Appendices
K.10.a.5.8.	14/9/18		Admitted sick 39 officers sick 2 wounded 1 (*includes 1 gas mustard)	
			To C.C.S. 34 32 2	
			To C.A.S. 18	
			Serious cases 1	
			To 12 S.F.A. 5	
			To Duty 9	
			Died 1	
			Remaining 13	
			Major Buchanan R.AM.C returned from leave to U.K.	
BRAS&DEMONT 15/9/18.			Handed over site at K.20.a.5.8. to 15 S.B.B.S. Marched to Bracquemont	
L.25.b.33.			+ took over from 4.5. F.A.	
6.00 a.m.			Admitted sick 17 wounded 60 (2 gas mustard) officers sick. Wounded 3	
			To C.C.S 13 58 1	
			To 12 St. A. 4	
			Duty 11 2	
			Remaining 11	
do	16.9.18		Admitted sick 9 wounded 58 officers sick 1. wounded 1.	
			To C.C.S 11 60	
			To 12 St. R. 6	
			Remaining 8 (wounded include 1 Off. & 1 S.O.R. W. gas mustard.)	
			P.O.W. 3 aerm & suspect	

WAR DIARY
or
INTELLIGENCE SUMMARY.
(Erase heading not required.)

Army Form C. 2118.

Instructions regarding War Diaries and Intelligence Summaries are contained in F.S. Regs., Part II. and the Staff Manual respectively. Title pages will be prepared in manuscript.

Place	Date	Hour	Summary of Events and Information	Remarks and references to Appendices
L.d.b.33	17.9.18.		Admitted sick 20 wounded 68 × Officers sick 1 wounded 2 To CCS 10 58 To duty 3 To 12 & 8 F.A 3 Remaining	
do.	18.9.18.		Admitted sick 16 wounded 2 (gas mustard) To C.C.S 8 To C.R.S. 4 (10 guns) To 12 & F.A 4 10. Remaining Started to Evacuate on M.D.S. cases going direct from ADS to CCS.	
do.	19.9.18.		Lt. WRAY M.A.C. rejoined from T. duty with 6th Tanned Mob. Lt. BURBER M.M.C. proceeded to 118 A.F.A. for temp. duty Admitted sick 16 wounded 18. (9 yellow cross) To CCS 6 8 To duty 1 (NYAN) To 12 & F.A 13 9 Remaining	
do.	20/9/18.		20 O.R. AATP proceeded to HQ 48 F.A. for temporary duty Admitted sick 18 wounded 6 (4 gas mustard) To CCS 13 9 To duty 4 2 Remaining 13 4	

Army Form C. 2118.

WAR DIARY
or
INTELLIGENCE SUMMARY.
(Erase heading not required.)

Place	Date	Hour	Summary of Events and Information	Remarks and references to Appendices
L25b33	21.9.18		Admitted sick 10 wounded 2 To CCS 7 3 To 46 F.A. 6 12 & 6.A 1 (shy water) Remain 9 3	
do	22.9.18		Admitted sick 9 evacuated 2 (gas mustard) To CCS 5 3 To 46 F.A 2 Duty 1 Remain 10	
do	23.9.18		Admitted sick 10 wounded 4 (1 gas ? gas crews) To CCS 6 3 46 F.A 2 - 1 To Duty 2 To 12 dc B 10 Remain	
do	24.9.18		Admitted sick 13 wounded 1 To CCS 8 46 F.A 6 To 12 & F.A 2.5 Duty 2 Remain 1	
do	25.9.18		Lt. EASY MRC transferred to 11 A&S Hy for Temp duty Admitted sick 10 wounded 3 (gas mustard) To CCS To 46 F.A Remain 1	

Army Form C. 2118.

WAR DIARY
or
INTELLIGENCE SUMMARY.
(Erase heading not required.)

Instructions regarding War Diaries and Intelligence Summaries are contained in F. S. Regs., Part II. and the Staff Manual respectively. Title pages will be prepared in manuscript.

Place	Date	Hour	Summary of Events and Information	Remarks and references to Appendices
L25b 33	26.9.18.		Admitted sick 19 wounded 1 (gun mounted) To 12 St.A 1 To duty 9 Remain	
L25b 33	27.9.18.		Admitted sick 11 wounded 5 (inclusion of 2 french civilians interviewed) To CCS 7 4 To 46 FA 5 To duty 46 2 Remain	M71/4
do.	28.9.18.		Lt. WRAY M.R.C. proceeded to 1/5 R. Scots. for T. centy. M7/3 Admitted sick 12 wounded 2. To CCS 8 2 (1 agent) To 12 St.A.P 8 4. Remain	
do.	29.9.18.		Lt. SHIRKEY M.R.C. is posted to 16 Scot. Rifles the strength of this unit accordingly. Maj. VICKERS. R.A.M.B. proceeded on leave to U.K. Admitted sick 8 O.R. 10 wounded Nil To CCS 1 To 46 FA 5 2 To duty 1 1 Remain 1 12.	M7/7
do.	30/9/18.		Admitted off. sick 1 O.R. 12. wounded O.R.M.1. 1 To CCS 1 4 To 39 St.A.P 1 O.R. (agent) Today 1 Remain 2	M7/7

H. S. Newbitt
Lt Col.
O.C. 47 F.A.

(6339) Wt. W160/M3016 1,500,000 10/17 McA & W Ltd (E 1898) Forms W3091.   Army Form W.3091.

Cover for Documents.

Nature of Enclosures.

War Diary of 1/1 Field Ambulance
for October 1918 by
Lieut Colonel H.C. MONTEITH. D.S.O. R.A.M.C.
Comm'g 1/1 F.A.

Volume 20
160/401 Vol. 39

SECRET
Oct 1918

Notes, or Letters written.

WAR DIARY
or
INTELLIGENCE SUMMARY.

(Erase heading not required.)

Army Form C. 2118.

Place	Date	Hour	Summary of Events and Information	Remarks and references to Appendices
BRAEQUEMONT L25 B 33	1/10/18		Admitted sick 9. To CCS 3. To 46 F.A. 9. wounded 1.	MAP 44 B.
L25 B 33	2.10.12.		Admitted sick 11. To CCS 4. To 46 F.A. 10. wounded 1. (gun wounded) To duty sick 1. Remaining - 5.	MR.
do.	3/10/18.		Admitted sick 1. O.R.B 1. To CCS 2. To 46 F.A. 6. To duty sick 1. Remaining - 4.	MR.
do.	4.10.18		Admitted sick to O.R. 2. To CCS 1. To 46 F.A. 4. wounded 4 (gun Y.C.) Remaining 1.	MR.
do.	5.10.18.		Capt. C. HARRIS R.A.M.C. posted to this unit from corps rest. Admitted sick 8. To CCS 2. To 46 F.A. 7. wounded 3. Remaining 1.	MR.
do	6.10.18		Lt. BEUKER M.R.C. rejoined from T. study k. 158th Rly. A.F.A. Admitted sick 8. To 46 F.A. sick 1. To CCS - 4. wounded 1. Remaining - 3.	MR.
	7.10.18		Remaining Other 1 sick off. To CCS 1 sick off. Remaining 5 sick. 2 sick O.R.s 4 O.R.s En Brancard En Brancard	MR.
	8.10.18		2nd Lt. H.G. Goodwill S.S.O. to today taken over temporary charge 45th Field Ambulance	

WAR DIARY
or
INTELLIGENCE SUMMARY

Army Form C. 2118.

Place	Date	Hour	Summary of Events and Information	Remarks and references to Appendices
BEACUZMONT	8.10.18		Major C. Buchanan to taken over temporary charge of 47" Field Ambulance	
			Admitted 10. OR's sick. To C.C.S. 11. OR's sick. Remaining 7. OR's sick	
			29. OR's W⁴. To 46 F.A. 4 OR's sick. 20. OR's W⁴.	Lieut Buchanan
			(Mt. GAS-SHELL.)	
	9.10.18		Admitted 7. OR's sick. To CCS 6 OR's sick. Remaining 7. OR's sick	
			To 46 F.A. 1. OR. sick. 20. OR's W⁴	Lieut B.
	10.10.18		47" Field Ambulance opened a Divisional Diarrhea Rest.	
			Admitted 1. Officer sick {1. Officer sick To CCS {21. OR's sick To 46 F.A. 4. OR's sick. Remaining 24. OR's sick	
			42. OR's sick To CRS 16. OR's W⁴	4. OR's W⁴. Lieut B.
	11.10.18		Inspection of Hospital by Maj General F.J. Gerrard. D.M.S. V. Army.	
			Admitted 31. OR's sick To CCS. 1. OR. W⁴. Died 1. OR. sick Remaining 31. OR's sick	
			23. OR's sick	3. OR's W⁴ Lieut B.
	12.10.18		Inspection of Hospital by Lt-Col. D.J. Young. D.D.M.S. 17th Corps.	
	"		Admitted 29. OR's sick. To CCS. 23. OR's sick To Seahir Rest. 1. OR. Remaining. 18. OR's sick	
			To C.R.S. {21. OR's sick To Duty. 7. OR's sick	1. OR. W⁴ Lieut B.
			{1. OR. W⁴	
	13.10.18		Inspection of Hospital by Maj General A.L. Reed. V.C. R.O.C. IV Division	
			Admitted {33. OR's sick To C.C.S {16. OR's sick. To Duty. 2. OR. sick Remaining {33. OR's sick	
			{1. OR. W⁴ {1. OR. W⁴	2. OR. W⁴ Lieut B.

Army Form C. 2118.

WAR DIARY
or
INTELLIGENCE SUMMARY.
(Erase heading not required.)

Instructions regarding War Diaries and Intelligence Summaries are contained in F.S. Regs. Part II. and the Staff Manual respectively. Title pages will be prepared in manuscript.

Place	Date	Hour	Summary of Events and Information	Remarks and references to Appendices
BRACQUEMONT	13.10.18.		Lieut. A.B. Eaby L.O.R.C. U.S.A. attached for temporary duty & instruction to No. 13 C.C.S. for 14 days. Major Lieut. E.T. Becken L.O.R.C. U.S.A. to the ore temporary medical charge of 1/5 Cordon H ors.	44 A N.W.
	14.10.18.		ADMT. 47 OR's sick. To C.C.S. 26 OR's sick. To E.R.S. 5. OR's sick. To Duty. HOT sick. 44 OR's sick	N.W. 2 OR's sick
	15.10.18.		Adm. 1. Offr sick. To C.C.E.S 1 offr sick. To Duty 3 OR's sick. Remaining 49 OR's sick	
	16.10.18.		Hospts Att. OR's Sgt at BRACQUEMONT 38 OR's sick Evacuated. Ambulance moved to Verquin. G.8.d.4.8. (sheet 36 C) Adm during station formed at I.9.a.2.8. (sheet 36") Lieut. Way. M.R.C. U.S.A. returned to unit from temporary duty & 2/9 Reg Scots. Adm 10 OR's sick. C.C.S. 37 OR's sick. To Duty. 22 OR's sick. Remaining N° 2 Lt. Bert Pratuetz injured from 45 RA.	
I.9.a.28	17.10.18.		H.Q. moved from Verquin to E. of MEURCHIN. I.9.a.28. Acc. During st. found at Sarvin in French Hospy. totally occupied by every as a Hospital. Adm. & evacuated 1 inch off. 1 O.R. in. & 14 sick Lt. Eury J.O.R. joined from 3rd KYR.	Monath
LA ROSIERE K12a 44 A N.E	18.10.18.		H.Q. moved to Neurville at K.7.d., rather built mode for avoid Brigade with 45 I.B. Moved on to La Rosiere, where A.D.S. also General Advanced cars at C.H. du Bois. L.7.b. Wounded S.O.R.	Bdy A N.E jury

Army Form C. 2118.

WAR DIARY
or
INTELLIGENCE SUMMARY.
(Erase heading not required.)

Instructions regarding War Diaries and Intelligence Summaries are contained in F. S. Regs., Part II. and the Staff Manual respectively. Title pages will be prepared in manuscript.

Place	Date	Hour	Summary of Events and Information	Remarks and references to Appendices
CAPPELLE F29a7.4	19/10/18		Moved from ROSIERE to CAPPELLE at 1400. Posts for advanced coys at GENECH A15 b & at OUVIGNIES A28 d Sheet 44. Casualties 2 wounded, at 1 French Division.	Sheet 57A/M NE
do.	20/10/18		Opened M.D.S. B room & Carantia. 2 O.R. wounded. 39 sick, 1 officer sick. 2 French wounded sick. Slight shelling the rest of day.	Sheet 44
BERCU B21c&8 (Sheet 44)	21/10/18		HQ F.A. moved to BERCU & opened M.D.S. here at 4 P.M. Casualties sick off 1. O.R. 24 wounded O.R. 3. Weather slight rain.	
do.	22/10/18		Remained at BERCU, some rain. Casualties officer 1, O.R. 19 sick - 12 O.R. wounded.	
do.	23/10/18		Casualties sick off 1. O.R. 20 wounded O.R. 11 Evacuated sick 6 entering 3 N.Y.D. gas mustard wounded 3.	
do.	24/10/18		Many civilian refugees arrived in collapsed from starvation; a considerable number of civilian population requiring medical and surgical attention. Casualties sick O.R. 21 wounded O.R. 5. Civilians wounded 1. A few H.V. shells fell in surrounding area during the night.	

Army Form C. 2118

WAR DIARY
or
INTELLIGENCE SUMMARY
(Erase heading not required.)

Instructions regarding War Diaries and Intelligence Summaries are contained in F. S. Regs., Part II. and the Staff Manual respectively. Title Pages will be prepared in manuscript.

Place	Date	Hour	Summary of Events and Information	Remarks and references to Appendices
BERCU B.21.c.8.8 (Sheet 44)	25.10.18		Casualties - Offr 20 O.R.!; wounded Offr 5 ; Civilians Sick - one Belgian; wounded - one French.	
do.	26.10.18		Casualties sick officers 3. O.R. 25. Sickness 4° MTY	
do.	27.10.18		„ sick O.R. 26. wounded O.R. 35, includes 30 gas mustard 2 civilian sick. Mums & diarrhoea from WEZ transported to MOUCHIN, & thence to LILLE. MTY	
do.	28.10.18.		Casualties sick 1 officer 17 O.R. wounded 1 officer 13 O.R. sickness with 4 MTY	
do.	29.10.18.		Casualties sick 1 officer 25 O.R. includes 5" influenza. wounded civilians 2 sick. - 63 - 61 gas mustard MTY	
do.	30.10.18.		Casualties sick 50 O.R.* wounded †59 O.R. Sickness 2 wounded (gas shell) * includes 37 P.U.O † includes 55 gas mustard MTY	
do.	31.10.18.		Casualties sick Off. 2. O.R. 35.* wounded off. 3. O.R. 6.† Units of wounded. * includes 13 P.U.O & 10 Influenza † includes 8 gassed (5 phosgene 3 yellowcross)	[signature] O.C. 47 F.A.

(6414) Wt. W3906/P1607 2,500,000 7/18 McA & W Ltd (E 3591) Forms W3091/4.   Army Form W.3091.

Cover for Documents.

Nature of Enclosures.

140/3461
Volume 41
V8240

War Diary of Lt. Pleasant by
HQ MONTEITH Bde Rice
Red Cross November 1918
for

SECRET Nov 1918

COMMITTEE FOR THE
MEDICAL HISTORY OF THE WAR
6 MAR 1919
Date

Notes, or Letters written.

47th FIELD AMBULANCE 1/12/18

WAR DIARY or INTELLIGENCE SUMMARY

Army Form C. 2118

(Erase heading not required.)

Instructions regarding War Diaries and Intelligence Summaries are contained in F.S. Regs., Part II. and the Staff Manual respectively. Title Pages will be prepared in manuscript.

Place	Date	Hour	Summary of Events and Information	Remarks and references to Appendices
MOUCHIN. B.21 c 6.8	1/11/18		Evacuated sick Off 1. O.R. 51 + Wounded O.R. 3. + includes 15 P.U.O. & 6 influenza. Evacuated 3 sick	MAP 44
do.	2/11/18.		Sick Off. 2. O.R. 37. Wounded O.R. 11. Evacuated sick. 3. 16 P.U.O. 6 influenza.	M [initials]
do.	3/11/18.		Admitted Off. 1 O.R. 35 sick. 80 O.R. wounded. 6 civilians sick. O.R. 35 sick, including 17 influenza & 5 P.U.O. + 2 died of wounds. 6 gas, 85 phosgene, 1 mustard.)	M
do.	4/11/18.		Admitted Off. 1. O.R. 3/ sick. 20 O.R. wounded. civilians 2 sick. — 20 sick includes 13 P.U.O. & 1 influenza.	M
do.	5/11/18.		Admitted Off. 2. O.A. 41 sick. 1 O.R. 3 wounded, 1 civilian sick. + includes 16 P.U.O. Evacuated sick 29	M
do.	6/11/18		Admitted Off. 4 O.R. 38 sick. 13 O.R. wounded 2 civilians sick. + includes 21 P.U.O. + 11 gassed yellow cross + green Evacuated 32	M
do.	7/11/18.		Admitted Off. 1. O.R. 48 sick. 1 Off. wounded 5 civilians sick. + includes 27 P.U.O. + includes 17 yellow cross gas. Evacuated O.R. 45 sick.	M

Army Form C. 2118.

WAR DIARY
or
INTELLIGENCE SUMMARY.
(Erase heading not required.)

Place	Date	Hour	Summary of Events and Information	Remarks and references to Appendices
MOUCHIN B21 c&	8·11·18		Admitted Oct. 6. O.R. 35 sick. Evacuated 2 sick + includes 17 P.U.O.	NYD
PETIT RONES B21 c.	9/11/18		Moved to Petit Ronnes 2 P.M. Admitted Off. 2. O.R. 57 sick. Wounded gas inhaled 1. 7 PUO 10. All evacuated	NYD
WASHES	10/11/18		Routine from →	NYD
HQ N 28d Sh.51 37			Moved from Petit Ronnes at 10 AM. Arrived ANTOING 3 P.M. HQ here for own hour, & moved to WASHES, arriving 8 P.M. 1 civilian wounded. 3 Off. & 17 O.R. sick.	NYD
WILLAUPUIS X 22 a. Sh.51 37	11/11/18		Routine from WASHES 9 AM. Arrived WILLAUPUIS 11 AM. M.D.S. established at convent. 2 off. & 12 O.R. sick.	NYD
do	12/11/18		Admitted & evacuated 1 off & 30 O.R. sick. 10 R. evacuated gas mustard + sick include 6 P.U.O.	NYD
do	13/11/18		Visit from DDMS I Corps. Transferred to III Corps 1800. Admitted & evacuated 15 sick, inclus. 6 PUO & 1 influenza. 1 wounded evacuated. Capt. D.L. Prentice RAMC transferred to Hanover to assume med. charge of 1/9 R.Scots. Lt. Bucher MORC, at present in Hosp., posted to this unit.	NYD

Army Form C. 2118.

WAR DIARY
or
INTELLIGENCE SUMMARY.
(Erase heading not required.)

Instructions regarding War Diaries and Intelligence Summaries are contained in F. S. Regs. Part II. and the Staff Manual respectively. Title pages will be prepared in manuscript.

Place	Date	Hour	Summary of Events and Information	Remarks and references to Appendices
WILLOPOIS	14/11/18.		Admitted & evacuated O.R. 29 sick. 1 wounded. gas mustard. MM2	
do	15/11/18		Lt. BERNER M.O.R.C. & Capt. HARRIS R.O.M.C. on strength of this unit. Admitted & evacuated sick 25. wounded 1. gas (burns) and include 3 influenza & 5 P.U.O. MM2	
"	16/11/18.		Lt. B.A. BARRISON M.O.R.C. taken on strength. Admitted 1 off. 29 sick. 1 Belgian. (P.U.O. 12. Influenza 1.) To C.C.S. 1. 23. 1. - Remainder 7 O.R. sick. MM2	
"	17/11/18.		Lt. R.A. HARRISON M.R.C. proceeded to 8th Div. for duty. Admitted sick 1 off. 14 O.R. evacuated 1 off. 9 O.R. Remaining 12 O.R. 1 Belgian wounded. Such include 8 P.U.O. MM2	
"	18/11/18.		Admitted 23 O.R. & officers evacuated 1 off. & 19 O.R. Remaining 16. P.U.O. 9. influenza 2 admitted. MM2	
"	19/11/18.		Admitted off 1. O.R. 28. evac. off. 1. O.R. 20. To duty O.R. 3. Rem O.R. 21. P.U.O. 12. influenza 2. MM2	
"	20/11/18		Admitted 40 evacuated 35. To duty 1. Rem 25. 3 Belgian Gsw sick evacuated. P.U.O. 14 influenza 3. Inspected by A.D.M.S. MM2	

Army Form C. 2118.

WAR DIARY
or
INTELLIGENCE SUMMARY.
(Erase heading not required.)

Instructions regarding War Diaries and Intelligence Summaries are contained in F. S. Regs., Part II. and the Staff Manual respectively. Title pages will be prepared in manuscript.

Place	Date	Hour	Summary of Events and Information	Remarks and references to Appendices
WILLAUPOIS	21/11/18		Admitted 0&1 O.R.21. Evacuated #1. O.R.19. To aus 5. Remaining O.R. 32. P.V.O. O.R.6. infantry 4. $evac'n$ (2 are wounded, 1 sick) evacuated M2	
"	22.11.18		Admitted OR 12. evacuated 24. Remaining 20. 16 PVO admitted	
"	23.11.18		Admitted 40ff7 YEOR evac'd. 400 40R. To aus BOR. Rem. 28 O.R. + PVS 3. Infantry 8. 6779	
AUTREPPE	24.11.18.		Marched to Autreppe arriving 1/pm. 17.5 stations taken over as a porter. Admitted O.R. 18. evacuated 10. To aus 2. Remaining 23. M2 6 PVO admitting	
do.	25.11.18.		Hospital instructed to pass in trucks & ASC's 187.8 W. Admitted 32. evacuated 27. To aus 2. Remaining 26. M2 16 PVO w. 1 infantry.	
do.	26.11.18.		Admitted O.R.2. O.R.24. evac'd. 87.2. O.R. 19. To aus O.R.10. Remg. O.R.21. 18 408 T.P.V.O. 677/	
do.	27.11.18		Admitted #1. O.R.35. evac'd #1. O.R.28. To aus 1. Remn 27. P.V.O. 13 O.R. infantry 2.	
do.	28.11.18		Admitted 27. evacuated 21. To aus 2 Remn 30. (P.V.O. 11) M22	
do.	29.11.18		Admitted 20. " 16. " 4 PV.O. 10. infantry 1. M22.	
			Pte JEANS K.O.G. Corps. taken on strength. Admitted 23. Evacuated 17. To aus 4. Rem = 32. (PV.O. 12) 6990 with 0C 67 F.A.	
do.	30.11.18.			I.C. Pet.

(6414) Wt. W3906/P1607 2,500,000 7/18 McA & W Ltd (E 3591) Forms W3091/4.   Army Form W.3091.

Cover for Documents.

Nature of Enclosures.

War Diary of 41/1st Ambulance
for December 1918
H.C. Monteith, Capt RAMC
O.C. and 41/1 FB Amb

Notes, or Letters written.

Army Form C. 2118.

WAR DIARY
or
INTELLIGENCE SUMMARY.
(Erase heading not required.)

Instructions regarding War Diaries and Intelligence Summaries are contained in F. S. Regs., Part II. and the Staff Manual respectively. Title pages will be prepared in manuscript.

Place	Date	Hour	Summary of Events and Information	Remarks and references to Appendices
AUTREPPE T1 d.99. Aug 38.	1/12/18.		Patients admitted 1 Off. 13 O.R. Evac^d 1 Off. 9 O.R. To du G. 4 Remaining 32.	Attention Lost
do.	2/12/18.		Admitted Off.2 O.R 4 Evac^d Off.2 O.R 4 To Aug 5. Remⁿ 28. Influenza 7 P.U.O 2	hosp
do.	3/14/18.		Admitted O.R 24 wound 18 To duty 6 Remain 28. Influenza 13 P.U.O.1	
do	4/12/18.		Admitted Off 1. O.R 30 wound. Off 1. O.R 27. Duty 2. Influenza 20. P.U.O.1	hosp Remain 27.
do.	5/12/18.		Admitted Off 1. O.R 22 wound Off 1. O.R 22. Influenza Off 1. O.R 14.	hosp Remain 26.
do	6/12/18.		Admitted 16 O.R. wound 12. Duty 2 Rem 28. 2ng Buchanan + party of 39 O.R. succeeded to civilians near WIHAUDRIS to extract 67 FA 80 NIZ. The King's visit hosp H.I.T. The King visited 15th Div^d area. Party of 2 Off. & 33 O.R. took the road wire-netting	
do	7/12/18		of this unit. Admitted Off 1. O.R.18 evac^d Off 1. O.R. 11. To duty 3. Remain 30 went. Influenza 11	
do	8/12/18.		Admitted 2 Off. 17 O.R. wound. 2 Off 14 O.R. To aug 5. 3 Rem 30 2 Off. 5 O.R. Influenza. NT_y	

WAR DIARY
or
INTELLIGENCE SUMMARY

Army Form C. 2118.

Place	Date	Hour	Summary of Events and Information	Remarks and references to Appendices
AUTREPPE	9.12.18		Advance party Staff Capt. & 5 I.B. to BRAINE LE COMTE to find suitable billets & hospital in our area.	
			Arrived O.R. 26. Evac.d 23. To duty S. Remain 28.	
			Lyharge 11 o.r.	M/Y
do	10.12.18		Admitted O.R. 34. Evac.d O.R. 39. To duty 3. Remain 22.	
			off. 2 off. 2	M/Y
			Lyharge to off. 2. O.R. 13	
do	11.12.18		Admitted off. 1 O.R. 26. Evac.d off. O.R. 27. To duty S. Remain 18.	
			Lyharge O.R. 8.	M/Y
do	12.12.18		Admitted 42. Evac.d 20. To duty 4. Remain 14	M/Y
do	13.12.18		" 37 " 42 " – " 19 off.	
	14.12.18		" " " off 1 O.R. 26 " off 1 O.R. 17 " – " 17 off.	
	15.12.18		" " " O.R. 17 " 24 " 9 " 7	
	16.12.18		Visited billets & hosp. in new area at Braine-le-Comte. off.	
do	17.12.18		Admitted 14 evac.d 19. To duty 1. Remain 1. off.	
			Marched to CHIEVRES 7 kilomtrs Weather fair	M/Y
			Admitted 8 evac 8 remain 3	M/Y
CHIEVRES	18.12.18		Arrived to SOIGNIES 24 Atlantic weather v. wet	M/Y
			Admitted 5 Evac.d 8 Rem: 2.	

Army Form C. 2118.

WAR DIARY
or
INTELLIGENCE SUMMARY.
(Erase heading not required.)

Instructions regarding War Diaries and Intelligence Summaries are contained in F. S. Regs., Part II. and the Staff Manual respectively. Title pages will be prepared in manuscript.

Place	Date	Hour	Summary of Events and Information	Remarks and references to Appendices
BRAIME-LE COMTE	19/12/18		Moved from Enghien to Braine-le-Comte. Took over École des Filles for Hospital & Billets. Patients evacuated 8. Remaining 10.	MAP B2011584
do	20.12.18		Admitted 5. evac'd 1. To duty 4. Remaining 10	MTD
do	21.12.18		Received equipment of ANTS. wing. Admitted Off 2. O.R. 6. evac'd Off 2. O.R. Nil. Remaining 16	MTD
do	22.12.18		Admitted Off. O.R. 5 evac'd Off 1. To duty 1. Remaining 10	MTD
do	23.12.18		Capt Jessel A.A.M.C. rejoined from Corps. Cas. attached Hd. Lt WRAY H.R.C. " " 71 Bde R.F.A. Lt. BRAIN R.A.M.C. & Lt. MARTIN M.G.B. reported for duty, & have been taken on strength. Admitted O.R. 3. To duty 1. Remaining 22	MTD
do	24.12.18		Admitted O.R. 2. Remaining 24.	MTD
do	25.12.18		Admitted 1. Remaining 25.	MTD

Army Form C. 2118.

WAR DIARY
or
INTELLIGENCE SUMMARY.
(Erase heading not required.)

Instructions regarding War Diaries and Intelligence Summaries are contained in F. S. Regs., Part II. and the Staff Manual respectively. Title pages will be prepared in manuscript.

Place	Date	Hour	Summary of Events and Information	Remarks and references to Appendices
BRAINE LE COMTE	26/12/18		Admitted Off. 1. O.R. 1. Remain 24. NYD	
do	27/12/18		Lt Martin M.R. attached to 6th M.B.B. for temporary duty. Admitted 8 E ORS 1. Remain 31.	
do.	28/12/18		Admitted No.2. Remain 33. Lethal given by Lt. Col. Wear Sgt Abelson NYD	
do.	29/12/18		Admitted 5 ORs. Remain 37. Move to A.U.O.2	
do.	30/12/18		Sgt. S. Buchanan R.A.M.C. received on strength from G.C.R. A(D)	
do.	31/12/18		Admitted 9 ORs. To No 5. Admitted 38. A.U.O. evacuated NYD
			Evacuated 11. ORs. 3. To Aug 7. Remain 39. Remain.	

H. H. Nesmith
Lt. Col.
O.C. 47 F.A.

15 DIV

BOT 1624

No. 47 Field Ambulance

Army Form C. 2118.

WAR DIARY
or
INTELLIGENCE SUMMARY.
(Erase heading not required.)

Instructions regarding War Diaries and Intelligence Summaries are contained in F. S. Regs., Part II. and the Staff Manual respectively. Title pages will be prepared in manuscript.

Place	Date	Hour	Summary of Events and Information	Remarks and references to Appendices
BRAINS le BOMTE	1/1/19		Strength attained 3, Privates 3. To-day 4, Privates 35. Minus 8. P.U.O. 5. remain. Lt. WRAY N.E., O.S.A. proceeded on leave to U.K.	
do.	2/1/19		Cols admitted 3, Privates 36. Sick 2, Privates 3, Privates 30. MONARTH DIED. Mange Privates 8, duty 4, company 4, P.U.O. remain 5. Gn.S.	
do.	3/1/19		Patients Privates 30, admitted 7, duty 4, remaining 35. Influenza = in = part 4, P.U.O. Privates 5, admitted 1, out 1. Convoy 6	
do.	4/1/19		Pte H.M. VICKERS took sick. Amb. Convoy. Influenza. SIX YEARS. Privates 35. Nil admitted 1. App. 2. D.D. Pvt. 141 + Dr. Influenza 2, P.U.O. 1. Remained to P.U.O. Convoy 6. Remain 30. Influenza sickness 6. Returned to P.U.O. Convoy 6. Admitted 7 remain 6. Lieut MARTIN reported sick for duty. Influenza case Ly IV T fever AC	
do.	5/1/19		Lieut Col: H.G. MONTEITH proceeded on leave B.E.F. Privates 29. Admitted 3, cases 3, due 3, Remain 30. Influenza - Privates 4, Admitted nil, remaining 4; P.U.O. Remain 6, out 1, Remain 5. APM.	

(3690) Wt W3500/P915 750,000 5/18 E 2858 Forms/C2118/10.

Army Form C. 2118.

WAR DIARY
or
INTELLIGENCE SUMMARY.
(Erase heading not required.)

Instructions regarding War Diaries and Intelligence Summaries are contained in F. S. Regs., Part II. and the Staff Manual respectively. Title pages will be prepared in manuscript.

Place	Date	Hour	Summary of Events and Information	Remarks and references to Appendices
BANNU-LE-CONTE	6/9		[illegible handwritten entries]	
Do	7/9			
Do	8/9			
Do	9/9			
Do	10/9			

Army Form C. 2118.

WAR DIARY
or
INTELLIGENCE SUMMARY.
(Erase heading not required.)

Instructions regarding War Diaries and Intelligence Summaries are contained in F. S. Regs. Part II. and the Staff Manual respectively. Title pages will be prepared in manuscript.

Place	Date	Hour	Summary of Events and Information	Remarks and references to Appendices
BRANFAY-COMTE	11/10		Patients - Remand 53, Admitted 70, Sick CCS 2, Duty 9, Remand 106.	
do	12/10		O.R.O. Remand 15. Major Remand 4, Sick 41, Remand 9. MM	
do	13/10		Patients - Remand 15, Duty 1, Remand 9, Sick 6, Convoy 17, Admitted 23, NCO-10, Convoy 7, Admitted 3, Sick 11, Convoy 1.	
do	14/10		Patients Remand 65, Admitted 5, CCS 2, Duty 5, Remand 63, Influenza 2, O.R.O. Remand 11, Admitted 1, Sick 15, Convoy 11. MM	
do	15/10		Remand 45, Admitted 8, CCS 4, Duty 3, Convoy 3, Influenza 2, O.R.O. Remand 11, Duty 1, Convoy 10. MM	
do	16/10		Patients - Remand 40, Admitted 6, CCS 1, Duty 2, Convoy 31, Remand 10, Convoy 1, Duty 1. Influenza 2, O.R.O. Remand 10, Admitted 6, Convoy 5, Duty 2, Convoy 2, Influenza 2. 6 Enemy 12.	
do	17/10		Patient Remand 22, Admitted 3, Duc 9, Duty 3, Remand 7, Influenza 2. O.R.O. Remand 12, Admitted 1, Int 1, Enemy 12. MM	

Army Form C. 2118.

WAR DIARY
or
INTELLIGENCE SUMMARY.
(Erase heading not required.)

Instructions regarding War Diaries and Intelligence Summaries are contained in F. S. Regs., Part II. and the Staff Manual respectively. Title pages will be prepared in manuscript.

Place	Date	Hour	Summary of Events and Information	Remarks and references to Appendices
BRAINE LE COMTE.	18/1/19		Patients - Remained 31, admitted 4, discharged 2, died 1, Remaining 32. P.U.O. Remained 12, Sick	
do.	19/1/19		P.G. Beaupinay, C. Duale in charge of the hospital the addition to the establishment of Colonel John B.F. WRAY F.C. MO. assumed charge from Lieut-Col...	
do.	20/1/19		Patients - Remained 32, admitted 3, discharged 1, died 1, Remaining 35. P.U.O. Remained 12, Germany 12.	
do.	21/1/19		Patients - Remained 35, admitted 3, discharged 4, Germany 34. Influenza 2, P.U.O. Remained 12, duty 1, Germany 1.	
do.	22/1/19		Lt. Col. M.S. MacEtt attached from here to U.K. Patients Admitted 2, To duty 4, Remaining 33. Influenza remaining 2. P.U.O. - 1 - 35 Influenza 1 P.U.O. 10	
do.	23/1/19		" 1 " 7 " 33 Influenza " P.U.O. 15	
do.			Influenza 1, P.U.O. 10 " 4 " 33 Remaining 15 P.U.O.	
do.	24/1/19		Admitted 4 To duty 1 Among 38. Influenza 1. P.U.O. 10 P.U.O.	
do.	25/1/19		Admitted 2 To sick 4 To duty 1 Remaining 33. Influenza 1. P.U.O. 10 P.U.O. Lt/Col. Monlett, Amj. Victoria + 12th Coy. Reserves to Brussels for review by the King of Belgium. Maj. Bay M.C. 46 F.A. assumed t/command of the ambulance. KSM.	

D. D. & L., London, E.C. (1450) Wt.W.300/P713 750,000 3/15 £ 2688 Forms/C2118/16.

WAR DIARY
or
INTELLIGENCE SUMMARY.
(Erase heading not required.)

Army Form C. 2118.

Instructions regarding War Diaries and Intelligence Summaries are contained in F. S. Regs., Part II. and the Staff Manual respectively. Title pages will be prepared in manuscript.

Place	Date	Hour	Summary of Events and Information	Remarks and references to Appendices
Braine le Comte	26.1.19	19	Arrived 19ff- 1 OR. evac'd 19ff- 1 OR. To duty 1. Run J 2. Jaylager 1. P.U.O. 9. 1772	
do.	27.1.19.		Gain 2.1. Premia 3.8. Inj. Violence received from Brussels, & heek cases evacuated from 3rd Div M3	
do.	28.1.19.		Admitted 8. Run J 3.8. Influ 1. P.U.O. 10.	
do.	29.1.19.		L.T.B.C. Hospital party returned from Brussels. Inj. day returned 648 F.A. M3 Capt. J. Anne & family moving to 4/R.9. Influ 9. Run J 1. P.U.O. 12. 1777	
do.	30.1.19.		Admitted 5. To duty 4. Run J 1. Run J 1. 27. -1. -13	
do.	31.1.19.		" 6 evac'd 4. 1772 27 Sean received a leave to K.J. France. Admitted 9ff. 1. O.R. 8. To duty 2 OR evacuated 1 Off -4 S.R. Run 39 OR PUO 14 Influ 1.	

Hewitt
Major
O.C. 47 F.A.

No. 44 Field Ambulance

Feb 1915

WAR DIARY
or
INTELLIGENCE SUMMARY.

Army Form C. 2118.

47 Fld Amb
Vol 4 3

Place	Date	Hour	Summary of Events and Information	Remarks and references to Appendices
B POINE LE COMTE	Feb 1/19		Patients admitted 5 evac'd 4 To Aus 4 Aus'? 30 Informal P.O.A.9	
do	2.2.19		" 4 Died 1 " 3 " 30 Pol EEE Area	
do	3.2.19		" 184 G.O.R. evac'd 147 SOR Totals 4 " 28 " 1 " 10	N.Y.D.
			Lt. Austin M.C. returned from leave to Paris	
do	4.2.19		Aus II Cl O.R.5 To Aus 2 (Iufluenza) Pulmonary 34 P.U.O.11	HOSP.COTT
			Injured A₂ ADNS III Corps	
do	5.2.19		2 cy. An. Vichon Rets. Jaundiced 6 O.R 3 Of Military Limit	
			Admitted Off 1 O.R.5 Was 2 Off 1 O.R.? Total O.R. 1 Pulmonary 3	P.U.B.19
do	6.2.19		" " 1 " " 7 " 1 " 3	" 19 N.Y.D
do	7.2.19		" " " 11 " " 4	" 23 N.Y.D
do	8.2.19		" " " 13 " " 2	" 53 N.Y.D.
do	9.2.19		Lt. Austin M.C. U.S.A. evacuated to No. 1 Aus. G.G.S	" 29 N.Y.Z.
			Junded 1 Off 12 O.R was 1 Off 7 O.R. To Aus 7 O.R.	
do	10.2.19		" " " 1 " 9 " 1 " 9 Rank 46 O.R P.U.O.22	M.Y.
do	11.2.19		" " " 1 " 9 " 1 " 8 38 " 22	M.Y.
do	12.2.19		" " " 1 " 13 " 1 " 14 34 " 27	N.Y.D
do	13.2.19		Lt Col Alen A.D.M.S rejoined from leave to S. France 27	N.Y.D N.Y.D
			Junded 13 Died 1 evac'd 5 Aus 8 Pul R 28	
			P.U.B 17	

Army Form C. 2118.

WAR DIARY
or
INTELLIGENCE SUMMARY.

(Erase heading not required.)

Instructions regarding War Diaries and Intelligence Summaries are contained in F. S. Regs., Part II and the Staff Manual respectively. Title pages will be prepared in manuscript.

Place	Date	Hour	Summary of Events and Information	Remarks and references to Appendices
BROINS le COMTE	14.2.19		Admitted O.R. 7. eva.ts 5. Total 12. Remain 26. P.U.O 18 temp 102	
do	15.2.19		7 7 19 2 - 14 - 102	
do	16.2.19		4 3 - 21 12 - 102½	
do	17.2.19		- - - - 23 6 - 102½	
do	18.2.19		18/8 O.R. 1 14 S.A. 4 2 25 13 - 102½	
do	19.2.19		9 3 4 27 29 - 102	
do	20.2.19		29/10 - 2-5 4 1 27 Influenza consumed 2 O.R. 4 O.R.	
do	21.2.19		5 4 - 9 34 P.U.O 17 Influenza Not.	
do	22.2.19		- 20 - 4 6 34 14 Not	
do	23.2.19		49 9 1-3 - 3 31 10 - 102	
do	24.2.19		9 9 3 37 7 - 102	
do	25.2.19		18 10 - 3 10 Influenza	
do	26.2.19		1F A&SACY MC DSA eyewad Influenza Army & is stack of 24 staying the P.U.O/Flu	
do			Brandard 26 aux 2 Rem 55 48 1 19 - 102	
do	27.2.19		17/Influenza 6 54 3 15 NYD Pyrexia 102	
do	28.2.19		5 8 6 45 3 15 NYD Pyrexia	

H.S Montieth
GL&GC
O.C 47 Field Ambulance

CONFIDENTIAL.

WAR DIARY

47th FIELD AMBULANCE.

March, 1919.

Army Form C. 2118.

WAR DIARY
or
INTELLIGENCE SUMMARY.
(Erase heading not required.)

Instructions regarding War Diaries and Intelligence Summaries are contained in F. S. Regs., Part II. and the Staff Manual respectively. Title pages will be prepared in manuscript.

Place	Date	Hour	Summary of Events and Information	Remarks and references to Appendices
BRAINE-LE-COMTE	1/3/19		Admitted O.R. 15 sick O.R. 3 To duty O.R. 9 Remain 2 Sick 53 Influenza nom 8 Wastage 14	
do.	2/3/19		" Off. 1 O.R. 7 " Off. 1 O.R. 4 " 3 12 44 " 8	
do.	3/3/19		" 14 6 10 42	
do.	4/3/19		" 10½ 5 3 42 3	
do	5/3/19		" 7 2 36	
do.	6/3/19		" 4 /civilian 10 35	
do.	7/3/19		" 3 O.R. civilian 4 33 2	
do	8/3/19		Capt. FRASER A.D.M.S. proceeded on seven days to ETREAT	
			Admitted 5 sick 3 2 Duty 12 26 3 1 man	
do	9.3.19.		" Off. 3 O.R. " Capt. 3 O.R. 5 19 2 1 m	
do	10.3.19.		Capt GRAHAM R.A.M.C. having proceeded to report 6 O.R.S Command army in reaches of 72 Reinfo	
			Admitted 6 " 1 Evacuated 3 army 19 O.R.S	
do	11.3.19.		" Off. 1 O.R. 5 " Off. O.R. 2 4 3 " 19 O.R.S	
	12.3.19.		Admitted 2 " Sick 9, 16 duty 5 Remain 7 S.R. Influenza covered	
	13.3.19.		" Off. no. 6 " Attack " H.R. " 3 "	
	14.3.19.		" " 1 " 2 " 2 " " nil	

Army Form C. 2118.

WAR DIARY
or
INTELLIGENCE SUMMARY.
(Erase heading not required.)

Place	Date	Hour	Summary of Events and Information	Remarks and references to Appendices
BRAINE-LE-COMTE	15.3.19		Admitted to R.2. Pres. R. [illegible] Ans. ward by Doctor McCall.	
do	16.3.19		Admitted to R.2 Pres. W. L. Influenza - no fever. Col. J.S. McCall Senr. Offr. in charge of Proceeded to England & Italy - no changes. Capt. R.C. Rae, R.A.M.C. returns from leave in France.	The End [signature]
do	17.3.19		Return to R.1 Pres. R.C.R. Influenza. nil	[signature]
do	18.3.19		Capt. C.A.G. Prino proceeds to port of embarkation for demobilization	[signature]
do	19.3.19		Admitted 3, Pres. 3 R. Influenza. nil	[signature]
do	20.3.19	" 2 " 2 " " nil	[signature]
do	21.3.19		Admitted & Pres. 4. R. nil	[signature]
do	22.3.19		do do -	[signature]
do	23.3.19		do 4 " 4 "	[signature]
do	24.3.19		Admitted 1 Pres. 1 R.	[signature]
do	25.3.19	" " Pres. 2 R. Influenza. Capt. WHITEHEAD, Capt. WHITEHEAD Capt. J. R. Bre. 2 R. Influenza left for party & takes on tonight for England.	[signature]

Army Form C. 2118.

WAR DIARY
or
INTELLIGENCE SUMMARY.
(Erase heading not required.)

Instructions regarding War Diaries and Intelligence
Summaries are contained in F. S. Regs., Part II.
and the Staff Manual respectively. Title pages
will be prepared in manuscript.

Place	Date	Hour	Summary of Events and Information	Remarks and references to Appendices
Brauve to Conde				
	26.3.19		Patient - evacuated 2 B.R. Sia. = 00 Afforage tout.	
	27.3.14		All patient admitted to Our Hosp. evac as direct admission from to hyp sia.	
	28.3.19.		Pass R.O.S.C.W. R.C.F. attached from to hyp sia.	
	29.3.19.		C.O. & office closed from to Adj's sia. Heavy fall of snow.	
			Capt. F. Sevens R.A.M.C & Capt. B.F. Way R.C. R.O. are about 9 days that to hyp but a place as sing to 4 of MO of Our.	
	30.3.14.		Nothing of note.	
	31.3.19.		do do	

A. N. Nunes
Maj.
O.C. 47 Field Amb.

Confidential

War Diary

47' Sikh Infantry

April 1919

Army Form C. 2118.

WAR DIARY
or
INTELLIGENCE SUMMARY.
(Erase heading not required.)

Instructions regarding War Diaries and Intelligence Summaries are contained in F. S. Regs., Part II. and the Staff Manual respectively. Title pages will be prepared in manuscript.

Place	Date	Hour	Summary of Events and Information	Remarks and references to Appendices
	1st April 1919		As from to-day also the F.O. Coss will take Ammunition. 9 no. D of I. Cyp.	
	2nd do		Nothing of note.	
	3 do			
	4 do		do	
	5 do		do	
	6 do		do	
	7 do		do	
	8 do		do	
	9 do		do	
	10 do		Visits by the Lieut. Col. McLaren O.M.O. III Army HQ. Brig Gen H.N. Sargent appointed as D.M.O. VII S.G. as from 22nd Army HQ A.F.M. Appointing 22.3.19.	
	11 do		Nothing of note.	
	12 do		do	
	13 do		do	

Army Form C. 2118.

WAR DIARY
or
INTELLIGENCE SUMMARY.
(Erase heading not required.)

Instructions regarding War Diaries and Intelligence Summaries are contained in F. S. Regs., Part II. and the Staff Manual respectively. Title pages will be prepared in manuscript.

Place	Date	Hour	Summary of Events and Information	Remarks and references to Appendices
BRAINE LE COMTE.	14.		Nothing of note	
	15.	do	do	
	16.	do	do	
	17.	do	do	
	18.	do	do	
	19.	do	do	
	20.	do	do	
	21.	do	do	
	22.	do	do	
	23.	do	do	
	24.	do	do	
	25.	do	do	
	26.	do	do	
	27.		O.M.O. had closed to Junction — O.M.O. Diary from reports at A.M.O. Lines	
	28.		Ordinary Coys now if I.A. supplied 7 clerks by D.A.D.O.T.	
	29.		Capt. Roberts posted to serve BEF. nothing of note.	
	30.	do	do	

A.D. [signature]
R.E. A.C. 47 3rd Res

CONFIDENTIAL.

WAR DIARY

of

47th Field Ambulance

Vol. May 1919.

****

Army Form C. 2118.

WAR DIARY
or
INTELLIGENCE SUMMARY.
(Erase heading not required.)

Instructions regarding War Diaries and Intelligence Summaries are contained in F. S. Regs., Part II. and the Staff Manual respectively. Title pages will be prepared in manuscript.

Place	Date	Hour	Summary of Events and Information	Remarks and references to Appendices
BRAINE-LE-COMTE	1/5/19		Nothing of note	HW
do	2.5.19.		do	HW
do	3. 5.19.		do	HW
do	4. 5.19.		do	HW
do	5. 5.19.		do	HW
do	6. 5.19.		do	HW
do	7. 5.19.		do	HW
do	8. 5.19.		do	HW
do	9. 5.19.		do	HW
do	10. 5.19.		do	HW
do	11. 5.19.		do	HW
do	12. 5.19.		D.A.G.C.R; 8930 2/0.5.19. recover cone of 2.6.5 XHH OR-1 Opr (Q.M.)	HW
do	13. 5.19		Nothing of note	HW
do	14. 5. 19		do	HW

Army Form C. 2118.

WAR DIARY
or
INTELLIGENCE SUMMARY.
(Erase heading not required.)

Instructions regarding War Diaries and Intelligence Summaries are contained in F. S. Regs., Part II. and the Staff Manual respectively. Title pages will be prepared in manuscript.

Place	Date	Hour	Summary of Events and Information	Remarks and references to Appendices
BRAINE-LE-COMTE	15/5/19		Nothing to note. (Sgd)	
	16.5.19.		Capt & Q.M. S. Davis rejoins from leave. Under instructions contained in D.A.Q.C.R. 3938 of 9-5-19 A/Sjt. A.H. VICKERS R.A.S.C. tendered commission of Capt & Q.M. to Capt & Q.M. S. DAVIS- R.A.S.C. Adv. Victim pay Rank.	
do	17.5.19.		10 M² D50104 Pte F CROSSAN, R.A.S.C. M.T. tried by F.G.C.M.	
do	18/5/15		Nothing to note	
do	19/5/15		do	
do	20/5/15		do	
do	21/5/15		Sentence of F.G.C.M. on Pte F CROSSAN promulgated (28 days F.P. No 2)	
do	22/5/15		Pte CROSSAN returned to 15 Div'l M.T. Coy.	
do	23/5/15		Nothing to note	
do	24/5/15		do	
do	25/5/15		do	

Army Form C. 2118.

WAR DIARY
or
INTELLIGENCE SUMMARY.
(Erase heading not required.)

Instructions regarding War Diaries and Intelligence Summaries are contained in F. S. Regs., Part II. and the Staff Manual respectively. Title pages will be prepared in manuscript.

Place	Date	Hour	Summary of Events and Information	Remarks and references to Appendices
Brique le Comte	26/5/15		Nothing to note	
"	27/5/15		"	
"	28/5/15		"	
"	29/5/15		"	
"	30/5/15		"	
"	31/5/15		"	

140/358-

8 AUG 1919

49th F.A.

June 1919

Army Form C. 2118.

47 Fd Amb 8/8/47

WAR DIARY
or
INTELLIGENCE SUMMARY.
(Erase heading not required.)

Instructions regarding War Diaries and Intelligence Summaries are contained in F.S. Regs. Part II. and the Staff Manual respectively. Title pages will be prepared in manuscript.

Place	Date	Hour	Summary of Events and Information	Remarks and references to Appendices
BRAINE LE COMTE	1/6/15		Nothing to note.	
do	2		do	
do	3		do	
do	4		17 Other Ranks demobilized.	
do	5		Nothing to note.	
do	6		do	
do	7		do	
do	8		do	
do	9		do	
do	10		do	
do	11		do	
do	12		do	
do	13		do	
do	14		do	
do	15		do	
do	16		do	

Army Form C. 2118.

WAR DIARY
or
INTELLIGENCE SUMMARY.
(Erase heading not required.)

Instructions regarding War Diaries and Intelligence Summaries are contained in F. S. Regs., Part II. and the Staff Manual respectively. Title pages will be prepared in manuscript.

Place	Date	Hour	Summary of Events and Information	Remarks and references to Appendices
Bourne la Comte	17.6.17		Nothing to note	
do	18.6.17		do	
do	19.6.17		Equipment loaded on vehicles	
do	20.6.17		Nothing to note	
do	21.6.17		do	
do	22.6.17		do	
do	23.6.17		Entrained at Bourne to Antwerp with Personnel and Equipment at 4 p.m. left at 19.50 p.m.	
Antwerp	24.6.17		Arrived at 6 a.m. and detrained vehicles which were driven in a convoy. Parked and Snr Personnel to Camp.	
"	25.6.17		Nothing to note	
"	26.6.17		do	
"	27.6.17		do	
"	28.6.17		do	
"	29.6.17		do	
"	30.6.17		do	

J. Cuffer Capt.
RAMC
30/6/15

16/30/3841
leaved

13 AUG 1919

L.y. 7.a.

July 1919

WAR DIARY
or
INTELLIGENCE SUMMARY.

Army Form C. 2118.

(Erase heading not required.)

Place	Date	Hour	Summary of Events and Information	Remarks and references to Appendices
Antwerp	1 July 19		Nothing to note	
do	2.7.19		do	
do	3.7.19		Equipment Michelin engines on trucks at 8pm 7/7	
do	4.7.19		Nothing to report	
do	5.7.19		do	
do	6.7.19		do	
do	7.7.19		Equipment trucks entrained for Boulogne 8/7	
Boulogne	8.7.15		Arrived at Boulogne 8am. To Marlborough Camp	
do	9.7.17		Left for United Kingdom transit chaperone. Train diary closed	

www.ingramcontent.com/pod-product-compliance
Lightning Source LLC
Chambersburg PA
CBHW080921230426
43668CB00014B/2168